THEY CALL IT THE CARIBOO

Cariboo Road Ranch showing round-up

They call it the CARIBOO

Robin Skelton

1980

Sono Nis Press

Victoria, British Columbia, Canada

Canadian Cataloguing in Publication Data

Skelton, Robin, 1925-
    They call it the Cariboo

    ISBN 0-919462-84-7 pa.

    1. Cariboo district, B.C. - History.
I. Title.
FC3845.C3S594   971.1′2   C80-091204-7
F1089.C3S594

COVER: *Alkali Lake Village.* Tourism B.C. Photograph

All other photographs courtesy Provincial Archives of British Columbia.

This book was published with the assistance of the Canada Council.

Published by
SONO NIS PRESS
1745 Blanshard Street
Victoria, British Columbia, Canada V8W 2J8

Designed and printed in Canada by
MORRISS PRINTING COMPANY LTD.
Victoria, British Columbia

To
Nellie and Reg,
and in memory
of Will Robins

AUTHOR'S NOTE AND ACKNOWLEDGEMENTS

My maternal grandfather's only son, Will Robins, settled in Cariboo in 1907, and throughout my childhood I frequently had news of him and of my cousins, and gazed in awe upon photographs of mountains, lakes and forests, and of my distant relatives on horseback. In 1963 I followed my uncle to Canada and visited Cariboo for the first time and was immediately fascinated both by the country and its history. I soon began to contemplate a book about Cariboo but it was not until 1974 that, with the aid of a Canada Council Explorations grant, I managed to spend a whole summer travelling there and writing down my impressions and the stories I was told. Other visits followed and at last, in the summer of 1977 I completed my first draft and proceeded, with the help of Charles Lillard as my editor, to prepare a second, and then the final version, which is now before you.

In writing this book I have been helped by a great many people. Kal Opré deserves special mention for encouraging me to do the work right at the beginning and for lending me many books. My wife should properly be credited as a co-author, for she made notes during many interviews and did a great deal of research for me. Without the hospitality and information provided by my cousins Reg and Nellie Rankin of Morgan Creek I would never have got the book off the ground, and I am also enormously grateful to my cousins-in-law, George and Jean Rankin and Gerald Rankin, for a great deal of information. Others who have been of great help in directing my attention to matters I might otherwise have failed to notice, and giving me information are Gilbert and Molly Forbes, she being herself a chronicler of the Lac La Hache area, Vivian Cowan, Douglas Huston, Dolly Madingley, Naomi Woodburn, Anne Mackenzie Stephenson, Clifford Lyne, Chris Foster, Clarence Roberts, and Avis Choate of the Clinton Museum. I am deeply indebted also to Harry Moffat whose family's day book shed much light upon Cariboo in the last years of the nineteenth century, to Kay Rines and the Quesnel Historical Society for allowing me to look through Cottonwood House papers, and W. J. Langlois of the Department of Aural History of the Provincial Archives of British Columbia who placed his magnificent collection of tape recordings at my disposal. I must also thank William David Thomas for lending me a number of scarce books, and, yet again, Charles Lillard for not only working with me upon the first draft but also for filling a number of gaps in my knowledge, as well as Margaret Reynolds for helping me acquire and select the illustrations.

There are a number of gaps in this book, I must admit, and many of my helpers will be as regretful as I that so many excellent and illuminating stories had to be omitted for reasons of space. I have, however, done my best to present my Social History of Cariboo in such a way that the actual experience of the people of Cariboo is not ignored for the sake of statistics.

In concluding this prefatory note I must thank a number of people and organizations for permitting me to make use of copyright material: Edith Beeson and Lillooet Publishers Ltd. for material from *Dunleavy*, the estate of the late F. W. Lindsay for material from his pamphlets, *The Cariboo Story*, and *The Cariboo Dream*, Gordon R. Elliot and Douglas and McIntyre for material from his *Quesnel*, Art Downs and the Foremost Publishing Company for material from his *Wagon Road North*, Fred W. Ludditt and the Mitchell Press for material from his *Barkerville Days*, M. G. Hurtig Ltd. for extracts from *Cheadle's Journal*, Margaret Ormsby and Macmillan Ltd. for an extract from her *British Columbia*, David R. Williams and Gray's Publishing for extracts from *The Man for a New Country*, Kay Cronin and the Mitchell Press for material from *Cross in the Wilderness*, Bruce Ramsey and the Mitchell Press for an extract from his *Barkerville*, and Hugh Wade and the Haunted Bookshop, Victoria for passages from *The Cariboo Road* by Mark S. Wade.

The University of Victoria   ROBIN SKELTON
Victoria, B.C.

Contents

Maps on pages 16 and 66

Photographs following page 80

PROLOGUE: THEY CALL IT THE CARIBOO

I have entitled this book, *They Call It The Cariboo*, but in point of fact, while this is true, it is as absurd as referring to "the Alberta" or "the Ontario." The name of the area was originally simply Cariboo and so, for a great many of its inhabitants, it remains.

It is appropriate that my title should be both correct and incorrect for almost everything about Cariboo is open to question, and almost every fragment of its history, every story of its inhabitants, exists in several versions. It is almost as difficult to discover two inhabitants of the area who will agree about any story as it is to find the motherlode of that gold which first caused the northern part of the area to be settled. Even the territory itself is ill-defined, for, apart from the lines drawn by political map makers around the Cariboo Riding for the purpose of elections, there are no easily defined limits. At first, in the late 1850's, Cariboo was taken to be the area north of Quesnel Forks and Keithley Creek. When gold was discovered there the tracks which led up to it were severally called "the Cariboo trail" and, later, "the Cariboo road." Those with a bent for geography seem to regard Cariboo as the whole of the Fraser Plateau between the Cariboo mountains on the east and Chilcotin country on the west bank of the Fraser, the northern limit being the Quesnel area, Fort George (later Prince George) being considered outside its boundaries, by some, and as just within it by others. The southern limit is variously defined. Some consider that Lytton and Lillooet at the northern limit of the great Fraser Canyon are the gateways to the Cariboo; others, like Bruce Hutchison, prefer to give Clinton the title. Still others name Cache Creek or, even Ashcroft.

To this series of confusions we must add those concerning the name itself. Governor Douglas, in September 1861, wrote to the Duke of Newcastle, then Colonial Secretary, of "the Cariboo country, in speaking of which I have adopted the popular term and more convenient orthography of the word, though properly it should be

11

written 'Cariboeuf,' or 'Reindeer,' the country having been so called from its being the favourite haunt of that species of deerkind." Gordon R. Elliott derives it from Carboeuf or Elk. Others have derived the name from an Algonquin Indian word "Xalibu" which means "the pawer or scratcher." Yet others suppose that the word has something to do with the Carrier Indians who inhabit the region, and that the word "Cariboeuf" referred to the Indian custom that a widow would carry ("cari") the cremated remains of her husband on her back in a satchel until the six ritual feasts for the dead had taken place, before disposing of the remains. This, like so many things about the Cariboo, seems unlikely. The Carrier Indians were so named, we have been told, by the French voyageurs for the reasons already given, and/or possibly because they served as porters, the word Carrier being a translation of the word "porteur."

Much concerning the Indians is also available in several versions. First hand accounts of them in the nineteenth century differ considerably from each other, and the historians and the anthropologists and the annalists and diarists all use different sets of tribal names. Sometimes the differences are explicable; many times they are not.

This type of confusion is in some ways a pointer to a central characteristic of Cariboo. It is a place which, as far as the settlers are concerned, began with dreams, with rumours, and with romance. The first aliens to find it were following a dream of a navigable waterway to the Pacific; later ones were obsessed by a vision of a land route across North America. All found the area both difficult to get into and difficult to leave, guarded by mountain ranges, unnavigable rapidly flowing rivers, and canyons and mountain passes that presented almost impassable obstacles. Even the tribes of Indians at its edges knew little of the country, and over and over again the guides turned back at the passes. The gold miners followed another dream, perhaps the most powerful dream of all, envisioning an Eldorado where untold amounts of pure gold could be picked up almost without labour in the creeks and rivers. In the 1850's Cariboo was alive with rumour, with tales of miraculous strikes in far places, with stories of huge nuggets and sacks of gold dust. This is the inheritance of Cariboo and it still colours the talk of the people, whether they are recounting stories of the old-timers or discussing events of the present day.

The fabulous is endemic in Cariboo, and those who live there delight in the eccentric. They tell of such characters as the miner who gave seminars on Plato, the lawyer whose office was a model T Ford, the Englishman who imported foxhounds to hunt the coyote, the old Chinaman who ran the rapids through the Fraser Canyon on a raft, his coffin beside him. Moreover, the events of past days were chronicled with real assiduity, both in oral and written form. The hotel register at Clinton not only gives the names and origins of the travellers but also adds details of the events of the time, a local death or funeral, the state of the weather, a good catch of fish. The journalists of the local newspapers were equally keen to record every event of interest, recording visitors, gold strikes, new arrivals. They wrote in a style Bruce Hutchinson has called "upholstered," full of euphemism and rhetoric. The Chinese were referred to almost invariably as "celestials," a meal as a "repast," and there are allusions to the good taste of the proceedings on almost every occasion. Indeed, as soon as the first wave of miners had flowed into Cariboo, the settlements began to develop a mid-Victorian devotion to the proper. Society was being invented, they realized. Society meant pianos (brought up on muleback through the Fraser Canyon), organs, and decorated dinnerware. It seems sometimes as if there were a competition to be the first person to have a piano, a harpsichord, a Paris dress, in Cariboo; the names of the winners of these competitions are faithfully recorded either by journalism or oral tradition.

It is not often realized that the majority of early pioneers always attempted, not to make a new way of life but to recreate the old one and to present, in a new setting, the dignities and observances of the upper middle class of the countries they had left. Conscious of this process, they saw each new aquisition as a symbol of a new stage in the growth of the country towards glory. This too was a dream, the dream of the rancher, the merchant, the hotel keeper, rather than that of the gold miner perhaps, though he, too, saw his wealth quite often as a means of achieving bourgeois opulence and social position.

These early settlers were conscious of making history as were the early explorers. There is a wealth of history and of poetry in the names of the rivers, creeks, mining claims and settlements in Cariboo—Murderers Gulch, Lightning Creek, the Aurora claim, Antler, Spanish Mountain, Grouse Creek, Jack o' Clubs Lake, Beaver Lake, Dog Creek, Horsefly, and Likely are a few of them. The poetry of the names, however, is as nothing to the poetry of the country itself. In the summer months journeying north from Clinton on the Cariboo Road after the harsh heat of the Thompson Canyon, with its tumbleweed and jack pines scattered over steep slopes of rock

13

that change hue from bone-white to purple to red as one travels beside the turbulent grey-blue-green river, you enter a country of rolling hills, firs, and grassland where many blue and green lakes lie still as mirrors, edged with bleached and alkali-encrusted earth and shaded by poplar and birch. The huge expanse of Williams Lake behind you, you climb a little and by-passing the twisting road down into Soda Creek are once again beside the wide rolling Fraser, where the gravel bars glare in the sun, and the dead trees at the river's edge testify to the power of the waters to rise and flood in the spring to an almost unbelievable height. Farther on, the hills are steeper, the rivers narrower and the terrain more difficult until at Barkerville, now an exact copy of the old town of the 1860's and 70's, the thickly wooded mountain sides, once denuded of all trees by the early miners, and the acres of stones in the artificially broadened creek bed have a theatrical presence. The new trees have hidden much of the past. Cameronton is once again bush, not a log remaining of all its cabins, and other settlements have vanished similarly.

There are many lost and ghost towns in Cariboo, and it is deeply moving to find in a tumbling house or cabin evidence of early hopes and dignities—an elaborate frontage to a falling store, a wilderness whose contents testify to the earlier presence of a garden, a window, now broken, that was proudly made at a time when glass was $3.00 a pane and the dollar was worth ten of ours.

Cariboo is at once tenacious and spendthrift of its history. Many old buildings have crumbled, sometimes together with their contents, but the stories about them remain, and the Cariboo Historical Society has done much to salvage the proud possessions and the working tools of the first settlers, placing them in Museums whose curators are generous with information on local history. Nevertheless even the eyes of the local historians brighten when they tell of places no longer to be seen, mines that are now a myth, and events of which there is only an oral record. It is as if the real Cariboo, the essence of it, can only be understood in terms of the lost, the unknown, the forgotten, the mysterious.

I return indeed to that quality of Cariboo which is for me the most fascinating, its dreamlike lack of definition, its romantic mystery. It is a country of uncertainties, of fables, and contradictions. Seeking a document at the Town Hall in one Cariboo centre I was told by a secretary that I could not see the town clerk. "We're in between town clerks at the moment" she said, and added, "I think." Her statement almost sums up what I feel about this book, for writing about Cariboo is writing about much more than a region and its history. So I would say, "this is a book about Cariboo—I think" and leave it to the reader to wander through these pages at his own speed and in his own fashion, determining for himself what is fact and what is fantasy, and perhaps, in this way coming to guess at a little of the splendour and confusion, the romance and the reality which they call "the" Cariboo.

CHAPTER ONE

Before the Gold Rush

When, in the last quarter of the eighteenth century, the fur trappers from Montreal, the voyageurs, first crossed the continental divide they found themselves in a land of fast running and dangerous rivers, that appeared to run north, west, south or even east again purely at whim, and of many lakes, all surrounded by mountains of various degrees of difficulty. There appeared to be no pattern of rivers or trails that could direct them towards the sea they knew lay to the west, or towards the great river which they knew flowed into the ocean from this region. Baffled, the majority of them retreated, and it was not until Alexander Mackenzie, having crossed the divide on June 12, 1793, found himself five days later on the banks of a river that the Indians called Tacoutche Tesse, and which we now call the Fraser, that the way to Cariboo can be said to have been found. Mackenzie, seeking an overland route to the Pacific, and knowing of the great Columbia River, naturally thought he had found its source.

Two days later, unfortunately missing the Nechako River which could have led him to the Pacific, he ran into the Northern Canyon of the Fraser and he and his lieutenant, Alexander McKay, together with their six accompanying voyageurs and two Indian hunters as interpreters, had to portage their twenty-five foot canoe, and its ton and a half of baggage. The strain was too much for the canoe and it began to split; as a consequence, while trying to run successive rapids and whirlpools a little later, it filled with water and the travellers were all nearly drowned. To the opposition of the terrain, was added the opposition of the inhabitants. At the meeting of the Fraser and Quesnel rivers they encountered a large number of Indians armed with bows and spears upon the river bank. Mackenzie landed, ostentatiously unarmed, and allayed their suspicions of the first white men they had even seen with presents of beads and mirrors and sugar for the children. The Indians warned him that the river ran "towards the midday sun" and was impassable in three places. On June 21 at a place called Stella Yah (later Fort Alexander) other Indians directed him to strike westward to a place where he would meet those people "who barter iron, brass, copper... beads for dressed leather, and beaver, bear, lynx, fox, and marten skins." Mackenzie did so, and travelled overland for fifteen days, leaving the canoe behind him; he was then taken down the Bella Coola River by friendly Indians and reached Bentinck Arm and the Pacific on July 20, 1793. He had achieved his goal of travelling overland to the Pacific, though not by the route he had envisaged. He had also been the first alien to enter Cariboo, though he had left it immediately.

The Indians who faced Mackenzie were Carrier Indians of the Dené race. The Dené (or Athapaskan) race occupied the large area of the country extending from the western shores of Hudson's Bay to the eastern edge of the Alaskan Panhandle, and from the borderlands of the Arctic Eskimo to the country of the Interior Salish and the Coast Salish of the Fraser River delta. The Dené of British Columbia were divided into several sub-nations, the Sekani and Nahani of the north, the Tahltan in the west by the Alaska Panhandle, the Chilcotin on the west bank of the Fraser River, and the Carrier or Yubatan (which included the Babines) of the Upper Fraser after whom the white men possibly (but only possibly) called their region Cariboo.

What sort of people were these Carrier Indians whom Mackenzie encountered, and what was their way of life at that time? The name "Carrier" was wished on them by others as was the name "Athapaskan" which simply refers to a language group, which includes also the more famous Navaho and Apaches of the south. They regarded themselves as belonging to the Dené race and the word Dené meant simply and proudly "Man." They were a not altogether peaceable people, we know, for in 1745 stories reached the coast of the Chilcotin group of the Dené massacring the inhabitants of the Carrier village of Chinlac at the meeting point of the Stuart and Nechako rivers. Mackenzie was wise to speak peace to these men of the race of Man.

War was not, however, a way of life for the Carriers. They did not indulge in the frequent forcible enslaving of other peoples as did the Haida of the Queen Charlottes who had an almost Viking propensity for descending upon their neighbours. There was warfare between the neighbouring nations certainly, and especially between the Chilcotins and the Carriers but it seems to have been sporadic and in the nature of bloody squabbles over hunting territories. In 1859 at a meeting at Lac La Hache in the Shuswap territory for intertribal games and a conference concerning the way to deal with the increasing number of white men approaching the region, Chief Dehtus Anahiem of the Chilcotins, advocated an alliance of the Chilcotins, Shuswap and Yubatan Dené in order to prevent the strangers from taking over their country. His speech, as reported by Alex P. McInnes who heard it from Peter Dunleavy who, with his companions Jim Sellers, Ira Crow, Tom Manifee, Tom Moffitt and John McLean, was present at the meeting, runs:

It makes warm the heart of the Chilcotin to come to this old time meeting place of the Shuswaps to visit with our brothers the Denés and the Yubatans and our cousins the Shuswaps.

These games are the chief attraction, for they keep us strong and brave, eager and fleet, not only for the hunt but to scare away our enemies. It is mainly for this last point that Anahiem of the Chilcotins has come to make talk and consult with his brother chiefs at this meeting.

For some time our scouts have been bringing us news of white men who are coming up our rivers. We have tolerated these men, thinking them to be weak minded and therefore entitled to the reverent regard which all Indians have for these weak ones as dictated by the Great Spirit. However, we have found out that these men are really not crazy and are washing out little pieces of yellow stone which they call gold and which they use for what we call Sunia (money), to use as we use skins to trade for other goods. The Indians of Lillooet have already been corrupted. It is said they have learned the white man's skill and are finding little pieces of yellow stone also.

The priests have told us to shun the firewater as we would the devil they have told us of, but how can we keep clear of their firewater, if we allow them to come among us and ruin our women with their diseases? Will we not be ruined, in turn, as other tribes far to the east about which the priests have told us?

Another thing, this sunia really belongs to us and the white men are taking it without asking for it. The priests tell us this is stealing. If we steal they tell us that their God will punish us. But these white men are stealing from us. Will their God punish them for this bad act or have they made a convenient arrangement with this God? Has he one law for the Indian and another law for the white man?

We must keep these white men out. We tribes must act together. If we do not act immediately we will only have to drive them out later. This will result in much bloodshed, for them and also for our own people. We must act now or we are lost![1]

Chief Williams (Willy-ams, Twilly-ums) of the Williams Lake Indians, though Chief Dehtus indicated that he should speak next, retired in favour of Chief LooLoo of the Yubatan-Denés. He said:

I have heard the serious words of the great Chief Dehtus of the Chilcotins. These words tell some strange things to my old ears—the danger to the

[1] Edith Beeson, *Dunleavy; from the Diaries of Alex P. McInnes*, 1971, pp. 63-65.

19

Indian from the whiteman, the danger to the whiteman from the Indian. But the strangest of these words are the telling of the spirit of love which these Chilcotins have for the Shuswaps and, more strange still, the great love and brotherhood they feel toward the Yubatan Denés. Do these words really come from the heart of our old hereditary enemy? Or do they, like (in) the past, come from the lips only, while the heart is black and treacherous and full of cunning tricks? Is it to make us become unwary so that our old enemies can at last conquer us, which they have never been able to do in the past?

I believe Dehtus speaks in truth, and every word of warning rings in my own heart and surely in the hearts of every Indian in our tribes. All the things he said are true, but what he tells us to do about them is false.

It is just as useless for our three tribes to resist these whitemen as it is for one of us to try to resist. We know that our resistance would only result in needless bloodshed and possible annihilation. The Indians can never win against the whiteman because of his numbers, his guns, his learning and his craftiness... All that I have to say is that as much as I have studied the whiteman and his ways, I do not know him yet. But I do know that my people must learn to live in contact with him. To attempt to stop him is impossible. Speaking for myself and my people, I say to you, we will not join forces in this useless war.[2]

There is another version of this conference. In this one the meeting was between the Carriers, the Shuswap and the Chilcotin, and it took place sometime after the miners had penetrated as far as the Quesnel River, and therefore after Dunleavy had struck gold on Horsefly. According to this story the Indians had already arranged for a general massacre of the intruders and had planned it to occur at the next full moon. The Indians were to gather on the banks of the Thompson and the Fraser and the Quesnel and shoot down at the miners working the river below. Chief Williams, however, opposed the scheme. He said that it would be better to trade with the strangers than kill them, for a massacre would be quite useless. However many were killed there would be many more following. It would be like the salmon run. They would come up river in their thousands. He pointed out that there were benefits to be gained from helping them and trading with them. He succeeded in bringing the assembled tribes to his point of view and from that time on there was no more talk of an organized Indian-settler war in Cariboo. The Indians acted as packers, carriers, and guides for the miners. They sold them dried salmon and flat cakes of dried berries. They taught many of them the medicinal properties of the various trees and plants. Many of the miners took Indian girls as common-law wives and these were most

[2] *Ibid.,* pp. 68-69.

often the daughters of men of high rank and of chiefs. Thoughts of war gave way to gestures of welcome.

Whether or not it was Chief Williams or Chief LooLoo (or Lolo) who brought peace to Cariboo, and whatever the exact nature of the argument that was put forward, there's no reason to doubt that the conference took place in 1859 and that it was a crucial occasion in the history of Cariboo and of what was to become British Columbia. It seems clear also, from all reports of this meeting that the Chilcotin and the Yubatan Denés were hereditary enemies who met together on occasion, and probably annually, for their own version of the Olympic games, and Lac La Hache provided one of those meeting places as did Williams Lake. It was not, however, sacrosanct territory at other times, for the large amount of spearheads turned up by the plough in this area testifies to the occurrence of more than one intertribal battle.

Chief Dehtus and Chief LooLoo saw the consequences of the coming of the white men clearly enough in 1859. Half a century earlier the danger was not so apparent. The tribes encountered by David Thompson in 1807 when he descended the Kootenay River were less concerned with trading skins and furs than with their inter-tribal squabbles. By that time Simon Fraser, working for the North West Company which, by amalgamating with the XY company in 1804, had developed enough strength to compete with the Hudson's Bay Company for the trade west of the Rockies, had already, with James McDougall founded Fort McCleod, and built Fort St. James as a trading post to compete with the Americans who had supplanted the Russians on the Coast. He had also founded Fort George at the confluence of the Nechako and the Fraser. In that year of 1807 he descended the "Grande Rivière" which was to be called after him, and refusing to be deterred by the warnings of the Indians at Stella-yah, or to accept their advice to travel overland to the Thompson, continued onwards, conquering rapids, whirlpools, canyons, until he reached the Fraser Canyon and its Indian tracks along the cliff walls, made of horizontal ladders and platforms of poles and twigs suspended from trees and rocks at the top of the precipice and sometimes insecurely tethered to others lower down. He and his companions inched their way through to Spuzzum, Yale and navigable waters.

Simon Fraser therefore was the first explorer to travel the length of the Cariboo country. He named the whole area below and above the canyon, including the Northwestern region "New Caledonia." From this time on, the Nor'westers and the voyageurs were everywhere in

21

Cariboo, and found the fur trade rich indeed. In 1811 Alexander Ross at a place called Cumcloups (now Kamloops) on the edge of Cariboo proper, found two thousand Indians eager to trade with him, and later reported that their enthusiasm was so great that he was able to get a beaver skin for only five tobacco leaves and twenty prime skins for a mere yard of white cotton.

Between 1811 and that historic meeting of the three tribes in 1859 the Cariboo Indians responded with enthusiasm to the advances of the white men. Missionaries came into the country with the voyageurs, and while the North West Company prohibited settlements other than their own wooden-walled trading posts or "forts," small communities did begin to form. In 1821 the rivalry between the Hudson's Bay Company and the North West Company which had sometimes been so intense as to lead to violence, ended and the two companies were combined, using the name of the older and more famous organization. This led to increased commerce not only between the fur factors and the Indians but also between the Indians themselves. The trading posts became meeting places where the tribes mingled as rarely before save on special occasions, and the lines of cultural demarcation so carefully drawn by later anthropologists rapidly became blurred.

It is from the accounts of the missionaries and the traders that we derive our knowledge of the Indians' way of life at this period. The Dené were a tall people, full faced with broad foreheads, and, in general, muscular and well built. They were expert fishermen, building weirs and barriers which guided the fish into a detachable funnel-shaped basket. They also suspended basket traps made from long spars of fir bound together with spruce roots in the shallower waterfalls. Dip nets were made from nettle fibre, the nettle stems being shredded and beaten into a fluff and then rolled into a yarn on the thigh before being spun into stronger threads by means of a spindle. Fish spears were also used. Some were three-pronged, the middle point transfixing the fish and the two outer ones, with in-turned barbs, holding it trapped. The barbs were made of bone or horn. Other spears had detachable heads to which a line was attached; when the fish was impaled the shaft would be withdrawn and the fish hauled in on the line. Some of the fish were dried and stored for winter use, as also were cakes made of mashed soapberries, cranberries, and blueberries, and a number of roots. The roots of the bracken fern were usually baked in underground ovens, but other roots, such as the bulbs of the sweet iris, the dog-tooth violet, and the red lily were eaten raw. Hair-moss or lichen, which hangs everywhere from the branches of the firs, was washed, pounded into a dough, and fried in grease. Wild onions and parsnips were also eaten.

All these foods were available in the summer and early fall. In the winter, while some fish were caught through holes in the ice, the main food source was different. Many kinds of deadfall traps and loop snares were constructed both for small animals, such as beaver, marten, otter, groundhog, hare, and muskrat, and for ducks and grebes which were caught by means of loops attached to submerged stakes. It is said that during the fall hunting season, a really expert hunter would swim up to bigger waterfowl while wearing a head-dress made of a complete bird, and then snare them with a line round the legs. Moose, caribou, mountain goats and sheep, wolf, fox, and bear, were killed with bows and arrows.

Unlike many tribes the Carrier cooked most of their food, roasting it or boiling it in bark vessels containing hot stones and water. Dry food was served individually on woven mats or hides; stews and soups were eaten from a common pot with spoons made of wood or bark. Usually the men ate first and the women and children afterwards.

Most of the trees and plants of the region were useful to the Carrier. Pounded alder bark provided a laxative, and a powder made from a fir tree fungus cured biliousness; both these were taken in water. Boils and other inflammatory eruptions were cured by drinking warm water in which young spruce shoots had been boiled, and the blotches and pimples of adolescence were treated with an application of mashed swamp cranberry. The leaves and the bark of the cranberry and of the bird-cherry were boiled to make a warm drink to cure internal haemorrhage; cuts were poulticed with chewed aspen roots. Black currant tea was as well known to the Carriers as to the white men as a cure for coughs and colds; so were the tonic properties of spearmint and wild cherry. Osier willow and aspen bark provided an ointment for sores, as did fomentations of the bark of the red willow. Many of these cures became known to the voyageurs and the early miners and settlers; in February 1864 the lives of several members of the Company of Welsh Adventurers under "Captain" John Evans, working on Chisholm Creek were saved by a prospector who diagnosed severe scurvy and advised the drinking of a "tea" made from spruce buds and twigs. The miners drank at least twelve cups a day and in ten days were back at work, several of them having been near death. The old prospector who told them of the remedy was

Pharker MacLennan, a Highland Scot; thereafter the Welshmen called him Dr. Spruce.

It was the spruce that was used most frequently by the Indians for their light canoes. The bark was stripped off the tree in the spring and moulded round a framework with the smooth side outward, the seams at the prow and stern being made with roots sewn around a strengthening length of wood, and sealed with a kind of pitch. Birch bark was also used, but less frequently. Tree-bark was also used to make the cooking pots; a single length would be folded into the correct shape, sewn with spruce root, and sealed with pitch, the rims being strengthened with lengths of willow. The cakes of dried berry mash for winter storage were made in a cylinder of bark with a hole in the bottom that was fitted with a filter made of twigs. The cylinder was filled with berries and the hot cooking stones were put on top of them. Thus the berries were simultaneously cooked and pressed, the juice running out through the filter into a bark dish. Some of these well-made vessels were decorated with abstract designs or with flower and leaf patterns, but on the whole the Carriers spent little time upon the decoration of utensils, or the creation of tools. Their stone implements were usually no more than stones that happened to be the right shape for the job. Arrow heads and fish hooks were carefully made, but the Carriers saw no sense in labouring on the making of stone mortars; found stones could be used as pestles and hides as mortars. The scrapers for cleaning hides were equally simple, usually being no more than sharp-edged stones that had been found in that state or broken deliberately, though in the later stages of preparing the hide more carefully chosen, and sometimes sharpened and serrated scrapers of bone and horn were used.

Some of this is probably due less to the Indians laziness than to their unwillingness to burden themselves with too many possessions as their way of life involved them in changing their living quarters at least twice a year. From May to September they lived in permanent or semi-permanent villages on the banks of a river or the shores of a lake where there was a good supply of fish. Here they built their lodges, the ceremonial lodge which was the chief's home and also the general meeting place, and other smaller lodges. The main lodge was rectangular, with four corner posts, and two roof beams to support the eaves. The walls were made of vertical slabs of spruce resting in grooves cut in logs laid along the sides as foundations. The peaked roof was built of spruce poles covered with sheets of bark. Everything was tied into place with thongs of willow bark. There was one door and a smoke hole. The bare earth of the sleeping area was spread with spruce branches.

The other lodges were similarly but more crudely constructed, the walls being made of poles laid on each other lengthwise in between vertical posts. Lodges made for winter use had the additional protection of a kind of enclosed porch made by leaning a semicircle of poles and saplings against the end wall, this porch having, of course, a second door opening. The inner door could be shut by lowering a slab of spruce suspended from the roof.

Usually, however, the Dené moved from these permanent buildings in September and built winter dwellings in the forest where there was enough wood for their fires, and where they were in good hunting territory. These winter dwellings were circular pits. Four beams were set in the earth outside each pit so as to meet in a point over the centre. These rafters were supported by other posts at the pit edges, and covered with brush, bark and earth. One entered the dwelling at the apex of the "roof" by way of a ladder made of a notched log or a log on which remaining fragments of branches were suitably spaced. A shelf of earth ran round the pit; this was used both for storage and for sleeping. These pits are nowadays referred to as Keekwillee, sometimes spelled "keekwilli," or Quiggly mounds or holes. A large tribe would denude a considerable area of forest during a winter season, and therefore it was usual for the tribes to seek different winter quarters from time to time, if not annually, though there are stories of some of these villages such as one beside Lac La Hache being used permanently.

Dependent as they were upon the natural world for all their sustenance, the Dené, like all other Indians in a similar situation, revered the animals, birds and fish they hunted. Long Baptiste, the Indian guide who led the Dunleavy party to their first gold strike on Horsefly Creek, objected strongly to one of the party throwing the bones of a doe they had just eaten into the fire. He is reported by MacInnes (who heard it from Dunleavy) as saying

Non! Non! No burn good bone. Injun plenty dog. They eat bone. No dog here. Sometam wil' fren fin' bone. Him eat. Good. Coyote all a tam come behin' where men go. Hongry, fin' bone eat. Tell Injun stanalia (Dené for thank you)![3]

He then threw back his head and howled, and was answered by first one and then another coyote. The Dené believed that the animal's

[3] *Ibid.*, p. 100.

spirit would become angry if any indignity were offered those parts of the carcass that were of no use to man, either for food, clothing or implements; they felt that gratitude was due to the animals for allowing themselves to be killed and exploited. Bears were given special attention. When a bear was killed the Dené spoke to it as if it were a close relation, offered it a pipe of tobacco, and apologized formally and frequently for having killed it. The bear's skull was always placed in a tree or in the fork of a tent pole as a mark of respect and to propitiate its spirit. The first fish to be caught in a new net was also given special respect. It had to be roasted on the fire rather than boiled; its flesh must then be removed without disordering the bones and the perfect skeleton burned on the fire. If these marks of respect for the spirit world were not shown that particular net would be certain to prove useless. Fish had to be lured by charms as well as bait. The hunter of animals also approached his task reverentially. He would take a steam bath to purify himself before setting out, and if the hunting expedition were crucial he would not sleep with his wife for a full month beforehand, not even using her drinking cup. Those setting snares would chew heracleum root, mix it with water in the mouth, and then spit it all out, saying passionately, "May I snare thee."

There were many rules about hunting. Game belonged, not to the one who shot it, but to the one who had first sighted it, to whom the animal had offered itself. Moreover the hunter was forbidden to eat meat from his own kill. He must either give it to a companion or, after skinning it, return to camp and tell others where he had left the meat. Even in doing this he was forbidden to boast about his success; he had to minimize it, to maintain that he had suffered very poor luck, even almost complete failure. In this way he did not risk offending the spirits by claiming as a personal success one which was truly due to the animal's own generosity of spirit.

The hunter of non-migratory animals could only lay snares in his own territory. Beaver grounds were owned in the way that range land is owned by ranchers. Those forced by hunger to snare animals outside their own territory or from another's traps, were obliged to dress the hide and give it to the proper owner. Migratory animals, however, belonged to the owner of the traps in which they were caught.

These rules of etiquette were fundamentally related to the Dené sense of an ordered universe in which territorial rights must be respected and the spirit world revered and placated. The Dené believed in a Creator spirit, "that which is on high," who was responsible for shooting stars, eclipses, and the changes of the weather. The world created by this god was inhabited by invisible spirits. Many of them were evil and caused sickness by entering men's bodies. Others controlled the animal kingdom and their co-operation was necessary for successful hunting. Animals, like men, had spirits distinct from their bodies, and these spirits, which left the body at death, were believed to be immortal. Sometimes the spirit would be restless within a man, and the man would fall sick; sometimes the spirit would leave the body for a time and the ensuing illness could only be cured by luring it back again. When a man died his spirit would go to live in an underground village that was usually thought of as lying on the other side of some large lake or wide river. These spirits of the dead could sometimes be persuaded to return and take up residence in the next child to be born in the family.

The way to influence the spirits was by way of ceremonials conducted by the Shaman. He could lure back a spirit to the sick body it had left by rubbing the sufferer's head with magical water, or filling his mocassins with down and hanging them overnight on a tent pole; if in the morning the down were warm it showed that the spirit had returned and that the patient would be completely cured once he had put the mocassins on again. Shamans were also witch hunters and would search out anyone who had harmed another person and put a piece of the victim's clothing, or a scrap of his hair or a nail paring in a place known to be frequented by evil spirits and leave them there with a curse.

For these activities the Shaman wore ceremonial dress that showed the nature of the spirit which gave him his power. Necklaces of bear's claws were frequently worn, and skins of animals or birds. He danced and sang to the accompaniment of drums made of hide beaten by the sufferer's family and friends, and often went into a trance. The shamans were not alone in having guardian spirits to help them. The male Carrier at puberty would attempt to approach the spirit world, hoping that his guardian spirit would appear to him in a dream as some particular animal, fish or bird. As with other races, this approach involved fasting and solitary wanderings through the forest. Once the dream had occurred, the creature who appeared in it was revered, and anything connected with it was regarded as a magical charm. Moreover, the hunter was forbidden to kill that creature, except when necessity commanded it, and even then only with the most humble and ceremonious apologies. The bows and arrows, the snares and the nets of the individual hunter were marked with a symbol of his guardian spirit and, after a successful hunting or fishing trip, the spirit would be thanked by throwing some gift, food or clothing, into the fire or into the river or lake.

Clothing was important to the Dené. The upper class of the tribe wore splendid garments, and these were prized family possessions. These upper class Indians belonged to the immediate families of hereditary chiefs. A commoner could not enter these ranks unless he raised his family status by a series of impressive potlatch ceremonies. In some tribes not even this would do. If you were not born into the ruling class you could never enter it. The Dené, like many other nations, also had a third social class, that of the slaves, though they do not seem to have been as numerous as in the tribes of the Tsmishian or the Haidas. Although the upper or ruling class was usually dominated by one hereditary chief, the community was always, in theory, ruled by a committee.

The hereditary nature of the ruling class might have resulted in the kind of inbred weakness which afflicted a number of European royal and noble families, had the Dené not been subject to a number of taboos concerning intermarriage. Dené society was matrilineal, descent being reckoned by way of the female line. Although all property was regarded as belonging to the male it could only be inherited by way of the females of that male's family. A man would inherit not from his father but from his mother's brother, his maternal uncle. If no male heir existed, a woman could hold the titles and privileges in question, and also the property, but only until she or one of her sisters produced a son. It was forbidden for anyone to marry a person of his mother's blood line, though he or she could marry a cousin on the father's side. Relatives on the mother's side were regarded as being kindred, however far afield they might be, and into whatever tribe they might have married. These clan connections were important, for any clan member was obliged to help and welcome any other member of the clan.

The dignities, privileges and possessions inherited by the young upper class Dené included territorial rights to fishing and hunting areas and ceremonial costumes. The ceremonial costume of the Carrier consisted of a head-dress, a breast-plate, and a shirt or cloak. The woman's head-dress was a coronet of hide on which upright pieces of wood or goose quills supported weasel skins. The man's head-dress was a cap of dentalia shells strung together with human hair, with a falling plume of human hair that reached to the waist and ended in tassels, the whole being crowned with a bunch of sea lion bristles. The crescent-shaped breast-plate was made of dentalia shells bound together with human hair, and the shirt or cloak was of caribou hide decorated with coloured quills of the porcupine, and tassels of young caribou hoofs and dentalia shells. The leggings were also of hide and decorated with quills and shells and fringes. The girls, according to Dunleavy in 1858, wore a breach cloth under their shirts, but were forbidden to wear leggings. "Indian, dey won't let dey womans wear no kin'a pants, savvy?" the buxom At-T'uss (black-headed chickadee) told Dunleavy at the 1859 games.

Certainly, matrilineal succession or no, the women did not wear the pants in the Dené tribes. As soon as a young girl began to menstruate she was secluded from the rest of the tribe, for it was believed that she housed evil spirits. She ate only dried food and water, and no freshly killed meat or fish in case she offended the spirits of the game or fish concerned. She drank the water through a drinking tube of bone in order not to contaminate the drinking vessel. Because it was bad luck for any man to see her face she wore a tanned hide head-dress which reached from her head to her waist, the front part of it being cut into strips so that she could see where she was going. One of her father's sisters would put this garment on her, and she might have to wear it for as long as four years. During the whole of that time she could only be visited by female relatives. Rings and bracelets made of animal sinew were placed on her fingers, wrists and ankles to stop the evil influences escaping.

Once the years of puberty were over and the time of courtship had begun she was scarcely more fortunate. Her own wishes were rarely considered. The man who wanted her would simply make gifts to her maternal relations and help them in every way he could over a period of two to three years, without ever mentioning his reasons. Then he would make his request formally and if it was accepted the girl would be told to spread her "husband's" blanket in a corner of the family lodge. Sometimes brides were bought outright by wealthy men. Divorce was not uncommon, but a man who married a divorced woman had to take due consideration of the fact that she always retained custody of the children she had borne; in some Dené tribes, (though possibly not the Carrier), a man could take another man's wife by defeating her husband in a wrestling match. Women were rarely left without some male support, however; if a man were to die his brother was obliged to support the widow and her children.

Among the Dené a new-born child was first of all washed and then swaddled in rabbit skins or moss and laced into a flat carrying-cradle made of bark. It would be washed daily in a tray of bark until it was able to walk.

Death was treated more ceremoniously than birth, especially when a chief had died. News was sent out to neighbouring villages while the widow, her hair cut off by her husband's nearest relatives sat by the corpse. While she sat there the visitors from other villages danced their tribute to the dead. The body, when the time came for cremation, was placed, face upwards on a pyre of wood. It was covered with a beaver-skin robe, wore new mocassins, and had had its face freshly painted. As the fire was lit the widow embraced the corpse until forced away by the heat and smoke. After a few breaths of clear air she returned either of her own volition or as a result of the forcible persuasions of her husband's relations, and continued to do this until it became obvious to all that she was in real danger. As the fire rose higher, the visitors from other tribes and clans threw gifts of clothing on the fire. The value of these gifts was carefully remembered by the dead man's kindred so that it could be repaid when a funeral ceremony took place in one of the visitors' villages.

After the fire had cooled the dead man's bones were gathered together and put in a bark container, which the widow then carried on her back in a decorated satchel of hide, only removing it at night and even then sleeping beside it. She carried this burden until the six mandatory potlatches had been given over the period of a year, the first two being in honour of the dead, and the remainder to honour the heir. Gifts were distributed generously to everyone present at only two or three of these ceremonies, though every Dené ceremony involved the presenting of minor gifts to a number of the guests.

The potlatch ceremonies of the Dené differed only in detail from those of other tribes. Instead of establishing their high status by giving away blankets and enormously valuable "coppers" (sheets of beaten copper) or portions of them, or blankets as did the Haida and Kwakiutl, they usually gave away ceremonial clothing. They did not have elaborately carved and inlaid feast dishes like some of the other tribes either. Nevertheless the intent was the same. A chief or other person could, on an occasion for celebration, establish his superiority by the lavish nature of his gifts, revealing himself to be both wealthy enough to give without apparent limit and powerful enough spiritually to be able to disregard material considerations. There was also an element of challenge and competition. The Chief who gave lavishly was challenging the chiefs of neighbouring tribes to equal or surpass his generosity at their own potlatches.

The spirit of competition was intense among the Dené Indians, and they greatly enjoyed sports and games of skill. When the three tribes of the Chilcotin, the Shuswap and the Yubatan-Dené met at Lac La Hache in 1859 for the historic conference already mentioned, there were intertribal and individual games before the speeches began. In the mornings they competed in archery, wrestling, knife throwing, shinny, and the throwing of spears, knives and torpedoes. In the after-noon there were foot races and horse races.

The Indians called the steel pointed feather-flighted torpedo "Lahausse." Dunleavy described it to McInnes thus:

It was made of the hardest wood, either birch or vine maple, three or four feet long and about one and a half inches in diameter at the largest part, all perfectly round and polished smooth. The largest part tapered from ten to twelve inches from the nose in a slightly curving line. Then from the swell again in a straight line to the tail end which was about an inch in diameter. It was a masterpiece of symmetry and perfect lining.[4]

Long Baptiste showed the Dunleavy party how the torpedo was thrown, and it flew with such force that an axe was needed to chop it out of the tree it had hit. "Keel kweek ten-ee-na (big animals)! Dem kweek keel man in war too, you bet!" said Baptiste.

The javelin and archery games involved the throwing up of a wooden hoop through which the javelin would be thrown or the arrow shot. The javelins had stone points, often of jade, and were decorated with beads and rabbit skin. The throwing knives called "nzizkl" were copper bladed and a little bigger than the normal hunting knife. Two other weapons which Baptiste showed Dunleavy, but which were not used in the games, were a foot-long stone club with a hole at one end through which a braided cord was tied, the other end being attached to the wrist, and a round rock varying in size from that of a hen's egg to that of an orange, sewn into a hide covering and similarly attached to the wielder's wrist. These were for use in war much as the medieval knights used spiked steel balls on the end of chains. "Cultus" (Dangerous) "Not for play!" said Baptiste.

Wagers were laid on the intertribal races, each gambler placing the article he was wagering on a pile, and much excitement and ribald amusement was caused by the Chilcotin placing a couple of pretty girls on their stack of goods. These girls, when lost to the Yubatan-Dené, were immediately ransomed but not without a good

[4] *Ibid.*, p. 46.

31

deal of preliminary horseplay. Gambling fascinated the Indians; their favourite game was Lahalle in which two players held two bones in their hands, one of them marked and one unmarked. These were moved from hand to hand and the opponent had to guess which hand held the marked bone. Neither the Chilcotin nor the Yubatan-Dené were above using the equivalent of loaded dice when the light of the day had gone and firelight made cheating easy. Jim Sellers, himself a gambler, was shown, after much persuasion, one bone in two parts so made that the marked portion could be slid into the other part and thus appear unmarked. Another trick was to mark only half the bone so that it could be twisted in the hand and only the unmarked side revealed; this could be done by touch as the marks were engraved, not painted on.

The 1859 games may have been untypical of the Carrier when they first encountered white men some sixty years earlier, for the fur trade had brought much intertribal commerce and some of the Indians wore clothes or cloth acquired from the Hudson's Bay traders, but the games must be assumed to have been going on fairly regularly for some years. A much more startling event of this occasion however, especially after Chief Dehtus' slighting reference to gold, was the way in which Baptiste convinced the Dunleavy party that he knew where there were gold nuggets as big as beans. According to McInnes, when Dunleavy said that they must start looking for gold the following day, Baptiste said

"Now you talk bout gol' Me I lak show you something, Messeur Pete" Throwing some more wood on the fire to make a light, he pulled a small buckskin sack from another buckskin pouch hanging from his belt, and took from it a small object that shone brightly golden in the firelight. This he handed to Dunleavy, saying "Dat one you col' gol' "
The object proved to be a plain circlet or ring that had been beaten out of a nugget of pure gold and then exquisitely carved in Indian lattice-work design.[5]

Baptiste explained that this was a family heirloom that had been handed down to the head of his family for many generations. This is the only known instance of a Cariboo Indian working in gold; all other reports speak of their thinking nothing of the shiny pebbles until the white men drew them to their attention. Baptiste's ring is, indeed, inexplicable unless one chooses to think of it as mythical, a ring of power, which would change the whole of Cariboo, leading, as it did, to the gold strike on Horsefly Creek, and to the gold rush which altered the Indian way of life forever.

[5] *Ibid.*, pp. 92-93.

CHAPTER TWO

Gold in Cariboo

Almost since the California Gold Rush of 1849 there had been rumours of gold in New Caledonia. In 1852 gold was brought to Fort Kamloops by some Indians and half breeds; the Hudson's Bay factor kept quiet about it; he wanted no disturbance of the fur trade. In 1856 and 1857 some Indians who wintered near Fort Colville where gold had been discovered in 1855, told the prospectors there that they had seen similar shiny pebbles in the Thompson River country, and a few prospectors followed up this clue, and to the extreme irritation of the almighty Hudson's Bay Company began to work on the Thompson. In 1857, John Houston took gold from Tranquille Creek, and the same year, the factor at Kamloops, having collected, much to his embarrassment, 800 ounces of gold, decided to send it down to the mint in San Francisco by the steamship *Otter*. The superintendent of the mint belonged to the volunteer fire department and at a fireman's meeting he is supposed to have said, "Boys, the next excitement will be on the Fraser River."

In the early spring of 1858 a group of prospectors reached the Fraser and made their way up river to Fort Hope. The Hudson's Bay factor, Donald Walker, was unhelpful and evasive, but he could not deter the men. One of them, James Moore, wrote later:

> The next morning we left Hope and camped on a bar at noon to cook lunch. While doing so, one of our party noticed particles of gold in the moss that was growing on the rocks. On the bar he washed a pan of that moss and got a prospect. After lunch we all prospected and got good pay dirt. We named the bar Hill's after the man who got the first prospect.[6]

The Hill's Bar strike was a rich one; it produced around two million dollars worth of gold. It also produced great excitement south of the border. In Puget Sound sailors jumped ship and workers deserted their mills to travel north. When the news reached California on April 3, miners, discouraged by their lack of success,

[6] Art Downs, *Wagon Road North*, 1960, p. 6.

either boarded ship for Victoria or trekked overland. The over-landers found the Indian warfare in the interior of Washington State a hazard, and so they altered their original plan of travelling up through the Okanogan and Okanagan to Kamloops and thence the Thompson River by the old Fur Trail, and travelled instead on newly cut trails to Fort Langley and Hope from Bellingham (then Whatcom), or took ship for the Fraser from Port Townsend or Victoria. The wave of humanity hit Victoria on April 22, 1858, and shortly afterwards the lower Fraser was a maelstrom of activity.

Nobody can be sure exactly which strike above the Fraser Canyon, in the region to be called Cariboo, set the miners moving in that direction. Dunleavy's strike on Horsefly has as good title as any. In May 1859 he and his party had reached the mouth of Chilcotin River where they were having as little success as Aaron Post, the first miner to reach the Chilcotin the previous year. A Shuswap Indian, Tomah, came upon them. The miners treated him with friendliness, giving him a meal and hot sweet tea, which he particularly enjoyed, accepting several full mugs. In return he told them that his friend Long Bacheese (Baptiste) would take them to a place where they could find bean-size nuggets, if he himself was unable to do so because of his work for the Hudson's Bay factor at Fort Alexander. He arranged to meet them in sixteen days at a lake called Lac La Hache which lay to the northeast; this was to be the site of the games which always took place before the Indians travelled to Kamloops with their furs. Tomah, it emerged, was the son of Chief LooLoo of Kamloops.

The party arrived on time, and after the games and the intertribal conference were over, Long Baptiste did indeed lead the Dunleavy party to Horsefly and there they did discover the nuggets as big as beans which had been promised. This is Alex McInnes' version of the meeting of Dunleavy and Long Baptiste. Captain Evans-Atkinson tells a different tale. According to him Long Baptiste was a Dené Indian six foot four inches tall, a giant of a man. He came to the attention of Dunleavy and his party at Kamloops, not Lac La Hache. The Dunleavy party had been led there by Tomah, who had met them as they were working hand-rockers on the Fraser River just above Pavilion in early 1858. Tomah had been a runner for the Hudson's Bay Company and knew some English and so was able to tell them that he knew where gold was to be found "as big as beans." He had showed his knowledge of gold by testing with a knife some coarse gold they had panned. He accompanied them to Kamloops

34

where they fitted themselves out for the expedition into the wilderness.

There were a good many prospectors in Kamloops at this time and also many of the hangers-on and parasites who always accompanied them. Two of these hangers-on were engaged in pressing rum upon two Indian girls when Long Baptiste came on the scene. He took the jar of rum from the men and smashed it on the ground, and told the girls to go back to their families. Then he deliberately turned his back upon the two men, who did not seem able to summon up the courage to start a fight with this formidable creature, and strode away. Dunleavy saw this incident and noticed that in Long Baptiste's hair attached to a leather thong was a gold nugget that had been hammered out into the shape of a ring and engraved. When they asked Long Baptiste about it he told them that the ring had belonged to his grandfather who had been killed by a grizzly at what is now known as Goose Creek on Cariboo Lake, which was his home territory. He did not know where the original nugget had come from. Being a Dené, however, he knew the area much better than Tomah, who was only familiar with the trail across country as far as Cedar Point at the outlet of Quesnel Lake, this trail being a very old and well known one running across country to the Fraser near Lac La Hache and then up to Horsefly by way of the McIntosh Lakes and so through Cedar Point to the Fraser at Fort Alexander and then through Chilcotin country right down to Bella Coola and the coast.

Tomah was left behind at Kamloops therefore and Long Baptiste led the Dunleavy party by way of the McIntosh Lakes into the river that was then called Wildwater but was later renamed Horsefly. The water was running high for it was still early in the year, but the party did some panning and found what is generally regarded as the first gold to be found by white men in Cariboo. Just as they were celebrating their find another party led by Neil Campbell that had left Kamloops twelve hours after them, arrived and gave them the news that there were hundreds more miners following. The rush was on.

Feeling that it would be wise to press on ahead, the Dunleavy party travelled on to the old Indian camping grounds at Cedar Point, an ancient way station on the trail. Here they spent some time. There was still some Solomon's Seal to be found there and Long Baptiste showed the party its value as a spring vegetable. He also dug up some of the small potatoes that miners later called the Goodwill Potato. These were very small, no bigger than a man's little finger in good ground, and about the size of peanut shells in gravel. These potatoes had been brought to the country by the Russian fur traders in the last years of the eighteenth century and given to the coastal Indians in trade. From the coast they had been brought inland. They were particularly valuable because they were impervious to frost and there was no need to peel them and they could not be overcooked. In later days they were often eaten raw by the miners in order to prevent scurvy. The Indians had planted some of these potatoes on the fringes of the camping ground and had let them multiply and run wild. Cedar Point would have been an ideal place to stay had it not been for the flies which were both numerous and voracious. Long Baptiste dealt with this by making a grease for the party to smear on their bodies, one of the ingredients being a fungus that appears only to be found on original growth cedar. He himself always greased his body, not only with this "fly dope" but also with other greases in which there was some skunk oil. This was a help in hunting, for the smell of the grease prevented the deer from catching the smell of man. He was an excellent hunter with bow and arrow and kept the party well supplied with fresh meat.

It was not long before other miners arrived along the trail from Kamloops. These were Spaniards, though it is not clear whether they had come out from Spain, or originated in California or Mexico. They reached Cedar Point at the same time as the Benjamin Mac-Donald Party which had travelled by way of the Fraser, Fort Alexander, and the Quesnel River. It was this group of Spaniards that staked and gave their name to Spanish Creek and Spanish Mountain. After a while the Dunleavy party moved on again.

The Dunleavy party was unusually fortunate in making friends with Tomah and Long Baptiste, for not all Indians were inclined to help the white men. Some, indeed, felt as much animosity as Chief Dehtus, and miners below the Fraser Canyon had been much disturbed during the previous year by the number of arrow-pierced corpses that had floated down the river. They were fortunate, also, in having good guides, for the country above the Fraser Canyon was a wilderness of forest, lake and swamp, and there were few trails.

It is difficult even to imagine now the difficulties faced by those venturers into the unknown. The trails to the lower Fraser and the Thompson diggings were rough enough, but those to the Upper Fraser were much more difficult. Some prospectors from America travelled up to Kamloops by way of the old Hudson Bay trail through the Okanagan and thence along another fur trail to Fort Alexander, but a great many, already working the bars of the lower Fraser, attempted the Canyon itself. One of these was Edward ("Ned") Stout, who, in company of twenty others in the summer of 1858 was attacked by Indians between Hell's Gate and Boston Bar. For a whole day they fought and then that night on China Bar tried to build some kind of fortification. It was not particularly effective. Dawn brought another onslaught with bow and gun. By the time a group of 200 other well-armed miners arrived to lift the siege sixteen men were dead and the remainder were all badly wounded, Ned Stout himself having been wounded in seven places.

Though this was the last big Indian battle on the Fraser there were a good many other incidents of the kind during the next twelve months. One anonymous miner quoted by F. W. Lindsay in *The Cariboo Story*, wrote:

In 1859 I was washing gravel with a rocker 20 miles above Yale. There was some fine gold but not a lot of it. This day I heard the report of a gun and saw a bullet hole in my rocker. I looked around to see where the noise came from and saw an Indian standing on a big rock across the river loading his musket. There was no place I could hide because I was out on a bar and my gun was up on the bank and I was very frightened as I thought I would be shot at any moment. Then I heard another shot and the Indian disappeared off the rock and into the swift water of the Fraser River. I had been very lucky, there was a party of white men working on the same side as the Indian and when they heard him shoot they watched and saw him aim his gun at me and they shot him before he could pull the trigger again. I left that bar that same day and I never mined alone on the Fraser River after that as it was very dangerous since the Indians were not friendly to white men.[7]

Much of the Indians' unfriendliness seems to have been caused by the belief of many newly arrived Californians that the only good Indian was a dead one. There were rough customers among those who came to the Lower Fraser in 1858. Indeed the group that settled round Hill's Bar included a gang who had been expelled from California by vigilantes. Their leader was Ned McGowan, and he and his partner John Bagley, a sometime politician in San Francisco, siezed the opportunity of a quarrel between the two resident magistrates to take over the newly swollen town of Yale. It was probably the McGowan rule of terrorism that caused the miners to form the secret protection society, the Lowhee Society of which Richard Willoughby (who later called his creek Lowhee Creek) was one of the founders. It certainly caused Governor Douglas, in Victoria, to think even more seriously about the problem of bringing law to the goldfields.

Not all the miners on the lower Fraser took the route of the unlucky

[7] F. W. Lindsay, *The Cariboo Story*, 1958, p. 21.

Ned Stout. Some journeyed up the river to Hope, climbed the Coquahalla, crossed Manson's Mountain to the Hudson's Bay headquarters for the Similkameen area, and then travelled north by way of Campement des Femmes to Nicola Lake and Kamloops. Some started from Yale and travelled to Spuzzum and Chapmans Bar (Keque-loose), and then over a 2000 foot height to Anderson's River which they followed to its source before reaching the Coldwater River and trudging across the Nicola region to Kamloops. The first of these trails was still in use by the Hudson's Bay fur brigade; the second had been abandoned; both were difficult.

There were, indeed, no easy trails to the upper Fraser, and there was not a single one that was good enough to enable supplies to be freighted to the growing company of the miners around Fort Alexander. Some miners attempted to bypass the Fraser Canyon by travelling along a route discovered by A. C. Anderson in 1846. This was partly a water route and partly a land one. The adventurers paddled their loaded canoes the length of Harrison Lake, to a point that became known as Port Douglas, and then fought their way along the Harrison River to Lillooet Lake, being obliged by the overgrown state of the river to wade up to their waists most of the way, towing their canoes behind them. After paddling the length of Lillooet Lake they portaged the canoes overland to Anderson and Seton lakes which took them to Lillooet, and to a hazardous trail over mountains to the banks of the upper Fraser. Sir James Douglas, in an attempt to ease the prospectors' passage through the "Harrison Jungle," sent the steamboat *Umtilla* on a trial voyage of Harrison Lake. It set out on July 25, 1859. On its next voyage it was filled with miners eager to co-operate with Douglas in cutting a trail to the Fraser by this route. Each miner paid $25 to Douglas as a kind of security or, as one miner put it, "in proof that I would not quit and would work." Douglas, in turn, promised free provisions, and when the road was completed, to repay the $25 in the form of provisions at the prices then current in Victoria. He also promised mules, which did not arrive; the road builders worked twelve to fourteen hours a day in hot, swampy, overgrown, and mosquito-ridden country, and it says much for their determination that by October 1859 the trail was almost completed.

Because of the Harrison Trail 1859 must be reckoned the year when it first became possible for Cariboo to be reached by mule trains from the lower Fraser. Once Lillooet had been reached, however, the journey had only just begun. There were two possible routes north from there. One which had been used by the Hudson's Bay trappers and carriers led along the west bank of the Fraser to Express Bay and then by way of Big Bar to Canoe Creek, so called because it was there that the Shuswap Indians on the east bank of the river ferried travellers across in their canoes. The Chilcotin Indians on the west bank lived farther away from the river. From Canoe Creek the route left the river and went inland following the trails between the various Indian villages and crossed the Dog Creek valley some ten miles from its mouth. There are two alternative explanations for the name Dog Creek. One is that it was so named by the travellers who were always greeted by the barking of a multitude of the Indians' dogs. Another is that it was named after a famous old warrior chief called Skaha, which means dog. From here the trail led in a fairly straight line to Alkali Lake and then through Springhouse and across Chimney Creek back to the east bank of the Fraser and on to Soda Creek. From there it led to Fort Alexander and joined the ancient trail that led through Beaver Valley to Quesnel Forks. A map of 1862 which calls this trail the Fraser River Trail disagrees in part with this account, showing the trail as going by way of Williams Lake and up through Davison's where it made a junction with another trail down to Fort Alexander, and then on to Quesnel Forks without ever touching the river.

Another trail took the east bank of the river from Lillooet to Fountain Creek and then cut over Pavillion Mountain to Jolie Prairie after which it proceeded by way of Green Lake, Lac La Hache, and Williams Lake to Davison's and then either down to Fort Alexander by way of Mud Lake (now called McLeese Lake) and thence up the Beaver Valley trail to Quesnel Forks or direct to Beaver Lake and so onwards. This was called in 1862 the Brigade Trail. There were also a number of variations on this pattern for a number of trails led from the Fraser to join the Brigade Trail. There was also a Thompson River Trail which started from Lytton, followed the Thompson to the western end of Kamloops Lake and then turned north and reached Green Lake, where it joined the Brigade Trail. This route was the one used by travellers who chose to get to the goldfields by coming up the Okanagan Valley and then heading west to Fort Kamloops.

The trail that turned out to be of most importance as the basis for a more permanent road was the Brigade Trail, at least as far as Fort Alexander. These trails were hazardous, and all circuitous. As one looks at the map one sometimes wonders why so many of them appear to proceed in a zig-zag fashion. The reasons are twofold. Firstly it was

39

necessary to avoid obstacles difficult to surmount and secondly it was vital to take a trail that led by way of lakes and valleys which could provide fish and game and good pasture for the pack animals. The trails were all, however, ferociously difficult. Lieutenant H. S. Palmer of the Royal Engineers who surveyed the trail from Port Douglas to Lillooet in order to determine how to turn it into a wagon road, wrote of the trails to the Cariboo in general:

It is difficult to find language to express in adequate terms the utter vileness of the trails of Cariboo, dreaded alike by all classes of travellers; slippery, precipitous ascents and descents, fallen logs, overhanging branches, roots, rocks, swamps, turbid pools and miles of deep mud.[8]

One of the miners, W. Champness, quoted by Art Downs in his *Wagon Road North*, described the journey thus:

Our route from Lillouet lay across the mountains to the Fraser River valley, near Lytton; thence up the wild and awful ravines in the district of the Thompson River, passing Loon Lake, and thence north, near Green and Axe Lakes to Williams Lake. This portion of our journey, being a distance of nearly 200 miles, occupied sixteen days, Sundays not included, as we were truly glad of a Sabbath rest.

Some portions of our route lay across mountain ranges from whose summits we enjoyed most magnificient views, and down whose steep pine-forested sides we had to lead our horses singly, and with the utmost care.

In other parts of the journey, especially in the river gorges, our track conducted us along the most frightful precipices. There was no help for this, as we could select no route more passable. The rivers flow oftimes through dark and awful gorges whose rocky sides tower perpendicularly from a thousand to fifteen hundred feet. By a series of zig-zag paths, often but a yard in width, man and beast have to traverse these scenes of grandeur. Sad and fatal accidents often occur, and horses and their owners are dashed to pieces on the rocks below, or drowned in the deep foaming waters rushing down the narrow defiles from the vast regions of mountain snow melting in the summer heat.

At Deep Creek, 10 miles from Williams Lake, seven of our comrades relinquished all further attempt to reach their proposed destination, being utterly discouraged by the excessive difficulties of the way and the unvarying tale of discouragement told by the parties of returning and unsuccessful miners. Truly, the numbers of these poor, broken-down fellows with their pale, pinched faces and tattered rags, eloquent of hunger and poverty, were enough to dishearten us altogether. Hundreds of such passed us during our journey in parties of from two to a score. Sorely tempted as we were to yield to despair, yet some of us were resolved to brave out to the end.

We thought we had now reached the lowest possible depth of difficulty, but not so, for after miles of deep mud and swamp we came to a region

[8] Quoted in Art Downs, *Wagon Road North*, 1960, p. 23.

where, for an extent of many miles, the earth was covered with innumerable thousands of dead and fallen trees, lying across each other in inextricable confusion and in every conceivable position. We were necessitated to travel over these fallen trees, stepping from trunk to trunk for a distance of ten miles. As may be supposed, this rendered us intensely fatigued and leg-weary, for it was, throughout, a series of acrobatic performances. Often we slipped between the fallen trunks and were nearly lost to view, having sunk two feet in a thick black swamp. Whenever one of us became thus 'bogged' he had to call for help, and was drawn out bodily by his comrades from his unpleasant position.[9]

In spite of these difficulties the prospectors continued to travel north, some of them no doubt persuaded by Kinahan Cornwallis' prophetic book of 1858, *The New Eldorado or British Columbia* published in London. As the name British Columbia for the new colony had only received royal assent on August 2 he must have published the book late in the year. It is astonishing to note that almost all the areas that he marked as "Supposed Gold Regions" on his map were subsequently found to be rich in gold. By this time Governor Douglas had become concerned at the number of Americans travelling to the goldfield and returning to America with their wealth without spending any of it in the colony. He therefore began work on a road from Hope to Dewdney which would divert the Americans, both coming and going, towards the Fraser valley, and he began turning the Harrison Trail into a more efficient transport system, the lakes being linked to each other by means of a road built by the Royal Engineers. By the end of 1860 navigation on the Harrison River had been improved and 28 miles of a wagon road from Port Douglas onwards had been completed. Steamer services were established on the lakes. The *Lady of the Lake* plied Lake Lillooet, the *Marzelle* Anderson Lake and the *Champion* Seton Lake. In 1861 Gustavus Blin Wright built a road from Lillooet that crossed a 4000 foot mountain and descended to a place known first as Cut-Off Valley or 47 Mile House because it was 47 miles from Lillooet, and renamed Clinton in 1863 to honour the then Colonial Secretary, Henry Pelham Clinton, the Fifth Duke of Newcastle.

By this time miners were pouring into the Cariboo by the thousand. Four out of every five of them were Americans, but there were also Australians, Welshmen, and some Cornishmen who were easily the most efficient workers, for they were familiar with tin mining and with the problems of recovering "stream tin" which is like gold in being alluvial, as well as with the techniques of sinking

[9] *Ibid.*, p. 22.

41

shafts in places threatened by water, and of making and timbering adits. Quite a number of these miners were also sailors. Of the early arrivals at Cedar Point, Jack Edwards, Jim Sellers and Neil Campbell were sailors. So was Billy Barker who arrived later and after whom Barkerville was named. These men were not technically "deserters" from their ships (the punishment for desertion was then death) but A.W.O.L. (Absent Without Leave). There was almost no way in which they could be caught, but if they were they were able to prove that they were only A.W.O.L. by showing that they still retained some article of issued clothing or equipment. This was acceptable as proof that they had intended eventually to return. These articles did not have to be carried about with them or worn; it was sufficient if they kept them in their cabins or among their gear though Billy Barker chose always to wear his sailor's belt. Sailors who were returned forcibly either to Navy or Merchant Navy ships and who produced this evidence together with a tale of having been drunk, or in an accident, were usually only punished with a few days confinement. It was rare, however, for this to occur. The authorities were not particularly keen on sending people out to look for absent seamen in Cariboo. The journey was much too hard to be worth the effort. One miner, Radcliffe Quine, wrote home on April 22, 1861

> I tell you it is a hard road to travel. You have to carry your own blankets and food for over three hundred miles and take to the soft side of the road for your lodgings and at daylight get up and shake the dust off your blankets and cook your own food for the day and take the road again. When you get in the mines you have to pay up to a dollar a pound for everything you eat as it has to be carried with mules and horses on their backs with a pack saddle.[10]

"A dollar a pound for everything you eat" is an understatement. Records show that at this peiod in the Williams Creek area potatoes were $1.15 a pound and flour $2.00, while butter was $5.00. One ingenious miner, Ned Owens, not having money to buy nails at $1.00 each, walked through the night from Goose Creek to Quesnel Forks 30 miles away and "liberated" a hundred nails that seemed not to be absolutely necessary to the efficient working of a number of sluice boxes, and then walked back again to make similar equipment and, together with his partner, take $16,000 out of the creek.

Mining, even the simplest kind of placer mining, needs equipment and the experienced miners travelling the Cariboo trails did not only carry blankets and food but also picks, shovels, gold pans, axes, pry-

10 *Ibid.*, p. 23.

42

bars (or crow-bars), and two sizes of auger as well as, inevitably, gold pokes and scales. The gold pokes were made of soft buck-skin, (for gold dust will leak through cloth) and in later years were often embroidered for the miners by Indian girls.

Way stations and small trading posts sprang up quite soon along the trail. Mules had to be watered every ten miles or so and men preferred sleeping under a log roof to sleeping on the earth. Franklin (Frank) Way, an American, after working on the river bars between Hope and Yale in 1858, gave up goldseeking and moved to the mouth of the Spuzzum River where he established a store and small hotel. He also constructed a ferry system across the river by stretching a rope across the canyon and linking a boat to it by means of a block and tackle. This business thrived, but in 1863 J. W. Trutch, with Halliday and Company of San Francisco as his contractors, built a suspension bridge two miles above Spuzzum. It opened in September 1863, having cost $45,000, and Frank Way, abandoning his now outmoded ferry, left Spuzzum and moved north, setting up another stopping place at Deep Creek, ten miles from Williams Lake and 164 from Lillooett. Thus various "mile houses" came into being, each mile house being given a number stating its distance from Lillooet. The term "mile house" was caused by Gus Wright placing a post to mark the completion of each mile along the Lillooet-Clinton Road, as he did also on the other roads he laid. Some mile houses are, however, numbered according to their distance from Yale on the second Cariboo road, and some are numbered from Ashcroft where the railhead met a new road some years later.

Before the gold rush began Clinton already had the beginnings of a settlement. Indians had made their keek-willi holes on a hill just south of the present town, and two fur traders, the Watson brothers, decided that this would be a good place to set up house. Jean Caux, a Catalonian known to everyone as Cataline, who was a packer for the Hudson's Bay Company fur brigade, and who later took his train of 16 to 48 mules along the Cariboo trail, had a way-station two miles away, so the brothers were not wholly isolated. When the Lillooet-Clinton road was completed they found that they had so many visitors that they needed a bigger house, and when two years later, they were told that a new road through the canyon would join the first road at the 47 mile post, they decided to build a hotel. They had just started work on this when Joe Smith and his wife and Tom Marshall, who had run a hotel at Port Douglas during the Fraser River rush, arrived looking for a new place for business. They bought the Watson's old house, completed the new one, and on New Years Day, 1861, the 47 Mile House opened for business and a town had begun.

Meanwhile, three hundred miles to the north, other and more ephemeral settlements were being created. At first the miners were finding satisfactory amounts of gold on the Fraser bars, on the shores of Quesnel and Cariboo Lakes, and in the Horsefly area, but no one had achieved a truly dramatic strike. The route to Horsefly by way of Lac La Hache did not attract many prospectors; they preferred to work the muddy Fraser above Fort Alexander, but the results were as disappointing as those now experienced on the lower Fraser where the bars had been largely worked out. Then, in May 1859 Benjamin MacDonald, a Prince Edward Islander, left Fort Alexander and paddled up river into the mouth of the Quesnel. On June 3 he panned the first gold, thus vying with Dunleavy for the title of the first man to strike gold in Cariboo. The following spring the disillusioned workers on the lower Fraser made their way up to the new fields, leaving the Hope-Lytton area to the horde of Chinese who, that spring, repopulated the area and, working with more patience than their predecessors on bars considered to be worked out and on abandoned piles of tailings, found much gold.

Fort Alexander was at first the main supply centre for the new fields. While a great many miners fought their way up the canyon, the mule trains travelled the Harrison trail and brought the necessary supplies to the fort. In 1860 Fort Alexander boasted a post office and several stores and saloons. The fort itself being on the west bank of the wide Fraser, however, was not an ideal way station for people whose way lay along the eastern bank. Consequently a settlement called Alexandria sprang up on the other side of the river, and it was not long before the fort itself was renamed Alexandria by A. G. Young, the Colonial Secretary. Gustavus Blin Wright's map of around 1861 shows Fort Alexander only. One map of 1865 shows Fort Alexander and Alexandria, and another gives the one name Fort Alexandria. However named, Fort Alexander-Alexandria did not remain an important way station or become an important centre of activity, for there was no gold there; the new centre was at Quesnel Forks where the two branches of the river joined, and a town was built in a ten acre clearing on the flat area separating the two branches of the river. In 1860 it had ten or a dozen stores, several boarding houses and liquor shops, and about twenty houses as well as a multitude of tents. In 1861 the government building, containing two jail cells, was erected.

By that time Fort Alexander had lost all its pretensions; it is said that, apart from the factor, two men only remained, T. La Roque and Charles Train. This pattern of sudden growth and sudden failure remained typical of Cariboo settlements for many years.

Quesnel Forks provided good "pay" but the miners were restless, and, in search of gold even closer to its source, and therefore coarser, less worn down by the river currents, made their way up the north branch of the river. Beaver Lake, to the southwest, was now an important stopping place for the pack trains who preferred the trail to the goldfields from Mud Lake to Beaver Lake to the old fur trail. There in 1861 Peter Dunleavy and Jim Sellers, with Moffat and Manifee to help them, opened a store, as did J. Deshields, having come to the conclusion that the needs of the miners could be exploited more profitably and safely than the mines themselves. Beaver Lake soon became a thriving trading centre, especially for the sale of pack animals, one of which might fetch as much as $300. Francois Guy (some say Frank Way) for example sold 58 mules and 4 horses there on September 1, 1861 for $14,000.

The whole area was now a whirl of activity. While Quesnel Forks was still in the building W. R. "Doc" Keithley and his partner J. P. Diller (some say George Weaver) found gold on a bluff above a creek running into Cariboo Lake. They built a chute to the creek itself to carry the dirt and washed it there in a rocker, but, while the results were good they were not outstanding enough to hold them there. It was a year later that the old bed of the creek and the richest gold was found. Nevertheless a horde of miners descended on the creek they had called Keithley and on Harvey Creek a little distance away, and in October 1860 there were already many houses, and gambling saloons were in full swing. By July 1861 F. Black and W. Carlyle's store at Keithley was doing a land office business and the settlement had become known as Black's Store, though some optimists wanted to call it, grandiosely, Cariboo City.

Even as the miners on the banks of the Quesnel were abandoning their new city and their now uninteresting diggings to the patient thousands of following Chinese, and making Cariboo City the new centre, the city's founder had moved on to another strike on Swamp River. He did not remain there long. In the fall of 1860 Doc Keithley, with George Weaver and John Rose and that Ben MacDonand who had first struck gold on the Quesnel River, each carrying 60 pounds of provisions and equipment, set out to prospect higher up Keithley Creek, through the narrow ravine where they found a new creek.

45

They made their way in the cold autumn weather up this creek for seven miles to its source and for the first time saw what was to become the heart of Cariboo. They were standing on the plateau which provided the waters of Cariboo Lake, and fathered the gold-bearing currents of Keithley Creek, Swamp River, and the Quesnel River itself. Moreover they saw that from the far side of the plateau other, and possibly richer creeks descended into unknown valleys. They crossed the plateau and clambered down one of these creeks, fighting their way through tangled brush, negotiating rock slides, and precipices. They settled at last by one particular creek which ran through a narrow canyon and began to pan. On either side of the creek there was gold. Some of it was even in plain view, lying on the exposed bedrock beside the torrent. Long exposed to the air, it had grown rust-coloured from oxidization of the iron in it; they called it "sunburn gold." One pan yielded $75 and another $100. It looked like a bonanza. This is one version of the discovery of Antler, which was thus named because there were a surprising number of shed antlers beside the creek. Another version states that John Rose, who had been grubstaked by Dunleavy who was then on Keithley Creek, made the discovery together with a companion. Rose was an educated, well-spoken American from Ohio. His companion's name is not known, but Mark S. Wade in his book, *The Cariboo Road,* tells us that he was killed by Indians on Bear Creek in 1862. He also gives the figure of $114 for the value of the first gold panned at Antler.

Whoever the discoverers were, it is generally agreed that they made a campsite and, undeterred by the first light fall of snow that the dawn revealed, continued to prospect and to stake claims. They built a cabin and worked hard. When it became necessary to travel back to Keithley for new supplies they did so by another route, travelling due south across flat land half a mile from their Discovery Rock to MacMartin Creek (where MacMartin himself was working), down MacMartin River and then up Swift River. It was a journey of fourteen miles, and the snow was now lying five or six feet deep. In Keithley their secret soon became known and that winter the miners deserted their Cariboo City for what was to be called Antler Creek, some taking the route over the top, and giving the creek and the plateau the name Snowshoe, and some travelling by the river route. The newcomers had no cabins made against the winter and at first they lived in holes cut into the deep snow drifts on the banks of the creek. In the spring of 1861 there were 1200 miners at work on the creek. Miners combined forces in small companies to work the

46

claims. By this time houses, cabins and stores had been built, though many, having been erected over existing claims, had later to be torn down. There was immense confusion. Some claims overlapped or coincided. Wrangles were numerous. In May 1861 the flat land below Discovery Rock was used by R. P. Baylor for a sawmill and called Sawmill Flat. In July 1861 Antler had sixty houses, and boasted luxuries hardly to be found elsewhere in Cariboo. Champagne was sold at $12 a bottle, and theatrical troupes such as Watson and Taylor's Minstrels were performing regularly. Antler was now so assured of its own prosperity that a group of suddenly rich miners decided it needed a race course. Several racehorses were ordered from England and arrived in Victoria in 1861. On the coast some thought it might be better to have a racetrack there, at Hastings, but they foresaw difficulties in getting the agreement of the owners, so the racehorses were taken up the Cariboo trail and a four-furlong course was laid out straight, edged with stones that were removed to clear the track. A thirty by forty foot "Casino" was built at one end. The date of the first race meeting is unknown but in later years the races were held between the first of July and Labour Day. Fred W. Ludditt believes that it was a visit by Sir James Douglas to one of these early meetings that so impressed him with the wealth of the Cariboo that he began his plans for the great Cariboo Road.

Antler certainly must have been impressive in several respects. "Argus," the correspondent for the *Victoria Colonist*, wrote on August 17, 1861, "Robberies are not infrequent in Antler. Recently $130 in gold dust and two pistols were taken from Cameron's Golden Age Saloon. A slight stabbing affair is also noted." Two days later he reported, "A band of minstrels performs here two or three times a week and together with the exciting recreations of bucking at *monte moule* and draw poker, tend to enliven us not a little. Money has lost its value in the mines, and a twenty dollar gold piece is looked upon much in the same way that a two-and-a-half would be in Victoria. It is an exhilarating sight to see natty pyramids of American double eagles changing hands in the saloons and impresses us with the idea that the country is safe and not played out." On September 19 the *Colonist* was of the opinion that Antler "bids fair to become the largest mining town in the sister Colony, and contains ten saloons, seven general stores, two blacksmith shops, a sawmill, a shoemaker and a butcher shop." On October 28 the report was of "the sporting fraternity" buying a house to turn into a hospital. Prices were high, of course. A box of matches cost $5 and flour was sold at over a dollar a pound. In the map of the Gold Regions of British Columbia of 1862 Antler and Quesnel are the only two mining settlements named in this area of Cariboo.

Antler did not last long. By the end of 1862, just as it had superseded Keithley, it was itself superseded by the discovery of Great Lowhee Creek by Richard Willoughby, H. Tilton, and the Patterson brothers who had struck it rich there in the summer of 1861.

The Willoughby story is typical of Cariboo. Richard Willoughby was born in Boone County, Mo. in May 1833, the son of an Indian-fighter and scout. When only eleven years old he took part in the Indian wars alongside his father, and in his teens he fought with the Texans against marauding Mexicans and Apaches along the Rio Grande. In 1852 he travelled the 2000 miles from Missouri to California as the leader of a 400 person wagon train, and made a small fortune mining gold in Hangtown. He spent the next few years prospecting and mining in Arizona and New Mexico but could find few companions in his work as the Indians were in a state of ferment and many miners were being killed. He returned to Missouri, but could not rest there, and so he led another wagon train back to California where he continued gold mining until 1858 when the rumours of the rich strikes of the Fraser reached him. As the only ship leaving San Francisco for Victoria was already fully booked he organized a band of twenty miners, provided them with pack and saddle horses from the proceeds of selling his mine, and on March 15, 1858 the party set out for the Fraser.

Willoughby's adventures on the journey were numerous. The party was ambushed by Indians on the Rogue River, and one miner was killed before Willoughby shot the chief of the marauders and the band scattered. Two days later there was another battle, and again the Indians were driven off. At Portland many miners were planning to travel north by way of Walla Walla and the Columbia River. At Walla Walla, however, the general in charge of the military, General Steptoe, forbade further travel as the Okanogan Indians under their chief, Tenasket, were on the warpath. Willoughby persuaded the general to let him go on with a small army of a hundred volunteer miners, and with this band he defeated Tenasket, and the adventurers at last reached Lake Okanagan. After a brief rest Willoughby and his party began prospecting at Hat Creek and in Marble Canyon after which they decided to descend the Fraser by raft. When the raft reached Hell's Gate Willoughby preferred to travel overland, but the others chose to run the rapids and many of them were drowned. At long last Willoughby reached the lower Fraser and took $20,000 out of Emory's Bar near Yale, and then lost all of it by a bad investment in another claim. He prospected all over the country after that, and found gold on both Ruby Creek and Silver Creek, but when, in 1861, he arrived in Cariboo he was almost penniless.

He found some gold on Quesnel River, and more on Keithley Creek, but when he started prospecting Burns Creek he had to rely on the storekeeper to give him his supplies on credit. He was almost at the end of his tether in July 1861, and then his luck changed. One day towards the end of the month he came into the Burns Creek store with enough nuggets to pay all his debts and to buy new supplies. He told the storekeeper it was Williams Creek gold, (Williams Creek having been discovered earlier that year) but the nuggets were quite different from those found in that creek and the storekeeper knew he was being teased. Willoughby hung around the store until evening and then set off back to his claim, followed, as he knew he would be, by many inquisitive and hopeful miners. After a while he stopped and waited for those following him to catch up. "Is everybody here?" he asked the late arrivals. "Not yet" he was told. "They are strung out over a mile or more." Willoughby waited patiently until everyone had arrived, and then said "Boy's, this is it! I'm standing on my claim. You can begin staking." Willoughby christened the creek on which he had staked his claim Lowhee Creek, after the society of miners to which he had belonged in Yale. He called his mine the Discovery Claim, and between July 27 and September 8 he took out 3037 ounces of gold. Before it was played out Lowhee Creek, which was no more than two miles in length, yielded almost three million dollars worth of gold.

In this fashion the miners moved across the country, from creek to creek, pursuing rumour and dream. As they shifted the towns rose and fell, each having its heyday of stores, saloons, and theatrical performances. When the miners moved on, so did the tradesmen, setting up new stores in new places. As the white miners left, the Chinese followed after, taking out more gold from the discarded workings, sifting over the huge banks of tailings. Buildings were torn down, either to prospect the land on which they stood, or for fire-wood. New way-stations opened upon the new trails, and then crumbled when the trails were abandoned. A shifting population of many thousands moved all over the area, supplied by the package trains still labouring up the primitive trail from Clinton but carrying now not only basic supplies, but also some luxuries which the luckier miners and merchants could well afford.

It is difficult for us today fully to appreciate the life of the goldfields in those days before the great Cariboo Road brought a few of the amenities we commonly think of as essential to anything approaching civilization. Popular fiction, and most history books, skate over those details which bring the picture to life, telling us curtly that "they built cabins" or that "they struck gold" and allowing us to imagine that building a cabin was as easy and painless as constructing a pre-fabricated dog kennel and that digging for gold was not unlike digging a potato patch or collecting pebbles. The facts are a little different.

Firstly the nature of the gold deposits must be understood. Gold is soft by comparison with other minerals and when the mountain ranges were first formed it was squeezed like toothpaste by the earth's movement into ribbons of varying thickness and pushed into crevices, so that it lay in long threads or "lodes" within the mountains. Gold is also heavier than other minerals so that when the huge glaciers of the ice-age began to melt and to carve out the riverbeds, scouring some valleys right down to bedrock, and in other places piling up mountains of rubble, the gold that it tore from the mountainsides, or that had already been liberated by the effects of wind and weather sank to the bottom of the moving waters, some of it to be covered by the settling clay, some by rocks, and some to be rolled down the creeks and rivers, the big lumps or "nuggets" becoming smaller as they were broken up, worn down, and ground by the rocks that tumbled with them in the torrent. Some nuggets, rolling along the river bottom, lodged behind boulders or stuck in crevices; some were deposited among the gravel piled up at bends in the river; some continued downstream for hundreds of miles and were broken down into flakes or even dust. When a river or creek changed course the gold was often left behind in the old channel and, as time went on, and the new channel was carved deeper than the first, this gold remained in the benches alongside the creek, in the river bank, or, if the creek's or river's diversion had been caused suddenly by earthquake or land-slide, some distance away from the water.

The prospector would first of all try to find bedrock beside a creek, and there he would gather gravel and sand and swirl the mixture around in the pan so that the gold settled to the bottom; carefully he picked out the bigger stones until only a kind of black sandy silt remained. This black sand is almost always present where there is

50

gold "in place," (or "placer gold," as it is called); it is made of magnetite and a magnet can be used to separate it from the gold flakes and dust it contains and partially conceals. This method of prospecting is fine for testing a prospect, but impractical for working a claim completely. Therefore the man who had staked his claim would use a "rocker" or "dolly." This is a wooden construction into which the gravel is placed together with water; it is then rocked by means of a handle and this sends the heavy metals and objects to the bottom of a tray which is perforated with holes so that the nuggets (if any) can fall through together with the sand and gold flakes and dust; the black sand and dust is trapped in a screen or blanket, the hairs of the blanket catching the "invisible gold" and the small pebbles are forced by the water along a sloping wooden tray which has projections or "riffles" that trap the heavy gold but let the water roll the lighter material onwards and out of the contraption. The nuggets are picked out by hand and then the sand in the blanket riffle is washed in a pan.

The hand-operated rocker can do a lot of work, but not as much as one operated by the force of water itself. Larger and more elaborate "sluice boxes" were therefore made and powered by the water flow, at first by means of diverting water along wooden flumes to a point above the sluice box and later by using Cornish water wheels to raise the water up from the creeks by which they were powered.

Neither of these devices were of much use if the gold bearing gravels and clays could not be found, however. Indeed those claims which could be exploited entirely by rocker and small sluice box were called "poor man's diggings" because even a poor man working by himself could make a profit out of them. The supply of poor man's diggings ran out quickly on most creeks and then more equipment and more labour were needed to search for whatever other gold there might be. Some gold might be found in the benches beside the creek or in an old channel now buried in the bank; miners would therefore cut tunnels or "adits" into the banks; this process was called "drifting." Other gold might be found deeper down, in or below the clay level on which the first gold had been found; this clearly meant digging straight down until one found gold in the clay or on the bedrock beneath it. Again more men and more equipment were needed, especially as these diggings were usually subject to water-seepage and continual pumping was needed to keep them dry. Sometimes, as in the Lightning Creek area, the mines were flooded, not with water, but with a thick liquid mud called "slum" which could not be pumped out and which defeated many miners completely.

When it was thought that there might be gold actually in the bed of a stream dams were made to divert the water into another channel; they were called wingdams; this was a favourite method of the Chinese miners. Another way of getting at the bedrock beneath a pile of rubble was to wash the rubble away by lifting water, by means of wheels, to a great height and then releasing it through pipes at such high pressure that the water would wash away the "overburden"; some mines were blasted out of the side of the creeks or the flanks of mountains by this "hydraulic mining."

The early miners did not use Cornish wheels, or any other kinds of wheel; they had not, and could not make, the equipment. They used all the other methods, however, stripping the mountainsides of trees to make their dams, their flumes, and their beams and pit-props for their mines, and logs for their cabins. The amount of lumber needed was incredible. Early photographs of Williams Creek show mountain sides entirely bare of trees, and a wide area of stone and rubble through which a small stream meanders muddily and weakly. The whole landscape has been devastated.

The earliest miners had only axes, adzes, and augers with which to build their cabins and their sluice boxes. They had no nails, and so dowel pins were whittled to fit in the holes made by the augers. The sluice boxes and rockers were first made with wood split by axe; later, sawn timber was used, logs being laid across a pit and sawn length-wise, one man in the pit below on one end of the saw, choking from sawdust, and the other above sawing from above in a cloud of mosquito and black fly. This "whipsawing" was one of the miners' least popular chores.

The vast majority of miners were, and remained, poor. Many died of accidents and sickness and malnutrition, though almost all of them were young strong men, few older than thirty-five and many not yet twenty-one, when they reached the diggings. Even those who struck it rich did not always live long to enjoy their wealth; some squandered it, dazzled by the possibilities of their sudden riches; some, worn out by their exertions, racked by rheumatism, died young. Those journeying up to the goldfields met a steady stream of disillusioned, ragged, and sick adventurers, all of whom advised them to turn back. A few did turn back, or stopped along the trail and turned their hands to store or hotel keeping; some turned to farming, raising hay for the passing animals, or raising cattle. The hopes of the majority, however, were still high. A new wagon road was on the way, and this would mean an easier life, more provisions, lower prices. Stories of rich strikes circulated rapidly round the camps and bolstered everyone's hopes. They also circulated abroad and the reports in the London and Californian papers and in the *British Colonist* in Victoria convinced many to attempt the adventure, and the imagination of the world seized upon the notion of a new Eldorado and would not be deprived of the dream. Thousands of miners, too, kept the faith, believing always that the next prospect would prove to be the bonanza they sought, moving on from digging to digging, from creek to creek, aiming to be the discoverer of the richest and most famous claim of all. Such a man was William "Dutch Bill" Dietz, a Prussian miner from California who had so far had only a little luck with his diggings and less with the Indians who had stolen his supplies at Lillooet when he first began the journey to Cariboo and forced him to return to Yale. In the spring of 1860 he set off again and early in February 1861 began the journey from Quesnel Forks that was to change the face of Cariboo and the whole of British Columbia.

CHAPTER THREE

Williams Creek 1861-1863

Antler was still booming and Keithley had scarcely begun to decay while Lowhee Creek was still to be discovered, when Dutch Bill made his discovery. The manner in which he made it is open to dispute, for there are several versions. Some say that he was staying *with one companion* at Maloney's Flat halfway between Antler and Keithley *on the river trail* when he decided to explore to the north. After wandering around for some time in the bush he tripped over a rock and literally fell upon a creek and immediately found gold. He didn't stake a claim at this time but went back to Keithley where he spent a couple of days drinking and talking and letting fall little hints. The result was that when he and his partner set out for Maloney's Flat again early one morning a great many other miners followed him. Dutch Bill threw off his pursuers before nightfall, but in the morning they saw his campfire, and made tracks towards it. Dutch Bill had still not staked out a claim, and was somewhat upset by the invasion. The newcomers, however, told him to eat his breakfast and that they would wait to stake their claims until he was finished. Some say that Dutch Bill's companion was Ned Stout.

Another version describes how Dutch Bill and *two companions* in February 1861, the snow on the ground, left Quesnel Forks for Keithley Creek and then went *over the divide* towards Antler where they found a creek which they decided to investigate. For various reasons this seems the more likely of the two versions, though the first one has charm to recommend it, and it is hard to give up that splendid picture of Dutch Bill at breakfast surprised by the unwelcome visitors.

There is, however, a third version, in which Dutch Bill was one of the several miners who, on arriving at Antler Creek, found there were no claims left to be staked and decided to travel farther up the creek.

They passed Discovery Rock and trudged up higher, passing a small stream later called Racetrack Creek, and turned right up the side of a mountain onto a broad treeless plateau. They called the place Bald Mountain Plateau. Dutch Bill had two companions, and others in the various parties were Vital LaForce, Michael Burns, Ned Stout and Michael Costin Brown. When Ned Stout got to the edge of the plateau it was almost dark, but they could just glimpse a creek far away below them, and then, as night fell, a campfire in the same area.

This brings us to the actual discovery on which, mercifully, all the authorities largely agree. The *Victoria Chronicle* of 5 November 1863 tells it this way:

On the following morning they (Dutch Bill and his two companions) eagerly commenced to prospect. They found prospects on the northwest side of the creek varying from ten to thirty cents to the pan near the bedrock. After that one of the party sunk another hold on the east side ... and obtained a similar result. Night coming on, and much time having been lost through having but one pick (the other having been left at Antler Creek because they thought that shovels would be more required for stripping off the snow), they abandoned their work for that day and lit a fire to cook supper. But Dutch William, restless and enterprising, left the others basking before the burning logs, and traveled up the creek until he found the bare bedrock cropping up in the stream. ... He tried one panful of gravel, but obtained none of the precious metal. He tried another taken from the side near where there was a high ledge, and to his great delight found himself rewarded with a dollar to the pan. The gravel was frozen hard to the rock and when detached with difficulty thawed in the cold stream. Time passed quickly, and he was soon obliged by darkness to return to his camp fire. He showed his companions the prize he had obtained, but they possibly hardly believed his statement, for they determined to return to the Forks.

The critical moments of history are rarely recognized by those who take part in them, and, as a consequence, only infrequently recorded accurately. Dutch Bill's discovery is no exception, though he himself seems to have had an inkling of the importance of his discovery for according to one of his two companions, writing under the pseudonym "Cariboo" in the *Vancouver Province* of 1895, he wanted his name to be immortalized by it.

"When we had our general meeting at the camp-fire according to arrangement," wrote "Cariboo," "we again compared notes and submitted our samples. The showing by Dutch Bill was the richest of the lot, about $1.50 (sic) to the pan, and on the motion of Mike Brown, it was decided to call the place William's Creek. Someone was about to propose another name, but Bill pleaded 'If you vill call it by me, I vill hoppen for you de very first case of vine vot comes into de counterey.' There was no opposition after this. 'Prosperity to Williams Creek' was drunk in tea out of tin goblets."

There is some confusion as to exactly what happened next. One story is that Dutch Bill staked a claim in a hurry, though he really wished for more time to prospect the creek thoroughly, and returned to Antler for more supplies and a pick, because his companions were insistent on getting back to the Forks, while Ned Stout, and soon after them, Michael Burns and Vital LaForce prospected the valley and staked claims in seven or eight feet of snow. The *Victoria Chronicle* wrote:

> On reaching Antler he obtained the co-operation of John Metz and two others, and the party, now numbering four, all returned to Williams Creek by a shorter road. . . . Two went in the canyon to prospect, and two began in the ground above; the former got a dollar to the pan in five feet of gravel, but those who worked in the higher ground failed to obtain gold in paying quantities. After being out seven or eight days . . . three started for Antler for provisions, one remaining to protect the claims taken up by Metz and William for their respective partners. Before making the secret known they had intended instituting a more thorough examination of the creek, that the discoverers might have had the choice of ground. William, however, found that his secret had been guessed soon after his arrival at Antler, and, leaving his companions to bring up the stores, he started back at daybreak for his new creek, making the distance, on snow shoes, in the wonderfully short time of three hours over an unblazed trail. But his strenuous exertions were unavailing; the whole population of Antler had tracked his steps, and within two or three hours of his arrival, the whole creek was staked off into claims over ground covered with eight feet of snow. He next packed a rocker from Antler, upon his back, and blazed the trail with a hatchet, that persons passing might avoid the danger which occurred from men daily being lost for hours. Keeping two of his partners at work at Keithley, to provide the others with means, he determined to put a flume in the canyon, which was the only claim he had secured. Money and provisions being scarce, this determined man with his mate sawed lumber from four in the morning until eight at night, and put up the first flume on the creek, 170 feet long, four feet wide and two feet deep. But when they obtained pay for their labor, they found that instead of fifty dollars they could only get twenty dollars per diem.

Whether it was upon Dutch Bill's return to Antler after only one night on the creek, or after the return of Ned Stout and company, after a slightly longer stay, that the other miners got the message, does not perhaps really matter. It is, however, clear that very soon the whole of the upper part of Williams Creek had been staked by the restless followers from Antler, and that it was not Dutch Bill, but one of the Antler miners, Thomas Brown, who first reached the nearest mining recording office at Williams Lake and recorded his claim with the overworked Gold Commissioner, Phillip Nind.

William Dietz had found the creek, but the creek itself, throughout that spring of 1861 was reluctant to give up its secrets. The miners worked hard, cutting timber, building sluice boxes, flumes, and cabins, and the creek itself fought them as the snows thawed, piling up log jams of trees torn from the upper reaches of the torrent, creating dams of tree roots and rubble, and flooding the staked-out claims. When the spring turbulence had subsided the gold began to be found, though not in those quantities the miners had hoped, and the name "Humbug Creek" began to be used. It was not until two miners called Abbott and Long who had a claim just above Dutch Bill's on the creek, had a stroke of luck that the real riches of Williams Creek became apparent. Once again there are two versions of the strike. One has it that Abbott and Long had cleaned up 50 ounces and wanted to go south for the winter; nobody else was ready for the trip, however, and they did not wish to travel alone through country that was being harassed by marauding Indians, so they decided to wait a while and spend the time by digging down through the blue clay on which they had found their gold, to the bedrock on which Dutch Bill had found his a little lower down the creek. Another version has it that, while Long was absent collecting provisions Abbott decided to pierce the clay and did so to such good effect that when his partner returned forty-eight hours later he was able to show him fifty ounces of nuggets. That winter in Victoria, Abbott was a happy man, astonishing the bartenders and the populace by hurling handsful of nuggets at all the mirrors behind the bars, and announcing that he had enough gold to buy all of Victoria if he wished.

Abbott's good fortune was shared by a 41-year-old Vermonter called Davis who noticed that Abbott and his neighbour Dave Gear had staked their claims a little carelessly; the law limited each individual's claim in size and there was a twelve-foot unclaimed patch between the neighbours. Davis immediately staked a claim there, and took out $12,000, acquiring in the process the soubriquet "Twelve Foot Davis." Later he became a trader, settling in Quesnel (Quesnel Mouth), filling scows with goods, and having them hauled up river and taken by wagon from Giscome Portage to Summit Lake, whence he would take them down to his customers in the Peace River country. He died in Slave Falls in 1893.

From that time on the miners began to dig through the hard blue clay and no longer regarded it as another form of bedrock. Only eighty men wintered on Williams Creek that winter, but the population was soon to increase. Abbott, Long and their third partner, Jourdan had reached Victoria on October 25 with $80,000 of gold which they carried in sacks on their backs, and this news was not slow to reach interested people everywhere. It had the more effect because of two previous arrivals of the steamship *Otter*, that of October 7 carrying $100,000 in gold dust, and that of October 14 carrying $150,000. When Abbott and his company arrived the *Colonist* reported that the ship carried seventy-two passengers and $250,000 in gold. As the snows closed in on Cariboo and the year ended, the gold recorded, which was certainly much less than that actually mined, reached a figure of two million six hundred thousand dollars, and the heyday of Cariboo was about to begin.

By no means all the Cariboo gold that year of 1861 came out of Williams Creek. In July, as we have seen, Richard Willoughby found gold on Lowhee Creek. In the same month Ned Campbell's party struck it rich on Lightning Creek. It is not clear whether or not they were the first to find the Creek; some say it had been discovered earlier in the year by Bill Cunningham, Jack Hume, and Jim Bell, and that Bill Cunningham named the creek saying, as he tackled its difficulties, "Boys, this is lightning!" Others say that Campbell found it in a thunder storm and called it Lightning for that reason. Although the slum was bad on the creek many claims were soon in full operation. Rich deposits were found on many of the smaller streams that fed the creek, the most notable being Last Chance Creek, so called because Donovan and his mate, on their retreat from the goldfields, weary and out of money, decided there to take one last chance. The prospects were good, and so they sunk an eighty foot shaft, and in one day took out as much as forty pounds of gold. Van Winkle Creek, named after a successful claim of the same name on a bar of the lower Fraser near Lytton, was also rich and a town sprang up where it entered Lightning Creek. This town grew rapidly and became the centre for the Lightning Creek area, and the government contemplated setting up a courthouse there and making the place the administrative centre of Cariboo.

Williams Creek had not yet shown its full power, however, and as the season of 1862 opened and a horde of new and returning miners descended on the area the pace of discovery quickened. Bill Cunningham had struck paydirt on a creek that was named after him in the early spring of 1861, and his claim was now proving the richest in the area. It is said that he took more gold out of the Cariboo than even Cariboo Cameron. On May 18, 1862 he wrote to a friend

Dear Joe,

I am well, and so are the rest of the boys. I avail myself of the present opportunity to write you a half dozen lines to let you know I am well, and doing well—making from two to three thousand dollars a day! Times good—grub high—whiskey bad—money plenty.

Yours truly,
Wm. Cunningham[11]

This letter, ironically enough, would have been posted in Van Winkle, which, by the summer of 1862, was really booming. Not only had it been accorded the dignity of a post office, but in August the Bishop of Columbia preached there every Sunday. Apart from the inevitable saloons, hotels and gambling houses, there were shoemakers, blacksmiths, and bakers, and family life in the goldfields had begun, for there were three married ladies with their children in the new little town.

Williams Creek, however, was fast catching up and those miners and merchants who had not left Antler for Van Winkle and Lightning Creek, now began to leave it for the town that in September was to be officially named Richfield by the indefatigable Lieutenant Palmer, now busy surveying Cariboo. By the spring of 1862 there were several saloons already built and more in the building. The claims were all taken up, however, and those who tackled the canyon below the town found nothing worth having. In the summer of 1862, however, Ned Stout decided to try the gulch of a stream running into the creek below the canyon. He found water-worn gold straight away and then dug down to discover the bright coarse gold that made this area famous. He continued to work his way up "Stouts Gulch," and was soon taking $1000 a day.

Stouts Gulch gave Billy Barker the clue he needed. He had arrived at the diggings earlier in the year, having jumped ship in Victoria on hearing of the Fraser River rush. Some say that he was impelled by a dream which included the words "Pay at fiftytwo." He was a 41-year-old Cornishman (some say a potter turned sailor, some say a sailor from his youth), and he left ship in Victoria harbour in early 1862. He was a short man, heavily built, and had slightly bowed legs and a bushy beard, its black already turning grey. He decided that the rimrock below the canyon had probably diverted the creek and that the old creek channel bed, if it could be found, would be rich indeed. He and his company staked their claim on August 13, 1862, built a shaft house and dug steadily down. It is said that at 40 feet they all despaired and then, deciding to have one more shot, brought out

[11] Bruce Ramsey, *Barkerville*, 1961, p. 6.

five dollars to the pan. The actual depth at which Barker found his gold is variously reported as 42 feet, 52 feet, and 55 feet; in any case he later dug even deeper down to 80 feet, found bedrock, and in forty-eight hours took over a thousand dollars of gold from one crevice.

When Billy Barker first struck gold the town went wild. A new field had been discovered; the future was bright, and all talk of Williams Creek being a "humbug" ceased. Bishop George Hills reported to his diary that "all went on a spree for several days, excepting one Englishman, well brought up." Billy Barker was not well brought up and for the duration of the party he roared from saloon to saloon his "signature tune,"

> I'm English Bill,
> Never worked, an' never will.
> Get away girls,
> Or I'll tousle your curls.

Six other Englishmen were working with Billy Barker. Art Downs gives their names as H. P. Walker, C. Hankin, R. Dexter, H. Gabel, A. Anderson and G. Henkin. Others say that the company included one of his shipmates, "Sailor" Jack Edwards, and two bodyguards, just in case anyone should attempt to return him forcibly to his ship. One of these is supposed to be Littler who was more generally known as the proprietor of Littler's Cabin, a port of call on the Keithley-Antler trail. Littler would certainly have been a good choice: Mark S. Wade tells us that he had originally been a pugilist in England.[12] He later acted for a time as a mail carrier, taking the mail from Barkerville to Quesnel Forks by way of the Antler-Keithley route. George Veith (later of Veith and Borland) succeeded him in this position. Littler may have had his problems as Billy Barker was, without doubt, a rumbustious character, and as the cabins grew up round his claim to create Lower Richfield Town, he became also a very wealthy one. He spent the winter in Victoria, where he met and married Elizabeth Collyer, a widow from London; when he returned to his mine he spent a good deal of time in the saloons, and a great deal of money, not only on grubstaking other miners but also on his new wife, who, when the gold ran out, left him. Billy Barker worked as a cook and did other odd jobs for the remainder of his days and ended them on July 11, 1894 in Victoria Old Men's Home, dying of a cancer of the tongue.

While Billy Barker lived it up in Victoria, that winter of 1862-63, the foundations of the third town to be built on Williams Creek were

[12] Mark S. Wade, *The Cariboo Road*, The Haunted Bookshop, Victoria, 1979.

being laid. A little way below the Barker claim and only nine days after it was staked, John A. Cameron, his partner Robert Stephenson, and a number of others, began work on another shaft down to bedrock.

The Cameron story, like the stories of Billy Barker and Dutch Bill, has several versions. One tells us that John Angus Cameron was born near Glengarry, Ontario and, as a young man in his middle twenties, together with his brother Alan, had done reasonably well out of both the California and the Fraser gold rushes. On his return home from these adventures he married Sophia Groves of nearby Wales (or Cornwall), and then the newly married couple set out for Cariboo. Another version states that Cameron had no previous mining experience but was a poor clerk with a young wife and a fourteen-month-old child who decided to better himself. Both these versions agree, however, that the couple arrived in Victoria on February 27, 1862 with little or no money, having sailed round the Horn from Halifax and that soon afterwards the baby died. Fortunately an old friend from Ontario, Robert Stephenson, helped Cameron get credit for provisions in Victoria before he himself left for Antler where he had a business.

Cameron arrived in Antler Creek later that spring. He staked one or more unsatisfactory claims on the upper part of Williams Creek before, interested by the success of Ned Stout, he decided to emulate him and sink a deep shaft below the canyon, staking the claim on August 22. It seems that the "Englishman, well brought up" may not have been the only one who did not take part in Billy Barker's cele-bratory binge on that and succeeding days. Art Downs, in his admirable *Wagon Road North*, prints a story by Robert Stephenson which may be as close to the truth as we can get. Stephenson remembered:

In July I sold out my business on Antler Creek and went to Williams Creek to get into what became known as the Cameron claim. Dr. Crane told me of the ground being vacant, and wanted me to go with him that night and stake it off. I told him I had a few friends I would like to take in with us. So I organized a company as follows: J. A. Cameron, Sophia Cameron, Robert Stevenson, Alan McDonald, Richard Rivers, and Charles and James Clendenning. I had to wait a day and a half on Cameron to come with us to stake the claim. Cameron was nearly not coming that morning to stake the claim, as he had a prejudice against doing so on a Friday, as he thought it was unlucky.

When staking, Cameron and I disagreed and quarrelled over the location, and if he had followed my advice the claim, instead of paying one

61

million dollars, would have paid double that amount. He would insist on single claims on the left bank of the creek and I wished to stake two claims abreast on the right bank. If my advice had been followed the Tinker claim would not have been heard of and it paid nearly as well as the Cameron.

After staking the claim we sat down to name it. This was August 22, 1862. Dr. Crane proposed that it should be called the Stevenson because I had got up the company. I objected to this and asked the privilege of calling it the Cameron claim, and so it was called.[13]

There is more than a touch of acerbity in Stevenson's account, and it is hard to understand why the obliging Dr. Crane did not get a slice of the pie, but his version is perhaps the most authoritative we have.

The miners worked hard on the Cameron Claim, but without any notable success and then Sophia Cameron fell sick of "mountain fever" (typhoid). Some time earlier she had borne a daughter who was either stillborn or died at birth. Although treated by a doctor who had come to Cariboo as a miner but returned to practising, she died on October 23. Cameron placed her corpse in a tin casket within a wooden coffin and she was buried beneath a deserted cabin; Cameron vowed to carry out her dying request to be buried in Ontario. Sophia Cameron had never taken to the life in Cariboo. Those who knew her tell of her complaining frequently of the roughness of the life, and also of her refusing to accept such local remedies as "spruce tea." She seems, indeed, to have been a rather neurotic and self-centred woman.

The temperature was thirty degrees below zero when Sophia Cameron died, and of the 8000 miners who had spend the summer on the creek only 90 remained to attend her funeral. Cameron, grief stricken and desperate, went on working. A day short of two months after his wife's death he struck gold. Robert Stevenson told the story:

On December 22 we struck it very rich at 22 feet. It was 30 below and Dick Rivers was in the shaft, and Halfpenny and I were at the windlass. Rivers called up from the shaft: 'The place is yellow with gold. Look here boys,' at the same time holding up a flat rock the size of a dinner pail. I laid down on the platform shaft and peered into the shaft. I could see the gold standing out on the rock as he held it. He sent the piece of rock up and I got one ounce of gold from it. Then Cameron started down the shaft, and while he was down I took my pick and went through some of the frozen stuff that had been sent up all morning and got another ounce before he came up again. Out of three 12 gallon kegs of gravel I got $155 worth of gold.

Sinking, we found bedrock at 38 feet. It was good all the way down from 22 feet to there, but the richest was at 22 feet. The coarse gold was at 22 feet, strange to say.[14]

[13] Art Downs, *op. cit.*, p. 15.
[14] *Ibid.*, p. 15.

While this account almost makes it seem that Stevenson was the guiding spirit in the venture and the true discoverer of the gold, and his partner, who was henceforth called Cariboo Cameron, little more than a spectator, it must be regarded as authoritative, though others give the date of December 2 as that of the discovery.

The Cameron company worked their mine all through that hard winter, and in the early spring Cariboo Cameron and Stevenson disinterred the coffin of Mrs. Cameron and put it on a horsedrawn toboggan and set off for Victoria. According to an old diary published in part by F. W. Lindsay in *The Cariboo Story*, the coffin had a fifty pound sack of gold dust on the top of it. The diarist met the two men at Pemberton and they all travelled together. The diarist says

> We made good time in the forenoon. The road was dry and fairly level. After lunch travelling became harder. The road became narrow, there was ice and snow on it and it was very slippery. Cameron walked ahead of the toboggan with an axe cutting brush and stakes. We used the stakes to hold against the toboggan to keep it from sliding off the road. Stevenson led the horse and I was trying to keep the toboggan on the road.
>
> My boots were very old and worn out which made them very slippery. Time after time we all went off the road. We would all go down, the toboggan, coffin and gold-dust and get ahead of the horse. The horse got onto the job. He would turn into the mountain, then the whole thing would stop. It took a long time to get it back on the road, over four hundred pounds. Finally I said to Cameron that I would carry the gold dust. He said, 'alright,' so I took it off the top of the coffin and after that I could keep the coffin from turning over and keep the toboggan on the trail. We got to Joe Smith's house a little after dark.[15]

Joe Smith's house was the roadhouse at Port Douglas, (or Douglas Portage as the diarist called it). The party sailed down Harrison lake on the *Henrietta*, whose shaft broke, so that it drifted with the wind rather than steamed. It was however, according to the diarist, "a fine trip, lots of good grub, good luck, and No. 1 Hudson's Bay brandy."

In Victoria, Cameron bought two claims that ran alongside his own company's and also the claims of James and Charles Clendenning, thus getting for himself five full shares in the mine. On March 3, 1863 he also gave Sophia a provisional funeral in Victoria. On November 7, however, she was again disinterred and on the 8th her husband boarded ship with the coffin for the journey home by way of the Panama Isthmus. At New York he succeeded with some difficulty in persuading the customs officers that the coffin did indeed contain a corpse, but the townsfolk of his wife's birthplace were more intransigeant. They believed that the coffin contained gold, and

---

[15] F. W. Lindsay, *The Cariboo Story*, 1958, p. 37.

again the body was disinterred and discovered to be perfectly preserved in the alcohol with which the inner tin coffin had been filled in Victoria.

Cariboo Cameron returned to Ontario with $300,000 in gold and a further $40,000 was sent on to him by Wattie, Stevenson and Steele whom he left running the mine. His three brothers Dan, Sandy and Alex got $20,000 each, and the two other brothers who had been in Cariboo with him received $40,000 and a farm apiece. He also endowed a scholarship for the family descendants at Queens University. In 1865 he married a girl called Emma (or Emily) Woods from Osnabruck Corners, and built a white marble home near Summertown for $60,000. This was the high point of his career. Thereafter luck was against him. His investments in timber and in the construction of the Lachine Canal failed. In 1888, together with his wife, he returned to Cariboo, but died before he had struck gold again. He was buried on November 7 of that year in the cemetery he himself had founded when he interred one of his own men, Peter Gibson, in the first months of the Cameron claim.

Not all the Cariboo stories end sadly. Richard Willoughby, on leaving Cariboo with seventy thousand dollars from his Discovery claim, and with another sizeable sum he had got from selling it, bought a pack train and is supposed to have put money into Barnards Express Company. He started a cattle ranch near Chilliwack in 1867, but could not rest easy when the Cassiar goldfield opened up, and mined there. He took twelve thousand dollars out of McDames Creek, and did well in the Omineca rush of 1869. In the 1870's he prospected in Alaska, and was finally rewarded by striking it rich in Nome, where he died in 1904, leaving an estate variously reported as being worth one hundred thousand or two hundred thousand dollars.

Willoughby was a man who could not get rid of the gold fever in his blood, and in this he was typical of many of the Cariboo characters who frequently attempted to return home and settle down, but failed to do so. An exception was Bill Diller (or Dillar), and his story reads like the plot of a Victorian melodrama. Born of poor but honest parents on a little farm in New York state, he rarely knew the luxury of reading a newspaper, but on one fateful day in 1858 he happened upon one which told of the gold to be found in the far off mountains of New Caledonia, as British Columbia was then called. He begged his mother to let him use her savings to travel to the goldfields, and promised to make his fortune there and bring it home with him to save her from poverty and anxiety. His mother gave him the money and the lad took ship to Panama, crossed the isthmus, took another ship to Victoria, and joined the rush. He was penniless when he reached Williams Creek, but refused to be downhearted. He found two partners and together they sank a shaft, and found themselves encountering slum. The green heavy-moving mud was everywhere, and they faced defeat. They refused to give in, however. They timbered their shaft so thoroughly that the slum was held back. At eighty-five feet they hit bedrock and gold, but only very little gold. They were in debt to all the storekeepers and the prospect looked grim. As a last chance they decided to tunnel, and after they had tunneled twenty feet they struck gold in incredible amounts. They took out over a hundred pounds of gold in one four-man night shift, and during the following months they took out forty thousand dollars worth of gold each week. In 1861 Bill Diller cleaned up and set out for home. He arrived at the farm to find all the furniture stacked out in front of the house ready for auction, and his mother crying quietly in her rocking chair. The auction was just beginning. Bill Diller had changed a great deal during his absence. He was no longer a youth, but a rugged, bearded man weighing 240 pounds, and so nobody realized the identity of the stranger who outbid all comers on every item, concluding his performance by buying the house and the farm buildings, and paying for everything in gold. Only when the auction was over did he reveal his identity, and give the deed of the farm into his mother's hands together with the remainder of the fortune he had made. Some years later the Dillers sold the farm and settled in New York City where Bill Diller became a leading citizen.

Bill Diller and Richard Willoughby provided Cariboo with two of the success stories that kept hope alive in the years after the first heady excitement, but the three men who could be considered the founding fathers of the new centre of the Cariboo goldfields were not so fortunate. All three of them died in poverty, William Dietz in 1877, Billy Barker in 1894, and Cariboo Cameron in 1888. All three, however, left towns behind them. Richfield was officially named in September 1862 at the newly built courthouse there, and Cameronton was christened in August 1864 by Rev. Ephraim Evans, with Judge Peter O'Reilly, Judge Cox, and Matthew Baillie Begbie in attendance; "Oh what a time we had" said the correspondent of *The Province*, "The following morning some of the boys were looking for a shoehorn to put their caps on." Barkerville was christened a little later. It was the only one of the three to survive.

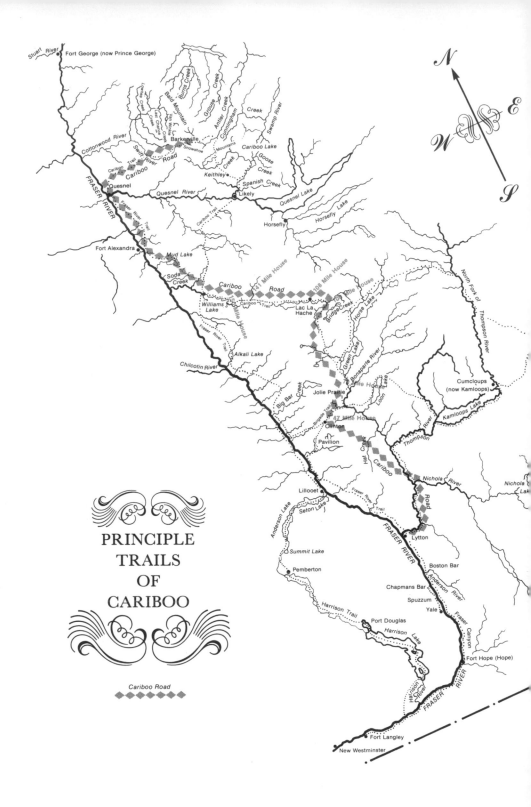

PRINCIPLE
TRAILS
OF
CARIBOO

◆◆◆◆◆◆◆ Cariboo Road

CHAPTER FOUR

The Cariboo Road

It was in 1862 that the town of Richfield, Dutch Bill's town, was named, and 1862 was a year of beginnings. In that year the great Cariboo wagon road began to become a reality. The road was contracted out to private bidders in sections so that as the work proceeded, until it arrived at Soda Creek in September 1863, the traveller found his route lay sometimes along a broad gravel road and sometimes along a trail. In October 1861 the Engineers had begun to survey and to blast out from the rock a road from Yale to Cooks Ferry, even while another contractor began work on the stretch from Boston Bar to Lytton; Gus Wright got the contract for the Lillooet-Clinton section, and then with J. C. Callbreath built the whole of the road from Clinton to Soda Creek and thence to Alexandria. From Soda Creek the traveller proceeded by sternwheel steamer to Quesnel Mouth; from there on he was left to the mercy of the trail to the goldfields, though a year later, in 1864, Gus Wright started a road from Quesnel to Cottonwood, and in 1865 took the road all the way to the three new towns of Richfield, Barkerville, and Cameronton.

It was this road from Clinton to Soda Creek, and, later, from Quesnel to the goldfields which established the pattern of the Cariboo settlements for years to come. As each mile of the road was completed one of Wright's men would unload from his hand wheelbarrow a stake bearing the number of the mile distance from Lillooet and hammer it into the verge. These mile posts served not only as markers but also as names for the various houses which began to be built along the trail. Some of these mile houses were originally places for the road crews to sleep and eat while working on a particular section; some originated in the need of the mule trains of the packers to have way-stations; some were created to serve the increasing number of wagon trains with places where oxen and horses could be watered and fed; others became inns for passengers on the BX stage coaches that travelled through the area.

It is not always easy to determine why one mile post became important and another one did not. Sometimes the road was a junction for other older trails, and therefore became busier than the average. Sometimes a particular Milehouse would become more popular that others. Existing houses and settlements were either enriched or desolated by the coming of the road. Williams Lake, for example, was already an established stopping place on the old trail when the road was being built, but Wright directed the road to by-pass it and Williams Lake lost its erstwhile importance, as it had already lost its gold commissioner and government offices to Richfield, and it was not until the arrival of the Pacific Great Eastern Railway at the close of the first world war that it revived to become once again the centre of the Cariboo. It has been said that the ill treatment of Williams Lake was caused by Wright's being offered a half share in Frank Way's Deep Creek ranch, and being refused a similar bribe by Tom Manifee whose property lay beside the lake. A more likely explanation, however, is given by Mark S. Wade in his book *The Cariboo Road*. Wade says:

Tom Manifee had a stopping place at Williams Lake and owned the property now forming the P.G.E. townsite. Manifee, as well as everybody else, knew that the proper way for the road to go was by Williams Lake and he looked forward to the reaping of a rich harvest as a natural sequence of the building of the road. Wright and Calbreath, the contractors, when they got as far as the 140, found themselves short of cash with which to pay the wages of the men working on contract; they lacked a few thousand dollars and felt the shortage to be an inconvenience. They went to Manifee and asked him to lend them the amount they required until they could get the money from Victoria. For some reason or other he refused, the contractors looked upon the refusal as a reflection upon themselves and said as much, and one word led to another until the affair developed into a first-class row, in which hot words were used on both sides.

The contractors were permitted, by the terms of their contract to take the road where they thought best and most expedient and when Manifee refused the accommodation they solicited they began to think pretty hard. Just before that time the Davison brothers had opened the 150-Mile House and when they heard, and such news does seem to get noised abroad, that Manifee had refused the contractors a loan, they saw their opportunity and jumped into the breach. They hurried to Wright and said: "You want a few thousands to pay off the men? All right, here it is. Help yourselves, but of course, you will bear us in mind, eh? You will bring the road past the 150 down to Williams Lake?"

Wright and Calbreath gladly accepted the loan and on the principle that one good turn deserves another, built the road past the 150, thus cutting out Williams Lake, and there it has since remained, although had the road gone by the lake and up the Fraser, the heavy pull over Carpenter Mountain would have been avoided and a much easier grade obtained.

The glory of the town of Williams Lake departed, but Tom Manifee still kept on his farm for a number of years, finally selling it to Pinchbeck and Lyne.[16]

Williams Lake was almost destroyed by the road; Soda Creek, on the other hand, was pretty well created by it. It was at that time the lowest navigable portion of the Fraser that also provided flat land beside the river suitable for steamboats to dock at. Here Wright established the sternwheeler, *Enterprise*. She was 110 feet long and 20 feet wide, with a very shallow draught. She had two boilers, each of them 10 feet long and 36 inches in diameter, and her 60 horsepower engines measured 12 by 36 inches. The engines and boilers were packed by mule to Four Mile Creek near Alexandria, where James Trahey, using handsawn and finished local lumber, built the boat for Gus Wright, who had Captain Thomas Wright as a partner. She was brought down the 56 miles of rapidly running river to Soda Creek, and set off on her maiden voyage at 4:00 p.m. on May 9, 1863; she docked at Quesnel the following day. The return trip was quicker; she reached Alexandria in two hours and took a further one hour and twenty minutes to arrive at Soda Creek. Freight cost $40 a ton, and each passenger and animal was charged $7. Thomas Wright was the captain on this voyage, and the pilot was Edmund C. Shepherd, a New Brunswicker, who had learned his trade in the riverboats of the Mississippi. Captain J. W. Doane took over the captaincy from Thomas Wright later that summer, but Shepherd continued to act as pilot.

As soon as the plan for the sternwheel route from Soda Creek to Quesnel Mouth was known it became very clear that these two places were due for a boom. In 1863 Peter Dunleavy, astute as ever, left Beaver Lake and set up a hotel in Soda Creek where he would be certain to get stop-over customers from those travelling not only to all the goldfields, but also up to Fort George and beyond. Another hotel run by Captain Robert McLeese, who worked for a time on the river boats, and who from 1882 to 1890 was a member of parliament for Cariboo, soon joined Dunleavy's, and the narrow strip of flat land beside the Fraser soon became one long street, Chinatown being at the downriver end where the road corkscrewed down through the dust past Soda Creek itself, where R. Collins built his flour mill powered by the rushing sparkling water; the landing for the *Enterprise* was established at the upriver end where, later, the ferry across the

16 Mark S. Wade, *op. cit.*, p. 162.

Fraser was also built. The now little-used road to Alexandria and Quesnel Mouth a little higher up the hillside behind the main street soon had its quota of houses, and a discreet mile and a half away from the junction of the road down to the village and the sternwheeler, there was a Sporting House, the date of whose foundation is unknown, though it was still a going concern twenty-five years later. Some sources maintain that Dunleavy's hotel was, in fact, owned by Jim Sellars and Tom Manifee of Williams Lake.

The rise of Soda Creek meant the fall of the already crumbling Alexandria, some twenty-one miles farther upriver. It had been founded in the early years of the nineteenth century as a fur-trading post at Stella Yah, the point at which Alexander Mackenzie turned back from the Fraser and named Fort Alexander. It was a gathering point for furs and a depot for supplies to be sent upriver by canoe to more northern forts. In 1821 when the Norwesters and the Hudson's Bay Company combined it was moved a few miles north, and then, in 1836 because of the increasing fur trade from the Chilcotins it was moved from the east to the west bank of the river. It later became a crucial port of call for those heading for the goldfields, either from the Kamloops direction or from the lower Fraser. By 1863, however, its importance had dwindled, and Lieutenant Palmer reported it as "a half ruined cluster of log dwellings roofed with mud."

The new competition from Soda Creek was too much for the old place, recently renamed Alexandria by A. G. Young, the Colonial Secretary. In 1866 a new Hudson's Bay store opened at Quesnel Mouth in the charge of Hugh Ross, and in 1867 the Hudson's Bay Company store at Alexandria closed forever, the land being used as a company farm until John S. Twan acquired the site from the crown. The old buildings, so dilapidated as to constitute a public danger, were pulled down by Twan in 1922.

While Alexandria dwindled, Soda Creek grew and those two astute gentlemen, Peter Dunleavy and Gus Wright, prospered. When it was proposed that the road to Alexandria, now very little used, should be extended to Quesnel, Wright was, predictably, less than enthusiastic. He not only owned the *Enterprise* which alone could transport heavy freight, but he may have had an interest in Way's Deep Creek Ranch which was strategically placed on the road south from Soda Creek at the exact point at which travellers could arrive after coming in on the night steamer and beginning their journey down the road. If the muddy awkward track from Soda Creek to Quesnel along the banks of the Fraser were to be replaced Gus

Wright would lose a lot of customers for both his enterprises. Nevertheless the road had to come and in the summer of 1865 the contract was awarded to Robert T. Smith, with Thomas Spence as inspector. Work began in·July and the road was completed by September. It was not long, however, before the heavy wagons had rutted the road and the rains had turned stretches of it into an almost impassable morass. Smith broke his contract by refusing to make "all necessary repairs" for the first year of the road's life, and Spence, on behalf of the government, took over the responsibility. Gus Wright and Frank Way had fewer customers at Deep Creek.

Wright was not, however, too dismayed. Since 1862 he had been sleighing goods from Quesnel to Cottonwood in the winter over the ten foot wide trail created by Allen Smith earlier that year, and by 1864 his sleighs were taking goods all the way to Richfield. He thus had enjoyed for several years, if not a monopoly, at least a very substantial amount, of the income from, all traffic from Soda Creek to the mines. In 1864 he built the road from Quesnel to Cottonwood for $85,000. Gordon R. Elliot tells us that

Employing 520 men, he boarded them all and paid choppers $74 a month and graders $60. Included in the 520 men were 300 Chinese paid only $45 a month. Wright bridged the Cottonwood River under a separate contract for $9000. The bridge was completed in November, 1864 ... Wright made an estimated profit of $40,000 on this road alone.[17]

In the winter of 1864 the goods were sleighed to Richfield from Cottonwood by Allen Smith and John Ryder, and in the spring of 1865 a regular stage line from Quesnel to Cottonwood was started by Humphrey, Pool and Johnston. There was still, however, another stretch of road to be completed before the dream of a road all the way through Cariboo could be realized. Gordon R. Elliot tells the story:

In April, 1865, Malcolm Munro of Victoria secured the contract to construct the road from Cottonwood to Richfield and commenced at once in order to complete the work by October. Unless the road were finished, the $45,000 contract was to be annulled. Munro built to Van Winkle only to be defeated by bad weather. He wrote to (Joseph) Trutch, then Chief Commissioner of Lands and Works, asking for permission to furnish bond and to finish the road in the spring. Trutch refused. Munro owed about $8,000 to his employees and $5,000 to local merchants. He gave bills of sale for all his equipment to three people and then left the district, went to jail in New Westminster and, finally, ended in bankruptcy court. James Duncan finished the road on his own volition and billed the government for $509.63.

[17] Gordon R. Elliot, *Quesnel, Commercial Centre of the Cariboo Gold Rush*, 1958, pp. 123-24.

Naturally, a cry arose on Williams Creek for a road from Richfield to Camerontown. This short route was surveyed by Spence and the contract awarded to Wright for the extremely low price of $6,700. Under the contract, Wright built as far as Barkerville. To stop the road there was ridiculous, but Wright asked $900 to continue it through Barkerville to Camerontown. This town on Williams Creek raised $500 and Wright finished the road.[18]

Although the road was now completed it did little to affect the fortunes of the good ship *Enterprise* in spite of Gus Wright's fears, and Soda Creek and Quesnel remained bustling river ports.

A few years earlier Quesnel Mouth had suffered a good deal from the exodus of its mining population, first to Quesnel Forks, and then to Keithley and Antler which could be reached without touching at the mouth of Quesnel River. When gold was discovered in the Williams Creek and Lightning Creek areas, however, it became strategically placed to serve all the mining settlements, being at one end of a rough ellipse of trails which connected all the important fields. Moreover after the building of the *Enterprise* it was the port at which all supplies from the south had to be unloaded.

In 1860 Quesnel Mouth had been prosperous. 1500 white miners were busy on the river bars, and pack trains were arriving steadily with flour at $1.25 a pound and bacon $1.50 in the stores. When the miners left for Quesnel Forks the Chinese moved in behind them, the first Chinese store opening for business in May 1860 and a second one in June. A gambling tent was put up at the same period. Charles Danielson, deciding, like Dunleavy, that the life of the middleman and merchant was preferable to that of the miner, settled there and raised cattle for butchering, and, later, turnips; with his profits he established a ferry across the river Quesnel. The government, believing a town was due to come into being, reserved a large area of land for its own use and for possible later sale at a profit for a townsite. The indefatigable Lieutenant Palmer quashed any notion that Quesnel Forks could be the new centre for distribution of goods and for the new road, still to be built, to the goldfields, by pointing out that the route from Quesnel Forks across the mountains to Antler and Richfield was simply impossible for heavy traffic and that a much easier route was that from Quesnel Mouth along the Cottonwood River through Beaver Pass. In 1863 the *Colonist* announced

At the mouth of Quesnel there is a town springing up which bids fair to be the largest interior town in B.C. The entire business of the present routes and of the projected coast routes, must eventually centre there.

[18] *Ibid.*, p. 124.

The land the government had reserved was surveyed, and in June 1863 three townsites were planned, Upper, Middle and Lower. On August 17 that year Lot 1, Block IV sold for 82 pounds sterling. Prosperity was clearly on its way. The industrious and ubiquitous Gus Wright, scarcely taking breath after his creation of the *Enterprise*, was busy organizing sleighs for the winter trail to Barkerville and building stables for the horses. Danielson's Ferry across the Quesnel had been augmented by another ferry owned by Cook three miles up river. Jerome Harper was building a mill. Some people thought that Quesnel Mouth (Quesnelmouth, Quesnellemouth, or Mouth of Quesnel) might become the new capital of British Columbia.

South of Soda Creek the results of the road were less dramatic, but just as important. The 47 Mile House where the road from Lillooet joined the new road through the canyon from Yale was fast becoming a community, and its success was recognized in 1862 when Queen Victoria gave it the name Clinton. The 70 Mile House founded by Gus Wright as a suitably situated stopping point while his road was building was also thriving, as were many other houses. These houses and villages, however, grew gradually over the next two or three decades; they did not have the overnight growth of the northern settlements but depended for their growth more upon slow accretion and the steady increase of the demand for the hospitality they could offer the traveller and the provisions with which they could supply the wagon trains.

By the end of 1863 the patterns of settlements in British Columbia had been established. Some towns would dwindle over the years; Keithley, Antler, and Quesnel Forks would die and Richfield and Cameronton would decay and merge with Barkerville. Van Winkle was to merge with Stanley before it entirely disappeared. But Soda Creek, Barkerville, and Quesnel would survive, the first two dwindling but the last named becoming a city of real importance to the region.

It was the dream of gold which created these towns and the road which led to them and created other towns as it did so; if we were to make a list of names of those who could rightly be called the founders of the Cariboo we know it would include not only Peter Dunleavy, Doc Keithley, William Dietz, Billy Barker, Cariboo Cameron, and Richard Willoughby, but also Gustavus Blin Wright and his overlord, the man whose imagination reached out to envisage a 400 mile road through some of the most treacherous and apparently impassable wilderness in the continent, the autocratic and thrifty ex-Hudson's Bay factor, Sir James Douglas.

The great Cariboo Road of the 1860's however, bore little resemblance to the highways of today. At eighteen feet, it was wide enough for wagon trains to pass each other, and could accommodate cattle drives of considerable size. It was, however, stony, dusty, muddy, pitted with holes, and constantly subject to slides, washouts, and other hazards. During the summer the dust was ferocious; cattle drives in particular would raise such a huge sand-brown choking cloud that citizens in Clinton would rush to close all doors and windows when the cattle were going through, and the houses did not have the conventional front porches but rather balconies above the dust level. Moreover, because the road had to be made quickly, it did not always take the most direct route. Rather than cut slowly and laboriously through hills Wright took the road over them; rather than face the problems of a bridge he would detour the road. Much of the territory was swampy and the road had to be built up, usually on a bed of logs laid side by side like the ribs in corduroy; often the rains would wash away the topsoil and gravel, and the road would be worn down to the logs themselves. The bumps on the roads and the rocky surface so belaboured the iron rims of the wagons that they expanded with the heat and mechanical tire shrinkers had to be provided at stopping places. Each wagon train took care to carry a jack to ease the wagons out of mudholes. The gradients were so steep and the wagons so heavy and cumbersome that each train had to be hauled by a team of oxen, horses, or (sometimes) mules, ranging from six to ten or even twelve in number. Blacksmiths were needed at each stopping place to repair broken chains, to reshoe horses, and even, on occasions, re-weld axles. There was no way of controlling each animal in a train by means of an individual rein, all reins being gathered together in the two hands of the driver, and cleanly separated from each other as with stagecoach driving. Therefore, highly trained lead animals were used on a single "jerk line" which could signal instructions by the number of jerks given. These animals were extraordinarily adept, could step over their own chains at sharp corners to keep the wagon on the road, and could even lead the team right off the road at sharp bends, so as to keep the wagon from rolling over the outside of the curve.

The wagon trains, hauled by either oxen or horses, were not the only traffic on the new road. Ever since the gold rush began mule trains had packed in provisions over the trails, and the most famous of these packers was Jean Caux, or "Cataline." He had begun as a packer on the fur brigade trails, and then turned to serving the goldfields, taking a train of 16 to 48 mules first along the rough trails and then along the road. It took him a month to reach the goldfields from Yale and he packed anything and everything from mine machinery to champagne, from crates of chickens to millinery. Cataline was a short, broad shouldered man, bearded, with shoulder-length hair. To establish his position he wore a starched white shirt, always, and it is said that his crew never contained any white men, but Chinese, Indians, Mexicans, and Negroes. He himself was a Spaniard from Catalonia. The mule train was led by a white bell mare, each animal walking free, not linked to any other in case one animal falling might bring down others over the precipices or into the swamps. A leading mule would be ridden or accompanied by the cook so that he would arrive first at the stopping place for the day and be able to prepare the meal for the cargo packers, one to every eight beasts, while the long, single file train came in and the mules, each carrying between 250 and 400 pounds of freight, were being unloaded. Cataline was famous for always sleeping in the open, wrapped up in a blanket, even when there was snow on the ground. He drank rum (or cognac) which he also rubbed into his hair, saying "a little inside and a little outside." He marked the conclusion of each trip by taking off his shirt, hanging it on a handy fence post, and buying a new one for the return journey. Twice during his career his mule train was almost destroyed by a series of accidents but, intent upon keeping to his packing contract, he hired Indian women who back-packed the loads to the end of the trail. The coming of the wagon road took much of Cataline's custom away from him, but he continued for a while and then moved up to the northern part of the country, packing in Northwestern British Columbia and was well known in Quesnel until he retired in 1913. He died in Hazelton in 1922, at the age of eighty (or ninety-three).

Cataline was not the only packer on the road. Frank Way, who also owned a stopping station on Deep Creek, packed as well, as did "Redhead" Davis, and there were a number of others. The most memorable packing venture of all perhaps was that organized by John C. Callbreath (or Calbreath) of Lillooet, who had partnered Gus Wright in the building of the Lillooet-Clinton road. Considering that mules could only carry 250 to 400 pounds, needed frequent stopping places for watering, someone had come up with the splendid notion that camels would be a superior packing animal. Callbreath, acting as agent for the syndicate of Frank Laumeister, Adam Haffy (or Heffley), and Henry Ingram, bought twenty-three Bactrian camels in San Francisco for $300 each. The camels had been used as pack animals by the United States Army in Texas and in the desert country of lower California. These camels could, the syndicate was assured, carry 800 pounds each, go for days without food or water, and travel thirty or forty miles a day. The partners estimated that they'd take in about $60,000 the first year, netting them a handsome profit in the region of $50,000 even when the cost of getting the camels to the Cariboo had been deducted. Unfortunately Laumeister and his friends had not studied the habits of the camel closely enough; they were unaware that camels are highly odorous, extremely bad tempered, and easily excited.

Frank Laumeister seems to have been the unfortunate who had charge of the actual operation. He accompanied them to Port Douglas on a barge towed by the *Flying Dutchman* sternwheeler. As they disembarked the camels began to show their true colours. One bit and kicked a prospector's mule and, in the following days it became clear that these camels were liable at whim to bite and kick anything that moved, including oxen, horses, and men. They could, it is true, carry immense burdens, but on the road their stench was such as to make other animals shy and bolt. On one occasion as Judge Begbie was conducting a trial on horseback and in the open air on one of his periodic journeys through Cariboo, the camel train came by and his horse bolted as did the horses of the other members of the court, carrying them all off into the bush. It is not recorded what happened to the prisoner.

For a time Laumeister tried to solve the problem by deodorizing his camels, a task which might make even Proctor and Gamble blench, but the scented water he used was ineffective. He also discovered that the camels' hoofs, while perfectly adapted for kicking, were not adapted to the jagged rocks of the Cariboo roads and trails. With a stubbornness, and an ingenuity, that does him credit, Laumeister fitted his camels with canvas and rawhide shoes, which did afford the animals some protection, but which soon wore out. By the end of the 1863 season the misnamed "Dromedary Express" was highly unpopular with everybody, including, one may deduce, Laumeister, Haffy and Ingram. Owners of other pack trains were grumbling loudly and talking of suing Laumeister for damages. In 1864 Laumeister abandoned the project and turned the animals loose, either on the flats near Cache Creek or in the San Jose Valley near Lac La Hache, it is not certain which, and there they eventually

76

died. Before they were all gone, however, Mark S. Wade tells us that "the proprietors of the hotel and store at 150-Mile House tried an experiment. It was observed that though the camels failed in winter, the cold proving extremely trying to them, they became rolling fat in summer, and Adler and Barry of the "150", (they held it on rental only) decided to kill and dress one for its meat. This was done and it was exposed for sale but no one would buy it, and the venture fell through. Others of the camels were taken by Henry Ingram, one of the partners in their importation to his ranch at Grand Prairie, about forty miles distant from Kamloops, and in 1881 there were three females living. In the spring of 1892 there remained but one, so feeble that, falling down, it was unable to rise to its feet again and the owner mercifully had the helpless creature shot by an Indian named Nopia. Mrs. King, a daughter of the late Mr. Ingram, informs me that an attempt was made to tan the hide of this animal but it was not a success. Because of its thickness it was used as a floor rug."[19]

Some of the camels wandered the territory for many years, bewildering and alarming those who occasionally glimpsed them. One man, it is reported, shot one under the misapprehension that it was an outsize grizzly, and thereafter was called "Grizzly Morris." The camel shot by Nopia may not have been the last survivor, however, for there is a story that another one turned up unexpectedly at Grand Prairie some years later. It died in 1905.

Perhaps the only people to equal Laumeister & Company's ingenuity, and possibly also their disillusionment, were those who are reported as packing their supplies on the backs of Newfoundland dogs.

Neither mules nor camels nor Newfies were available to all the travellers on the road in the sixties. Men still back-packed into the country, and two ingenious men built a trundle barrow that would carry 400 pounds. It consisted of a platform with two shafts fore and aft and a central wheel about four feet in diameter. One man would pull on the forward shafts and the other push on the ones aft. The inventors of this contraption were two newcomers from Australia, an Englishman called Downs and a Swede called Oleson who had been shipmates on the voyage to Victoria. They stopped for a rest at a point north of Alexandria, 209 miles from Lillooet, and liked the place so much that, after a short experience of the mines, they returned there and created what is still known as The Australian Ranch. Downs died there of overwork, and Oleson returned to

[19] Mark S. Wade, *op. cit.*, p. 81.

Sweden at the beginning of the new century. The Yorston brothers bought the place, together with 135 head of cattle, for $10,000.

Downs' and Oleson's trundle barrow served better than another more complicated contraption introduced first in 1871 by F. J. Barnard and J. C. Beedy. Their advertisement in a Victoria newspaper on March 23, 1871 was headed "STEAM TO CARIBOO." Beneath this enticing legend was a picture of a 3 wheeled machine that looked like a cross between a tractor and a steam roller dragging two wagons, and under that the announcement that

> The British Columbia General Transport Company Will place Four of Thompson's Patent Road Steamers on the route between Yale and Barkerville in the First Week in April, and will be prepared to enter into Contracts for the conveyance of Freight from Yale to Soda Creek in Eight Days. Through Contracts will be made as soon as the condition of the road above Quesnelmouth permits.
> Rates of Passage will be advertised in due time.

It seems that, in fact, two not four of the machines were imported, together with two drivers for them, Andrew Gray who later ran the Marine Iron Works in Victoria, and James McArthur who worked in Barkerville for a time, and then also settled in Victoria where he worked for the Albion Iron Works. The machines were wood-burners and stacks of wood were built along the road from Yale to Soda Creek to provide fuel. Unfortunately, however, the steep hills on the road from Yale made the water level in the vertically mounted boiler vary a great deal and thus caused overheating and stoppages. Moreover the big wheels with their rough tread damaged the road to an unacceptable extent. All in all, R. W. Thomson's "Patent India rubber-tired Road Steamer" fared less well in British Columbia than one must assume it to have done in its native Scotland. It took three days to get from Yale to Jackass Mountain, pulling 6 tons of freight, and there it stopped. The experiment was over.

This must have been almost the only occasion when Francis Jones Barnard made a fool of himself. He began Barnard's Express at the very start of the gold rush, and almost immediately outdistanced or swallowed up his would-be competitors. The first of these was "Billy" Ballou from Victoria, who ran the "Pioneer Fraser River Express" to the diggings on the lower Fraser in 1858. Ballou was an Alabaman of French ancestry. He fought in the war between the United States and Mexico and was wounded several times, though not seriously enough to slow him down. In 1849 he moved to San Francisco and thence to the Californian goldfields where he started the first express business in the region, charging a thimbleful of gold dust for carrying each letter or packet. In December 1849 he sold out to the newly organized Adams Express Company, and together with Sam L. W. Langton started the "Yuba Express." Shortly after fighting off a gang of thirteen robbers near Mountain House on the road from Marysville to Downieville, he left the business to his partner and became a merchant, first in California and then in Olympia in Washington Territory. In late 1857 or early 1858 he saw some gold that had been sent south from Victoria and decided to visit the city. After studying the situation there, he went back to San Francisco and organized an express service from there to the lower Fraser. He then returned to Victoria and set up *Ballou's Express*, transporting mail and newspapers (at a dollar a copy) from there to the lower Fraser, and linking up with Freeman's Express that was running an express service between Victoria and San Francisco. He started this venture in June 1858, and in September faced competition from D. C. Fargo who ran an express service from Yale to Lytton. Ballou soon took over the Fargo business. *Wells, Fargo and Company* then established an office in Victoria and provided a connecting service for *Kent and Smith's Express* which ran between Victoria and Lytton. Ballou joined up with them and took over the business. In 1859 the *W. J. Jeffray Express* came into being, but collapsed under the pressure of Ballou's competition. In 1861 F. J. Barnard took over the Jeffray company and extended its operations, taking mail and newspapers beyond Yale as far as the northern mines, at first packing it in on his back and then leading a packhorse. In July 1862 Barnard was given the government contract to carry mail from New Westminster to the mines by way of Williams Lake and Ballou gave up the struggle. He sold out to Dietz and Nelson in 1863. Dietz and Nelson, however, had been collaborating with Barnard since 1861, and so Barnard now had something approaching a monopoly of the express business from New Westminster to Cariboo. In 1867 (or 1868) Barnard bought out Dietz and Nelson and in 1871 the Provincial Legislature passed a private bill incorporating *The British Columbia Express Company*. F. J. Barnard held half the stock and the remainder was divided equally between Steve Tingley and James (or Jamie) Hamilton, who died in Victoria not long afterwards, Steve Tingley acquiring his stock. In spite of the bill, it seems, however, that in 1872 the new name used was the F. J. Barnard Company, and it is said that it remained known by that name until 1879 when Barnard himself retired and the management of the concern was taken over by Steve Tingley, when it became known as *The British Columbia Express Company*, or, more familiarly, as the *BX*. In 1886 (or 1888) Tingley bought out Barnard who had suffered a stroke in 1880 and whose son, F. S. Barnard, later Lieutenant-Governor of British Columbia, was now dealing with his business affairs. In either 1896 or 1897 a syndicate consisting of John Shields, Peter Ryan, Charles Millar and J. Kilgour of Toronto took the mail contract away from the *BX*, whereupon Steve Tingley sold them the business of which Millar soon gained total control. The *BX* continued in the old way, with James B. Leighton as manager until 1913 when it again failed to get the mail contract, which was acquired by the *Inland Express Company* operated by James C. Shields of Vancouver. Thereupon the *BX*, with Leslie Cameron as manager, modernized itself, replacing the stage coaches with trucks and automobiles, and an era had ended. Francis Jones Barnard died in 1889, and Steve Tingley in 1919.

It would have been hard to prophesy Barnard's future eminence and his importance from his beginnings. He was born in Quebec City in 1829 and christened Francis Jones Barnard. In 1853 he married Ellen Stillman and moved to Toronto in 1855 where he operated an unsuccessful business. In 1859 he left Toronto for Victoria, travelling steerage round by Panama, leaving his family behind him. He arrived at Yale with five dollars, and immediately set to work cutting and splitting wood. He mined for a short period but soon sold his claim. He then took the position of town constable, after which he worked as a purser on the steamboat *Fort Yale* which appears to have given him the idea of starting an express service. The *Fort Yale* had been built for $26,000 (or perhaps $31,000) by Yale citizens in order to bring people to their town instead of to Douglas by way of the steamboat *Lillooet* which had been built to increase Douglas' trade. The *Yale* did not last very long. She arrived at Yale from Victoria, where she had been built, on November 26, 1860, and there was a great celebration. She took only seven and a half hours for the return voyage to New Westminster which caused more celebration. On April 14, 1861, as Francis Jones Barnard was sitting at the dining-room table, at Union Bar, two miles above Hope, the *Fort Yale* blew up. The wreckage was swept down river past Hope where the survivors were rescued by Indians. Many people died, including a host of Indians and Chinese and Captain Jamieson, who had been in the pilothouse which received the full force of the explosion of the boiler directly beneath it. Barnard was blown clean out of the dining room onto the rails of the rapidly sinking boat and was rescued from

The Great Bluff, Thompson River

59 Mile House, Cariboo Road, 1895

Wheelbarrow in the Cariboo

S.S. **B.C.** Express *and S.S.* **B.X.** *tied at south Fort George*

B.C. Express Co. Stage at Quesnel or Soda Creek

Enterprise *at Soda Creek*

William Barker

Main Street, Barkerville, before the fire

Main Street, Barkerville, after the fire, September 1868

St. Saviour's Anglican Church, Barkerville

Sir Matthew Baillie Begbie

Richfield

The flumes of the Cariboo goldfields, Barkerville

The Calvenos Claim, Lowhee Creek

Cameron and Waitie Claim, Camerontown

Mucho Oro Claim

Sheepshead Claim, Williams Creek

Quesnel Forks

150 Mile House, Cariboo Road. The Cariboo Trading Company

the water by Indians. Shortly after this catastrophe he began his express business, carrying letters at $2.00 each delivery and newspapers which he sold, like Ballou, at a dollar apiece.

In 1862 he had enough money to buy horses for a pony express, and when the road opened he was ready with horses and wagons, and Steve Tingley as his driver, and a two-horse wagon made the trip from Lillooet to Alexandria every ten days. It was not until March 12, 1864 that the first real stagecoach began; it left Yale at five o'clock in the morning with James Down (or perhaps Charles G. Major) holding the reins of the two to six horses. Two horses were used on the easy stages and four or six on the difficult ones. It took approximately 50 hours to get from Yale to Soda Creek; the horses were changed every 18 miles, and usually so quickly that there was no time for passengers to do more than enjoy for a few moments the cessation of the jolting. Steve Tingley was the driver on the way back. The coaches stopped roughly every thirty-five miles for the passengers to have a meal. Overnight stops were often cut short if the coaches were carrying mail and passengers had to catch up on their sleep in the swaying, rocking vehicle.

The coaches first used were of the Concord type and imported from California; they were fitted with springs made of layers of leather on which fitted the "rockers" which supported the body of the coach which was painted bright red, the trim and running gear being yellow. Riding in a coach was not unlike being in a small boat in a choppy sea, and passengers were not infrequently seasick. For this reason, or for more idealistic ones, women were always given the seats they preferred, and were always the first to be seated; this applied whether the woman was duchess or squaw, and at mealtimes, when the driver always took the head of the table and saw to it that the passengers were well served, the women sat at his right hand and, later, were given the choicest accommodation available.

According to the botanist J. McCoon, in 1864 it cost $130 for the journey from Yale to Soda Creek, meals being 50 cents as far as Felker's "Blue Tent" stopping-place half way on the journey; there and thereafter meals were 75 cents. A night's lodging usually cost fifty cents. In 1872 the fare was halved and the journey for this amount was from Yale to Quesnel, which took around sixty hours. The service was now twice, instead of once a week, though mail, as distinct from express letters and parcels, was only carried on one of the journeys. In 1865 the fare for travellers was reduced. It now cost only $125.00 to journey from Yale to Barkerville. Barnard charged a

81

dollar a pound for express parcels, a dollar for each express letter, and fifty cents for a newpaper. Although, in 1865, Barnard still had the government mail contract, many folk preferred to use the express service as there were more deliveries. Barnard provided envelopes with *Barnards Express* printed on them for express letters. These envelopes could be bought at any office of the company, which meant almost every mile house of consequence, for a dollar each. In 1868 the fare was again reduced to $85 and the rate for express parcels dropped to fifty cents a pound.

Barnard did not always have it all his own way. In 1871 Gerowe and Johnson of Victoria got the mail contract and a price-war ensued. After ten months they gave up the fight and sold their business to the *BX*. Four years later, in 1875, James and Edward Pearson, who had been running a freight service for some time, began a Yale-Barkerville stage line, and another price war followed. It is said that the fare for the journey went down as low as ten dollars. After a year of this the Pearson brothers, two Englishmen who had come to British Columbia in 1862 by way of the Horn, left the field of battle, defeated. We are told they came from Stockford, which, as Stockford does not exist, may be a mistake for Stockport, Stockton, Salford or Stamford.

For this enterprise many horses were needed, for fresh ones had to be ready and waiting at every stage. No less than 150 horses were always in a state of preparedness and another 250 were waiting "in the wings." In 1868 Barnard sent Steve Tingley down to California to bring 400 (perhaps 500) horses, mares and stallions, up to the newly founded BX ranch which is now Vernon. There the horses were bred and from the resulting herd of 2000 the best horses were chosen for work on the stages. Some say that Tingley went as far as Mexico on this buying trip.

Coaches were, however, no use in the winter when even the southern part of the Cariboo is blanketed with three to four feet of snow, while the northern part suffers falls of from six to ten feet. Nothing daunted by this problem, Barnard organized sleighs to replace the coaches in the winter and Wayne Huston, one of his more notable drivers was especially famed for his handling of a four-horse sleigh. The sleighs, like the coaches, varied in size; just as there were six-horse mail coaches and four-horse covered and open coaches, so there were small sleighs and sleighs which could accommodate fifteen people and their possessions.

The commencement of any journey by stage was an impressive spectacle. Willis J. West wrote in the *B.C. Historical Quarterly*:

These stage horses were never really broken. They were trained for staging alone and had to be handled in a way they would understand. To illustrate this the custom observed in preparing a stage and its horses for leaving a station had to be carefully and expertly carried out to ensure a safe departure. When the mail, express matter, and baggage had been loaded and securely lashed onto the stage, the passengers were requested to take their places. Then the driver with his treasure-bag took his seat and all was in readiness for the horses to be brought from their stable. First the wheel team was led out by the hostler who backed it into position on either side of the stage-pole and passed the lines to the driver. After this team was ready with harness and rigging adjusted to the satisfaction of the driver, the swing team appeared and the same procedure was followed. Finally the two leaders, the freest and most spirited horses in the six-horse team, were brought out and after the horses had indulged in much restless prancing, the hostler would eventually succeed in completing the 'hooking-up' of the team and would then quickly back out of the way. At this moment the driver released the brakes and the horses lunged forward, starting the stage on its way to the next station. Some teams when leaving a station at the beginning of their drive would behave in a most alarming manner and fill timid passengers with fear. The horses would stand on their hind legs and would seem to be so wildly entangled that a serious accident appeared inevitable. They would continue these antics until they had travelled 100 yards and then they would settle down to a brisk trot. In their natural health and vigour they could not refrain from these exuberant demonstrations.[20]

The stage drivers required great skill to handle a team of six horses on the rough Cariboo Road, and Tingley, when he was in charge of the operation was justifiably cautious in his hiring of drivers. Wayne Huston used to delight in telling of the first time he tried out for Tingley. Aware that he was being closely watched he grabbed all the six sets of reins in a bunch in one hand, and set out, expecting and receiving a roar from Tingley to "Come back." He did so immediately and presented Tingley with the picture of the ideal driver, each rein held correctly by the proper fingers in each hand. Tingley looked at him. "Go ahead!" he said, and Huston went ahead, grinning.

Huston was one of many skilled drivers who worked at one time or another for the *BX*. Mark S. Wade gives the names of Ned Tate, Ned Parsley, John McLeese (Captain Robert McLeese's nephew), Alex Tingley (Steve's brother), Harry Moffat, Sandy Locke, E. E. Bell, William Parker, L. Hautier, Louis Brousseau, Fred Tingley (Steve's son), John Hamilton, R. E. Smith, C. Westaby, W. Brash, F. Peters, W. Everson, A. C. Minty, J. M. Yorston, Robert Yorston (who

[20] Art Downs, *op. cit.*, p. 30.

bought the Australian Ranch), and Sam Marwick. These drivers did not only travel the main Cariboo Road. They also travelled the auxiliary roads to Quesnel Forks, Horsefly, Big Bar, Dog Creek, Alkali Lake and the Chilcotin. The *BX* also served the Okanagan, securing the mail contract for that area in 1874 and keeping it until 1881. In the early 1880's the *BX* also took mail from Spences Bridge to Kamloops by way of Nicola. Numerous express agents were also needed at the various stopping places. Barkerville was served, at one time or another, by Robert Poole, James B. Leighton, and the store of the Buie Brothers. J. M. Yorston supervised the branch routes to Quesnel Forks, Horsefly and the Chilcotin at 150 Mile, which was a busy and important junction.

Six horses were the maximum for stage coaches, but ten or more might be used for hauling a train of two or three freight wagons. When it came to bull teams, however, the number was likely to be twelve yoked pairs, twenty-four beasts in all. Each bull pair was harnessed in a cedar wood yoke from which two hooped collars or "bows" of maple wood depended; from the centre of the yoke an iron chain connected with the yoke of the pair behind. The driver or "bull-puncher" had a long bull-whip and at the beginning of the journey, while inspecting the oxen and their yokes, looking for chafings and sores, and testing the security of the chains, he would wear this around his neck. The inspection over, he would climb aboard the first of the three wagons, shout the names of the leading bulls, and start them pulling. Then he would divest himself of the whip and send it snaking out over the team, and crack it like a thunder clap. A good bull-puncher or bull-whacker, such as the gentleman variously named I. W. Strout and "Dirty Harry" Strousse who had the distinction of making the last bull-team journey up the road from Ashcroft on September 2, 1899, and who had the further and more remarkable distinction of being an ex-theological student, would wield the whip with such delicate precision that he could crash the whip behind the ear of any one of his twenty-four bulls without touching a single hair of its hide. A bull team would make 20 miles on a good day and 12 on a poor one.

Up the Cariboo Road, then, from 1863 to the end of the century, the stagecoaches, mule teams, and horse-drawn and bull-drawn wagon trains, careered, lumbered and plodded in their attendant clouds of dust, and along the way there were those ready to cater to them with pasturage, with hay, with meals, with lodgings and with blacksmith services. These mile houses served the fraternity of the

84

road faithfully until the coming of the Pacific Great Eastern Railway and of the automobile made the older methods of freighting unnecessary. Even then, however, in the twenties and thirties, there were still some wagon trains on the Cariboo Road, and they were still stopping at mile houses which had, under one owner or another, served travellers since the road first began.

CHAPTER FIVE

The Stopping Places

The buildings of Cariboo were as different from the buildings of today as was the Cariboo Road from our modern highways. At first the adventurers into Cariboo attempted to make do with tents, but these proved to be inadequate in many ways. They provided little protection against marauding men or animals, and were worse than useless in the harsh Cariboo winters. In the early days, of course, few of the gold seekers remained in the area during the winter months; they would travel to Victoria or the lower Fraser when the winter snows began, and only return to the diggings in the spring. Nevertheless, they found it necessary to build cabins that were strong enough to survive the elements during the time they were away, so that they could leave what equipment they had behind them in the goldfields. These cabins were built entirely of logs, Fred Ludditt describes their construction as follows:

The logs used in constructing the walls of the cabins were 'saddled' at the corners; that is they were cut to fit snugly together. In the earliest cabins a 'square-cut' method of saddling was used; in later cabins a more elaborate type of saddling, the 'dove-tail,' was common. The logs used in the gables were held together by wooden dowels. A hole was bored through a log and into the log below with an auger, and a dowel was driven through to pin the logs together.

When the logs reached the height of the door the larger auger was used to bore a hole into the bottom log and one into the top log before it was put in place. These holes were at the extreme right or left of the door sills. A small pole was shaped and set in the hole in the sill and the top log put in place, the pole fitting into the hole in the log at the door head and jamb. This log was firmly held by several dowels, and the pole then served as hinges for the door, the door being morticed and pinned to the pole.

In the opposite end of the cabin a hole was left in the wall from the floor. It was generally four feet high and about five feet wide. In this space the fireplace was built with clay and boulders, with the chimney being built up past the roof on the outside of the cabin. This served as both stove and light in winter evenings.

The roofs consisted of poles about five inches thick. They were split and laid in two layers on the roof. In the first layer, the round side was turned down, and in the second layer the round side was turned up, with each pole overlapping half of the pole beneath. The cabin was then chinked with moss and sometimes clay throughout.[21]

The furniture of the cabins was as primitive as the cabins themselves; beds, tables and stools were made from logs and poles; wooden pegs on the walls were hung with rudely fashioned traps, snowshoes, and other implements. Ammunition boxes served as tables and seats. A single iron cooking pot would be by the fire, along with the necessary minimum of tin mugs and "eating irons." The food was simple, the staples being bread, bacon or pork, beans, and tea (heavily sweetened). Salt was essential. Green vegetables were impossible to come by until the Chinese began to make their market gardens down the trail and early miners suffered a good deal from scurvy, and from typhoid (or "mountain fever"). There were no drains, or course, and the sewage dumped in the primitive earth closets was subject to water seepage and polluted the water supply Only simple medicines were available and there were no doctors apart from those who had given up the profession for prospecting; some of these turned back to practising medicine when they saw the desperate need of their services.

Many would-be gold seekers turned from mining to providing the miners with services. The first and most obvious need in the early days of settlement was the need to provide food and shelter for the travellers along the road, and it was not long before there were many road houses or mile houses as they were then called, along the roads and trails to the goldfields. These places were at first little more than large cabins, or even groups of cabins, but over the years they developed all the characteristics of proper hotels, complete with bar and, in at least one case, a poolroom. Famous road houses in the sixties were those at 70 mile, 83 mile, 100 mile, and 150 mile. Later 122 mile achieved a considerable reputation.

The reports of the travellers of the earliest days tell of many mile houses and stopping places. Harry Jones of the Company of Adventurers, in his recollections of travelling the road in 1863 describes the pleasure of travelling through Lac La Hache Valley where there were "wild strawberries" and where they stopped at the house of "Mr. Eddy of England, a very interesting old gentleman who could talk on any subject almost," of Mrs. Jones, a widowed

---

[21] Fred W. Ludditt, *Barkerville Days*, 1969, p. 66.

Irishwoman whose husband, Tom Jones, had been Welsh, of Murphy's 141 Mile House, and of the 150 Mile House owned by "Dais (Davidson) Brothers." Sent back to Lillooet by "Captain Evans" from Soda Creek to get more provisions he slept on the floor at 83 Mile House wrapped in his blanket. Travelling north again he used the 111 Mile House, and again, Mr. Eddy's and Mrs. Jones, and 150 Mile House. At Deep Creek Ranch he had a disturbed night "as the proprietor (Frank Way) and his friends played cards all night and made more noise than a half dozen thrashing machines." Mr. MacDonald (Jones' travelling companion, whom he had met on the road just before 150 Mile House), at different times during the night, asked them not to make so much noise. The answer from the gamblers was "we could go outside if we did not like it."[22]

Some of the Mile Houses were more crowded and more rowdy than others. Frank Way of Deep Creek had a deserved reputation as a roisterer and practical joker. On at least one occasion his sense of humour helped him turn a profit. Mark S. Wade tells the story:

In the fall of the year 1865, the Western Union Telegraph Company wintered a number of their horses at Deep Creek, and purchased the grain for feed from Frank Way. After a good deal of bargaining as to price, in which it was a case of diamond cut diamond, one shrewd Yankee against another, an agreement was finally reached on a basis of eight cents a pound. As a goodly quantity of grain was involved, Way suggested that a box four feet by four feet be constructed with projecting side pieces to serve as handles. This was to be filled with grain, then weighed, and taken as a standard measure to be used in the delivery of the quantity bargained for. One weighing would suffice for the whole transaction; it would be simply a case of so many measures containing so many pounds equalling such a total. This was accepted and the box was quickly made and weighed, all this taking place at the granary which was across the road, opposite the house. The weighing of the empty box over, Way put into effect a scheme he had planned beforehand.

"Come and have a drink while the men are filling the box!" he suggested, and as this met with unanimous approval all hands adjourned to the bar excepting Way's employees, who were busy shovelling grain into the box and as they shovelled they tamped it down hard and firm. Over at the bar, one drink did not satisfy and there was another, and Way encouraged delay. When the men at the granary had tamped down the grain as compactly as possible they filled in a top layer of loose grain and then one of them went over to the bar. "The box is full now," he announced, and he returned to the granary, closely followed by Way and the company's representatives. The box was then duly weighed, the net weight carefully noted by both parties to the bargain and Way smiled with inward satisfaction. The box of

22 F. W. Lindsay, *The Cariboo Dream*, 1971, p.

tamped grain resulted in a much greater weight than if the grain had just been shovelled in loosely—as was done subsequently and Way got the best of the bargain by a considerable amount, the company paying for a good deal more grain than they actually received.[23]

Harry Jones, in 1863, was lucky in having some money and in being able to pay his way; other travellers were less fortunate. A year earlier another prospector whose diary is quoted in F. W. Lindsay's *The Cariboo Story* reported on May 27, 1862, "Shot 1 rook and 1 hawk for dinner. Quite a treat, being on short fare. 1 lb rice between 5 men for breakfast. Walked 15 mi. Tented on farm land. Bought 12 lbs flour and 6 lbs beans of a packer." On June 3 he "Bought fish and duck of Indians" at Williams Lake. Had he in fact had the money to pay for lodgings he might not have fared very much better, at least as regards accommodation. W. Champness wrote of one stopping place in 1862 "Whilst staying here we were very crowded, as the small building was filled with miners by day and night, sleeping under the table and benches as well as on top of them, and all over the floor."[24]

The mile houses were not always busy, of course, and some of the most northerly could become very lonely places during the winter months. This was especially true of those nearest the goldfields. John Boyd, who operated both Coldspring House and Cottonwood House at Cottonwood wrote to J. F. Hawks on 26th January 1879:

Dear Sir,
Yours of 21st Just came to hand enclosing Mr. Girod's order on me. Which amt. please find enclosed as follows five Twenty Dollar B.B.N.A. (Bank of British North America) bills no. as follows 0225, 0248, 2409, 0410, 0455 also one ten Dollar bill no. 1580 two Dominion one Dollar bills no. 03668, 03975 and one American Half Dollar Piece. Now if any or all of the above are lost hunt them up.
No travel since you left. but Angus and the Mail down and the Mail up. Wish we had them Hours. Come up again with your own Teams and bring them if you have no business. come for Humanity Sake. We are it appears completely shut up here a little more snow has settled since you left but the weather has been Mild and the snow has settled therefore does not loom up so high but still high Enough to be continually looking at. So come up and bring Judge Heath with you. if Either of you has the least regard for us poor "Mortal's"

On the same day, clearly very much aware of the unlikelihood of any casual visitors until the spring thaw, he wrote to "Messrs Pinchbeck & Lyons, Williams Lake"

[23] Mark S. Wade, *op. cit.*, pp. 166-67.
[24] F. W. Lindsay, *The Cariboo Story*, 1968, p. 8.

Gents
   If Either of You are Coming up this way within the next three months and
you can make it convenient bring me a half dozen of your best hens.

by doing so

you will much

Oblige Yours

Very Respectfully

John Boyd

The firm from which John Boyd ordered these hens was not, in fact,
Pinchbeck & Lyons but Pinchbeck & Lyne. William Pinchbeck had
been the first appointed constable in Cariboo, and on giving up this
position he went into partnership with William (Billy) Lyne and
bought Tom Manifee's place beside Williams Lake. There he ran a
dairy farm and a grist mill on the land which now is occupied by
Williams Lake airport. The partnership was dissolved in the early
eighties and in 1884 or 85 Billy Lyne married Angelique Dussault,
the daughter of a French Voyageur, Joseph Dussault, and his Indian
wife. He then settled a piece of land at Nine Mile, which was so called
because it was nine miles from Soda Creek. Being a blacksmith by
trade he began by setting up a blacksmith's shop to serve the
freighters, and himself lived in a tent. The next building to be put up
was a stable, as the horses often had to be housed for a couple of days.
After this he built a bunkhouse to accommodate the drivers and
packers, and only then did he build a house for himself, his wife, and
their small children. In time he enlarged the bunkhouse so that he
could accommodate more travellers and thus the place became a
noted stopping place or mile house. When this trade slackened off he
built a sawmill and began ranching. He worked hard and every now
and again would find that he had to get away and would disappear to
Vancouver or Ashcroft on a spending spree, leaving Angelique in
charge. She was equal to the task, and certainly equal to emergencies.
   On one occasion, when her husband was away, she heard a team
coming along the road from the Williams Lake direction and also
some other inexplicable accompanying sounds. She went out and saw
that an Indian known as "Wild Jack" was riding his own horse alongside the stage and beating the driver with wild cries. He was wearing
only a loincloth and was painted all over. As she knew the man, she
called out to him and asked him what the matter was. He left the
stage driver alone and rode up to her and told her that he was on the
warpath and was going to kill all the white men. She said "You won't
kill me, will you?" and he said he would not because she was his
friend. "Is that a promise?" she asked. He said that it was a promise,

90

and added that when white men made a promise they kissed a book, but "We have no book. Me kiss you!" Angelique was not too enthusiastic about this as the man was frothing at the mouth. "I'll shake your hand" she said firmly and so they shook hands. He then realized that the wagon was getting away from him and already almost over the rise and on the road down into Soda Creek, so with a whoop, he went after it hell for leather. It is not recorded whether he caught up with it or what happened after that.

Some of the mile houses may have been lonely during the depths of winter, and many of them may have been a bit short on comfortable beds, but all seem to have been plentifully supplied with food. An average meal would include fresh beef, various kinds of pie, plenty of cabbage and beans, tea and coffee, and sometimes cakes. The food was usually all laid out and the travellers were invited to help themselves to as much as they wished. Some houses rapidly became small farms as well as stores, and several provided entertainment, especially in later years. Dances were frequent during the winter months, and some dances might go on for two or three days. C. C. "Dick" Allen, in the *100 Mile House Free Press* of 2 December 1970 recalled a dance at 150 Mile House at the New Year of 1922-23 which so filled the place that he had to sleep on the floor. The mile houses were indeed, right from the beginning, social centres as well as way stations, and the bigger mile houses could almost be called settlements in themselves, for they would consist of a number of buildings, including barns, a blacksmith's forge, a store as well as accommodation for travellers. They were often run by ex-miners, or by men who had been side-tracked on their way to the fields. One party of prospectors lost one of its members as soon as he saw the grass "high as a horses belly" round 47 mile; he settled there immediately. Another ex-miner, quoted by Art Downs, wrote to his father in Pittsburgh that he had quit mining and boasted

I have got a house for travellers and a store with grub. I have 3 tons of flour, 1000 pounds of coffee, sugar, butter, and beans, 600 lbs of pork, 90 gallons of schnaps of different kinds, and all kinds of tobacco and clothes. I have 7 head of cattle, 3 steers, 9 sheep, and a chicken house.[25]

The same inspiration clearly struck a good many people as the Cariboo Road grew into being. At 47 Mile House, where Gus Wright established a tollgate to pay for the expenses of his road (a penny a pound for freight, a shilling per animal, Indians and government equipment free) craftsmen and merchants were soon busy. Black-

[25] Art Downs, *op. cit.*, p. 30.

smith McLennan was one of the first to set up shop, and was quickly followed by a harness maker, and a storekeeper. The original hotel of the Smiths was followed by the erection of another hotel; astutely the Smiths put in a sawmill powered by a water wheel and made a profit out of supplying cut lumber to a competitor whose emergence was, after all inevitable. The first log cabin store of the Greenbaum Bros. was bought out by F. W. Foster of Lillooet who foresaw the increasing importance of the new settlement, and the Chinese, pouring into the area from the lower Fraser in the wake of the white miners, set up a store, a restaurant, a rooming house, and, inevitably, a laundry, as well as a handsome sporting house. It was a well appointed place and provided with a piano and much sheet music for vocal and auditory pleasure as well as with the necessary equipment and personnel for more private delights. By 1863 when the road from Yale met that from Lillooet at the 47 Mile House the settlement became generally known as The Junction, and only when the Smiths, obedient to Queen Victoria's ukase, changed the name over the door of their hotel to Clinton did the new name begin to stick in people's minds. Clinton was fortunate as a stopping place in that it was the point at which the up stage met the down stage and passengers and freight were moved from one coach to another. Thus the stops at Clinton were longer than most and there was more opportunity for commercial transactions to take place and liquid refreshments to be imbibed. By 1868 the population had swollen enormously from that of 1861 when Mr. and Mrs. Smith and Tom Marshall were the sole permanent white inhabitants, and when the first Clinton Ball was held on New Year's Day 1868 there were quite enough local ladies to make a success of it without the enthusiastic influx of others from Lytton, Lillooet, Lac La Hache and the ranches in the area. The dance went on till dawn, and the company had taken the trouble to dress in the height of fashion. Ball gowns had been imported from San Francisco; the men wore dress suits and kid gloves. Some ladies, it is said, even changed gowns several times during the course of the evening. It was not merely an expression of confidence in Clinton itself, and in the coming prosperity of the Cariboo in general, it was a proud claim that civilization and high society existed in these wilds.

There is no record how long that particular ball lasted; later ones were known to go on for as long as a week, those obliged to leave to perform necessary chores being replaced by others and then returning themselves, having established baby-sitters and other substitutes at home. In the next years two more blacksmith shops were established, another general store, and the government agent received a fine residence and was provided with a courthouse and jail to manage. A bigger schoolhouse was needed and Ed Norton, already manufacturing handmade bricks, got the contract, but miscalculated as to the costs, and went out of business as soon as the building was completed.

Cattle drives were now coming through town. Colonel Palmer and others drove the herds up from Oregon and got a good price per head. Others drove the herds up the road to the goldfields or to the towns that supplied them. Cattle ranches were already spreading across the green rolling plains of the valley, though the ranchers were troubled somewhat by the herds of wild horses which roamed all over the country from Clinton up to the Lac La Hache Valley. The young men herded the wild horses into "box" canyons by means of fences or "wings." Some they broke and sold locally; others they drove elsewhere. Gilbert Forbes of Lac La Hache recalled driving wild horses over to the railhead at Ashcroft and selling them at twelve dollars apiece early in the new century.

Clinton must have been an exciting place in the sixties, seventies, and eighties, but it was still as reliant upon the travellers to the goldfields for its prosperity as were the mile houses farther north, to whom it sold so much of its merchandise.

One of the most important mile houses was 150 Mile. The Davison brothers settled there in 1861, and it soon became clear that, as they were 45 miles from Horsefly, 54 from Quesnel Forks, and on the roads leading to Dog Creek and the Chilcotin, they were in as strategic a position for trade as was Williams Lake. When the new road came through 150 Mile became a regular stopping place for all; the Davison brothers sold it to A. S. Bates who rented it to others for a while and then, in 1870, took it over himself and soon had a store, a blacksmith's shop, and 400 head of cattle as well as a hotel which included a billiard table that had been installed before 1868. Jim Griffin leased the property in 1875 and in 1876 it was taken over by Gavin Hamilton, Chief Factor of Hudson's Bay at Fort St. James who wanted to move near to the Mission School run by the Oblate Fathers not far away, because of his large family. Hamilton gave the place up to Veith and Borland in the middle 80's and they eventually sold it to an English company for $90,000. In its heyday 150 Mile was a noted place of entertainment with a great deal of poker being played and large bets being placed on the results of horse races and dog fights.

100 Mile House began as a camping place for the fur brigade.

When the rush started Thos. Miller saw the place's possibilities and built a mile house there in 1862-63. In 1874 it was owned by Nelson and Charlton, and the accompanying store was run by Carter. A telegraph office opened there in 1877, later moving to 115 Mile. In the middle eighties a brother of Gavin Hamilton (either James or Thomas) took it over. It passed through the hands of William Allen next, and then those of Sydney and Frank Stephenson. In 1912 G. C. Cowan bought it in his capacity as agent for the Marquis of Exeter, and the Marquis' son Lord Martin Cecil took it over in 1930.

The Letterbooks and Daybooks of the mile houses, stopping places, and stores of the Cariboo of the last quarter of the nineteenth century, though rarely giving much detail, nevertheless provide a fascinating picture of the way of life of the time. One such daybook is that of Lansdown Farm which was a stopping place and place for changing horses on the road south from Quesnel not far from Alexandria. Harry Moffatt, who began the series of daybooks, which run in an unbroken series from their beginnings to the present day, came to Cariboo from Pembroke, Ontario, aged twenty-three, in the year 1875. He married Jennie Roddy, an Irish Catholic, and the girls of the family were all raised as Catholics and the boys as Presbyterians. He first worked with survey crews for the C.P.R. and then became a road superintendent and it was he who discovered that snow-blocked roads could be made passable by rolling the snow flat with a field roller, not the usual stone-crushing roller used for roads. He became a stage driver and later went into business for himself as a teamster, freighting goods up to Barkerville from his farm which was also a stopping place for stagecoaches. He was frequently away from home and on these occasions his wife kept up the daybook. When her husband had been absent for more than a few days she ceased to refer to him as "Harry" but called him "Moffat", later, as his absence continued, altering this to "The Boss." She was not averse to putting down her feelings in the daybook as well as her accounts and there is one entry which reminds one of John Boyd's dismal letter to J. F. Hawks; on December 31, 1893 she wrote "I tell you or whoever wants to know this has been a long day." The passing scene was recorded faithfully if brusquely: "April 3rd 92 Wild Geese passed over," "Sept 16th, 1891 Three Chinaman went up on mountain today for to cut hay." On November 20, 1891 there is a laconic note, "Chinaman got $150.00 left for China."

Most of the Chinese working in Cariboo during these years returned to China once they had made a reasonable amount of

94

money, the young ones in order to marry and the old ones to die. Thus, although Cariboo had a vast Chinese population, some working in the mines, and others running businesses, serving as cooks and housemen, and working as market gardeners, only a minority can be said truly to have settled in the country.

There was a constant stream of travellers along the road in the nineties as in the seventies and eighties, and the Moffat daybook records some of the more notable:

26th August 1891. One passenger on stage —
School teacher for Quesnelle

June 6th 1891. Passengers going down

John Bowron   Gold Comm Cariboo
James Stone   Postmaster
James Reid   Senator
Mr. Hancock   England

August 15th 1892. Judge Riealy

Family news was included, as well as matters pertaining to business

Sept 6th 92   Roddy born
Nov 21st 92   Dentist Jones, Barkerville came here Saturday afternoon and left Sunday A.M. after fixing Ryland's teeth
June 2 93   Bought hogs from Dunleavy
Oct 10 1893   Bought steel skate from Duke of Sutherland when on way down. He having come threw (sic) Fort Edmonton
27th May 1893 Duke of York 3 Meals & bed $2.00

This last named duke was not, it seems, entitled to his soubriquet, being a local and notorious tramp.

The mile houses of the last years of the nineteenth century were not only stopping places but news gathering centres; it was at the mile houses that travellers exchanged information of all kinds. Many of them also developed into settlements, as did 47 Mile and 100 Mile. Some of them remained in the hands of one family for many years; others passed from owner to owner. Some of them began as ranches and became stopping houses; others reversed the process. Some were connected with the Barnard's Express itself. The 108 Mile House was first owned by Bill Roper, then (in 1884) by William Walker, and then by Steve Tingley and his two sons, Fred and Clarence as a way-station for the company. It was managed by Clarence until the end of the century.

Lac La Hache, like 100 Mile began as a stopping place for the fur brigade. Archibald McKinley, the son-in-law of Peter Skene Ogden, the Hudson's Bay factor at Fort St. James from 1835 onwards, was working for the company at Fort Alexander in the mid forties and travelling from there to Kamloops with the fur traders, when he discovered the green sparsely wooded grassland of Lac La Hache and decided to settle there. He staked out his lot in 1862-63 at the east end of the lake where he built a cabin to house himself and his wife, three sons, two daughters, and Julia Ogden, his widowed mother-in-law. The log cabin soon proved inadequate and was made part of a new two-storey building for travellers, who proved so numerous that more land and cattle were needed. In 1870 he was joined in the area by his nephew by marriage, Isaac Ogden, who opened the only general store and fur depot of any importance between Clinton and 150 Mile. Isaac also acted as Indian Agent for the area. He died in 1927 and was buried in the cemetery of St. Joseph's Mission near Williams Lake.

So, from 1863 onwards the new road created settlements and problems and opportunities, and while the mile houses and their attendant settlements changed hands and fortunes, at each end of it grew bustling towns. When "Captain" Evans and Harry Jones and the rest of the Company of Adventurers started their journey north in the spring of 1863 the road had got within 8 miles of Soda Creek and had still to reach Alexandria, but Soda Creek was already lively. Peter Dunleavy had established his popular Hotel there, having moved from Beaver Lake and left the place in the hands of Jim Sellers, who had taken Agat, the Indian girl he had met at the 1859 games, as his common-law wife. Her children became prominent in the area, and the present Chief Sellers of the Soda Creek Indians and his father before him, are descendants of Agat. Tom Manifee bought a ranch on Mud (later McLeese) Lake; he may have also been the Manifee of Williams Lake who quarrelled with Gus Wright, though it seems unlikely. Tom Moffit (or Moffat) gave his name to Moffats Creek, married a Shuswap girl and settled down to ranch, probably near Alexandria. John MacLean, whose temper had always been quick, and who had a history of trouble with Indians, whom he treated arrogantly and roughly, was already dead; a Chilcotin arrow had killed him while he was panning a bar on the Fraser south of Williams Lake. Ira Crow, thought by some to be a negro, but described by McInnes as a "typical lean and lanky all-round California miner" seems to have disappeared, though an Ira Crow was buying stores in Soda Creek in 1870; local tradition also has it that Edmund Shepherd ran a man called Ira Crow out of town for paying undue attentions to his wife.

Dunleavy himself, of all the partners, was clearly the man of success. When Harry Jones arrived at Soda Creek with his new friend MacDonald, and Dunleavy who had been forewarned by a letter from "Captain" Evans welcomed him, and showed him the dining room and told him when the bell for supper would be rung and arranged to take him next morning to the *Enterprise*, he clearly impressed the young Welsh prospector as he impressed many. McInnes describes Dunleavy as follows

He was about five feet nine inches tall and would weigh in his prime about a hundred and seventy five pounds. Of light complexion, he had fair straight hair and blue eyes. Mostly he would wear the Yankee beard, or chin whisker as it was then called, sometimes with a moustache but usually not. I have seen him clean shaven too.

After he quit active manual mining for a businessman's life, he was never seen except in a white shirt with a stiff starched front—the 'boiled shirt' of the time, but without collar or tie—unless the occasion demanded a coat. His vest was always open except for one or two buttons at the bottom and it carried a gold watch and heavy chain and gold-mounted magnifying glass. But so rarely as to be almost never, did he wear a coat in his own house. And there were many Americans like him in those days who seemed to consider the boiled shirt stood for everything in the businessman's conventional dress. (He prided himself on his personal appearance, but had his own notions of what a gentleman should wear.)

Yet among his occupations, he was first, last and all the time a miner. He would grubstake anyone in whose character he had confidence to go prospecting on a 50-50 basis, and it mattered not at all to him that the man knew nothing about mining. To his friends who would remonstrate with him he would say,

"What's the odds? It's all a gamble anyway. I love the element of chance in it, and I'm willing to pay for it, besides they say 'a fool for luck.' So if he's a fool as a miner and I'm a fool for staking him why then there's two fools. So we should have double luck. That's sound logic, isn't it? Anyway it's what I'm betting on."[26]

Thus was the proprietor of the Colonial Hotel at Soda Creek in the summer of 1863, welcoming the prospectors and the other travellers, escorting them to the newly launched *Enterprise*, and, it is said, quietly becoming owner of almost all the land the length of thriving Soda Creek, the northern gateway to the fields of gold.

[26] Edith Beeson, *op. cit.*, p. 14.

CHAPTER SIX

From Soda Creek to Quesnel 1860-1870

Soda Creek in the sixties was a thriving settlement. Dunleavy's Hotel, store, and farm were busy, as were Robert McLeese's hotel and store. In 1863 Soda Creek residents complained that it was stupid for Williams Lake to have the central post office for the region, especially as the settlement had been bypassed by the new road. Soda Creek's post office opened in 1864, as did other post offices in Quesnelle-mouth, Van Winkle, Keithley, and Quesnel Forks, and on Williams Creek. Until this period the greater part of the necessary supplies for the goldfields had been packed in from the south, and, while now the freight trains made supplies easier and prices cheaper, it was obvious that some produce could be raised locally. Williams Lake had already begun to grow grain in the area that later became the Stampede Grounds, and Alexandria had been growing it since the early nineteenth century, and had even ground its own flour in the years 1842-48. When the Hudson's Bay Company abandoned Fort Alexander the farm was leased for a while to Archibald McKinley of Lac La Hache who had once served there, and then in 1880 it became the property of Alexander Douglas MacInnes. Other farms and ranches were springing up in the area. In 1861 G. Weaver and J. May established a ranch at Mud Lake (now McLeese Lake), and two years later Robert McLeese also (with J. T. Lenay and Robert Stoddart) began to farm in the valley. McLeese, like Dunleavy, sold his farm produce through his own store in Soda Creek. Other important farms between Soda Creek and Quesnellemouth were the Australian (begun in 1863 by Andrew Olsen, W. H. and Stephen Downes), and the Bohanon Ranch, which was created by Samuel H. Bohanon by combining the earlier holdings of V. Mackenzie, Sam Brierly, A. Saunders and Charles Kersley (the settlement is now called Kersley) late in the decade. All these farms had Soda Creek as their main centre, though the Mud Lake settlement was also becoming impressive. Alexander Saunders had a store there, presumably to sell his produce, and Sellers, Hamilton and Company had a big house. The amount of grain being grown in the area made the provision of flour mills essential. Gus Wright planned a big one for Quesnellemouth, but couldn't get the government subsidy he wanted. Jerome Harper and J. H. Scott built one in Clinton in 1868. Before both these, however, John R. Adams, having taken over the project from W. H. Woodcock, had his grist mill working on Soda Creek itself, at the lower end of the village, and actually on the Indian reservation. This mill (which continued to operate until 1947) has been called the first flour mill in Cariboo, though William Pinchbeck and Billy Lyne were operating their grist mill at Williams Lake as early as the middle sixties. Pinchbeck had been the first constable in the area and on his retirement settled down to growing grain beside Williams Lake. He applied and obtained, for sixty pounds a year, a licence also to operate a distillery. His product which is reported to have been not unlike vodka and extremely powerful was usually referred to as Williams Lake Jawbone, it is presumed because it made people extremely talkative, or possibly because it felled men as effectively as that Jawbone of an ass which is celebrated in the bible; it was much in demand by the miners of the time. He may have been more interested in distilling than in milling, for in 1868 R. A. Collins, who bought Weaver and May's Mud Lake Ranch and two other farms from R. L. Brown and John Oscar Smith thought it worthwhile to build another flour mill four and a half miles south of the Soda Creek mill at Deep Creek.

It is clear that Collins, McLeese and Dunleavy intended to be as self sufficient as possible. This is typical of the pioneering families of Cariboo at this period, and, indeed, well into the twentieth century. Farmers were also freighters, hoteliers, and blacksmiths. Some, like H. H. Moffat of Landsdowne at Alexandria, in the nineties, raised potatoes as well as cattle and horses, ran a stopping house which was a staging post for Barnard, and dealt with merchants along the road from Soda Creek to Barkerville. Billy Lyne of Nine Mile Ranch south of Morgan Creek in the eighties, not only provided a staging post, hotel, and blacksmith's shop but also a lumber mill, the first in the Soda Creek region. Much can be learned of the activities and the trade way of life of the settlements in the last early days of the Soda Creek settlements from the daybooks of the stores. McLeese's Day Books for 1867-76 reveal that a great deal of produce was bartered and much was paid for by work. In 1870 Ah Choy, a Chinese cook, paid his bill by working for ten and a half months at fifty dollars a month. In 1868 a Mr. Watson settled his account by working for $2.50 a day. In 1868 Dunleavy & Co. paid their account with beef at 15¢ a pound, oats at 5¢, and two boxes of cigars for $12.50. In 1870 Ah Sing paid a bill of $33.50 with gold dust, and in 1871 Van Valkingburg & Co. paid for their purchases with sheep. Some customers took a long time to pay their bills, and were charged interest by the store. Chas. McHurdy owed $20.50 in October 1868; by December 1876, after ninety-eight months' interest at two percent, he owed $76.09. The entry in the daybook is marked "taken to Victoria," which means of course, "to court." Malcolm McLeod & Co, were more fortunate; they bought goods to the amount of $415.58 in October 1869 and in November 1870, the interest on the debt having amounted to $84.42, paid off the whole with $500 in gold dust.

While most of the goods listed in the daybooks are clearly necessities, some are not. In 1868 an order by mail to Thomas Briggs resulted in the receipt by the hotel of 2 casks of absinthe for $29.00, 1 case of brandy for $225.00, and 2 bottles of champagne for $66.00, as well as 112 lbs of butter for $89.60.

It is easy to understand why Soda Creek in the sixties and seventies was so busy. Until 1865 the only means of transporting goods easily over the last stage of the journey to the goldfields was by Gus Wright's riverboat, the *Enterprise*, and that made Soda Creek an important centre. Even after the road to Alexandria had been extended to Quesnel many travellers preferred the entertaining river voyage to the discomfort of the roads. The voyage appears to have been made especially entertaining by the personality of Captain Doane, if we are to rely upon the diary of Dr. Cheadle who accompanied the Viscount Milton on a trip across Canada in 1862-63.

Thursday, October 15th—My Birthday but I forgot to keep it. A long ride with tired horses; dined at Frank Way's 114-mile, he has farm valley 4 miles long and 1/4 wide; over 200 acres; a considerable part of this growing oats & barley which is cut principally for hay. Then, leaving the valleys, we crossed timbered hills, descending by a sinuous & very steep road into the valley of the Fraser once more at Soda Creek to wait here where there were a few houses, for the steamer at noon tomorrow. House kept by a Yankee. All 'Docs' & 'Caps.'

Friday, October 16th—Steamer came in about 2 o'clock bringing a host of miners 2 of whom were very drunk & continued to imbibe every 5 minutes; during the time we stayed in the house they must have had 20 drinks. The swearing was something fearful. After we had been on board a short time the Captain, finding out who we were, gave us the use of his cabin, a comfortable little room, & supplied us with cigars & a decanter of cocktail, also books & papers. We were fetched out every few minutes to have a drink with some one, the Captain taking the lead by standing champagne all round. We had some dozen to do before supper; no one the least affected, Milton and I shirking in quantity. The 'Cap' told us the boat was built on the river, all the timber sawn by hand, the shaft in 5 pieces packed up on mules, cylinders in two, boiler plates in same manner. Boat cost $75,000.!

Saturday, October 17th—As we did not leave Soda Creek until 4 & the boat makes very slow progress against the powerful current, we had to anchor for night after doing only some 10 miles. At daybreak went on 4 or 5 miles, & then delayed by the dense fogs which prevail on the river in the early morning at this season. Passed Fort Alexander about 10. No great trade there now; depots of furs from the north; 20 miles from Soda Creek. Country more level and under usual Fraser benches, & low wooded hills; river banks sandy; few rocks; River about size of Saskatchewan at Edmonton; Coal found on banks. Continually called out to have a drink.

Sunday, October 18th—Arrived about 9, at Quesnel mouth, a little collection of about 20 houses on the wooded banks of the Fraser. Quesnel at the north side of the Fort. Large new stores & cards all lying about the street. A drizzling rain all day. We made up our pack and set out. Captain Done met us in street half seas over & insisted to treat us to champagne, & c., at every bar in the place. At last escaped & walked to 4-mile house. ... We stayed there all night. Packers playing cards. Proprietor one of the Canadians who had come overland and down the Fraser last year. Gave fearful account of hardships especially on the raft.

On their return to Quesnel from the goldfields Cheadle and Milton found that the *Enterprise* had been laid up for the winter. Nevertheless they chose to call on Captain "Done" and experience his hospitality once more:

Wednesday, November 4th—Steamer stopped & hauled on to the bank—row boat going down tomorrow to Yale which will take us to Soda Creek. Numerous Chinamen keep stores here. Chinese & English signs, "Kan See washing, ironing & Bakery" ... &c. &c. Called on Captain Done on the Steamer. Cocktails every five minutes, & champagne lunch afterwards. Happiest man I ever saw. Steward tells me he takes a cocktail every ten minutes when on board. Very jolly fellow. Had to give a keg of brandy to his men before they could haul the steamer on shore. Gave them a champagne dinner on being paid off today, & we heard them singing away below deck. Paid $10 for passage in boat to Soda Creek.

The journey to Soda Creek by water was not as comfortable in winter as in the summer. Dr. Cheadle's account of it is little short of horrendous:

Thursday, November 5th—"Captain" McBride got his boat, a large strongly built 6 oar, ready to start about 11 o'clock & we, together with some 40 other passengers, embarked; very crowded; no room to sit comfortably; like flock of penned sheep. He said he had taken 50 in the same boat last year, & ran thro' to Yale, where he intended to go this time if he could get sufficient passengers. It was a miserably cold, raw, cloudy November day just such as we have in England, & snowing fast, & we were dreadfully starved in spite of several whiskey bottles which came out very soon after we started, & were all emptied before we got very far. The river was unusually low, but we ran all the "riffles" successfully until we came to one below Alexandria, when McBride was induced to take the wrong side by the affirmation of a passenger that the steamer always took that course. Here we stuck fast in a tremendous stream, & could not get her off; there was therefore nothing for it but for some of the men to jump overboard & lighten the boat & help to push her off; several volunteered at once, & carried some of the passengers ashore on their backs, the water being only knee deep. One unfortunate little man got a gigantic miner on his back, & losing his footing, both fell overhead into the water & got thoroughly soused, the small fellow tumbling 3 or 4 times before he could get on his legs against the strong current. Water like ice & day cold enough. Milton & I in the most cowardly manner stuck to the ship & taking the drenched men on board again & wrapping them in blankets, we went on until it was almost dark, when the "Cap" suggested camping for the night. Several daredevils urged going forward, but as we were still 10 miles from Soda Creek, & the river so very dangerous, they were overruled by the more sensible, & we put ashore at a large pile of wood belonging to the steamer with which we made free to kindle some enormous fires which were kept going all night. The Captain produced plenty of bread & butter & a flitch of bacon, which with some tea went very well. Milton & I each had a blanket lent us in addition to our own one each, & he constructed a covering of pine boughs which with plenty of brush to lie on made very snug quarters for the night. I collected lots of small pine boughs, & with my feet to the fire, & a good stock of logs to replenish it, spent a very comfortable night.

Friday, November 6th—Most of the men up before daybreak. Snowing heavily, & I kept my head under the blankets until dawn. We did not start until quite light & made Soda Creek in about an hour. There were several bad places in the river, rock sticking out in the rapids, which made us very thankful we did not try them in the dark. Had breakfast at Soda Creek, left our baggage there for the express to bring forward, & then walked quietly on to Frank Way's (Deep Creek) where we spent the night.[27]

A few days later, while staying at Davidson's Lake Valley Farm fourteen miles south of Deep Creek, Dr. Cheadle tells of another encounter with the river.

Saturday November 14th—A number of men arrived on way down from William's Creek. Came down in canoes. One laden to water's edge with 14 men swamped in rough water of first riffle 2 miles below Quesnel; 7 men lost; of the others, 5 clung to canoe & got ashore, one was thrown on beach by an eddy, with money & blankets all safe. Another swam ashore, but obliged to

[27] *Cheadle's Journal of Trip Across Canada 1862-63*, 1931, pp. 259-60.

102

drop his blankets containing the dust when within a few yards; 3 or 4,000 dollars lost; 5 belonging to Prince of Wales claim. Adam Ross (in whose cabin we stopped on Lightning Creek) told us that his partner (whom we also met there) was one of those lost altho' a good swimmer. He delayed a day at the mouth in order to try & get a companion to go by Bentinck Arm & thus escaped. I remember the riffle well, a tremendous rush of water & very rough so that even our large boat shipped water.[28]

At the time Dr. Cheadle wrote his diary and revealed for us the hazards of the river journey between Soda Creek and Quesnel Mouth that city had become one of the busiest centres of Cariboo south of Barkerville. While it was still, in terms of permanent buildings, little more than a village, it was subjected to a constant stream of people travelling to and from the goldfields. Not far from the town itself hundreds of Chinese were working Nine Mile Bar; the two ferries were constantly in service, and Jerome Harper's mill was under construction. That winter the *Colonist* commented:

> Mouth of Quesnelle. What a change! The few scattered huts and shanties that in the month of June last collectively struggled for a name—for to call it a town or hamlet would be a libel on the language—have all disappeared and are replaced by excellent buildings, fronting on a good street. Everything looks clean, orderly and business-like. Messrs. Brown and McBride, G. B. Wright, Laumeister and May have control of the business of this future entrepot of the mines. The Streamer ENTERPRISE has been a great success this year. Captain Doane, her commander, is a universal favorite with all classes and creeds.

Newspaper prophecies about Cariboo had up till this time rarely proved accurate; many settlements had been touted as future cities and had lasted only a few summer months: this time, however, the *Colonist* was right. Though in 1862 there was only one store to welcome the overlanders and by 1865 the town still only consisted of one line of buildings facing the Fraser, there were two hundred regular inhabitants, half of them Chinese, and the considerable transient population was catered to by several trading posts, hotels, and restaurants. The population was very mixed. The main hotel, the Occidental, was run by Thomas Brown and Hugh Gillis from Great Britain. One of the two butcher shops was operated by Russians; the drugstore was opened by an old Chinese and largely stocked with oriental remedies. The Kwong Lee & Co. store began in 1865, and in 1867 the Hudson's Bay Company built a store, a dwelling house, and two warehouses.

There were also a livery stable, two blacksmiths' shops, a sawmill, a post office, an office of Barnard's Express and a barbershop. There

[28] *Ibid.*, p. 261.

103

was a brewery operated by James Kerr and James Duhig. The main banks of the area, however, remained in the Barkerville district; the solitary Quesnel bank, a branch of the bank of British Columbia, was founded during the gold rush period, but closed on October 27, 1866 and thereafter the citizens of Quesnel used Barkerville banks until they closed at the turn of the century leaving no bank at all in Cariboo proper, until 1909.

Life in Quesnel in the sixties and seventies was not, however, all business. The strip of land between the buildings of Front Street and the river was used for races, and on July 8, 1865 Frank Way won the first race with his "Boston Colt" and received a $200 prize.

Quesnel was determined, clearly, to enjoy itself and not to be denied its place in the sun. On September 14, 1865 at 3:00 p.m. the telegraph cable from New Westminster which had reached Yale on August 26 and which had been laid along the river through Soda Creek and Alexandria reached the town. This line, the Collins Overhead Telegraph, had been planned by Perry McDonough Collins, and was intended to be part of a line linking North America to Europe, the line running from Chicago through British Columbia and Siberia. In 1866, the first successfully laid transatlantic cable from Ireland to Newfoundland spelled the end of Collins' venture, but the line to Quesnel remained and in 1868 Thomas R. Buie, at a cost of ten thousand dollars, extended it to Barkerville, which it reached on July 4th. The line did not, however, pay its way, and in 1869 when the government ceased to maintain and operate the line to Quesnel, it was abandoned. When the government gave up the line to Quesnel, J. L. Hughes, the Clinton postmaster and telegraph operator, and Yates, the operator at Soda Creek, decided to keep the line open between their respective offices, and maintain it. They did this for twelve months but then were forced out of business by the work it required and the poor returns. Thereafter for some years there was no telegraph service in Cariboo.

It is not difficult to understand why both government and private business found it impossible to make a profit out of the telegraph. The maintenance of the line must have presented enormous difficulties, as, initially, did the creation of it. Edmund Conway spent the winter of 1865-66 in Quesnel preparing to take the telegraph farther up river and later described his achievements of the following summer in such a way as to give a very clear picture of the problems not only he but all builders of roads and railways in British Columbia had to face. He wrote:

We constructed the Telegraph Road, and line to latitude 55.42 N and longitude 128.15 W. The distance from Quesnel, by the road, is computed at 440 miles, and by the wire 378 miles. There are 15 stations built, a log house, with chimney, door and windows, 25 miles apart. We built bridges over all small streams, that were not fordable, corduroyed swamps. All hillsides too steep for animals to travel over, were graded, from 3 to 5 feet wide. The average width of clearing the woods for the wire, is, in standing timber, 20 feet; and in fallen timber, 12 feet. All underbrush and small timber is cleared to the ground, thus leaving the road fit for horses, travelling at the rate of from 30 to 50 miles per day. Double wires are stretched across all large rivers. . . .[29]

By 1868 the telegraph service in Cariboo was well established. There were offices at Clinton, 83 Mile, Soda Creek, Quesnel and Barkerville. In 1865 there was a temporary office at Frank Way's Deep Creek Ranch, the operator being Robert Burns McMicking. He was one of the Overlanders of 1862 who had travelled from Fort Garry (Winnipeg) to Edmonton in Red River wagons, and then gone over the mountains with pack animals. He had been one of the party who had travelled by raft down the Fraser to Quesnel, arriving on September 1, 1862, three of the company having been drowned on the way. McMicking was later responsible for bringing the first Bell telephone to Victoria and for giving the city electric light. It may have been his stay at Deep Creek which gave Frank Way his idea. Business in Cariboo had fallen off, and there were fewer travellers on the road, and Way was deeply in dept. He decided to abandon Deep Creek to his creditors, but was certain that once people got wind of his departure the telegraph would be used and he would be capiassed, which is to say arrested and his possessions siezed, at either 83 Mile or Clinton. He therefore cut the telegraph line three miles south of Deep Creek. Yates, the operator at Soda Creek, on discovering that the line had gone dead, set out to find the break. He found and repaired it, but then discovered that the line was still out of order. He searched further, carrying with him the regulation length of between twenty and thirty feet of telegraph wire to deal with difficult breakages. Eight miles south of the first break he found that his wire was inadequate. Two hundred feet of line had been cut off and removed. He went back to Soda Creek and picked up his equipment and drove as fast as he could to 150 Mile which was well below the break. There he cut into the line and telegraphed to 83 Mile for the people there to send him wire. There was not enough. He therefore telegraphed Clinton, which could provide enough wire, but not until the up-stage

[29] Gordon R. Elliot, *op. cit.*, p. 52.

105

arrived in a few days time. Yates had no idea of the culprit, nor of the reason for what must have seemed pure vandalism, or Frank Way, who by now was well on his way, would have been in trouble. As it was, he reached Yale in safety, sold his horse and buggy, got onto a steamboat, and continued his journey. He was not seen in Cariboo again. His Deep Creek Ranch was taken by his creditors, and after some years it became the property of the government who made it an Indian reservation, which it remains.

Frank Way was not the only man in difficulty in the middle sixties. The gold rush was now over. The supply of placer gold had dwindled, and more and more capital and machinery were needed to mine the deeper deposits. Some of the settlements vanished; most of them dwindled. As a consequence those who needed stores and supplies and who were not working on Williams Creek, found it more necessary than before to turn to Quesnel, so the businessmen in Quesnel prospered. In 1868 Quesnel received another boost from the fates, for "Twelve Foot" Davis found gold in Arctic Creek on the upper Omineca River. Vital LaForce and Michael Burns then discovered gold at Vital Creek and the Omineca Gold Rush had begun. Though Quesnel was 230 miles from the new mines it was well situated to provide a staging post for supplies sent up through the interior. Gus Wright and Edgar Marvin of Victoria were so convinced of the importance of the new fields that, using the engines from an old Lillooet Lake streamer, *The Prince of Wales*, they had James Trahey build a sternwheeler which they named *The Victoria*. It ran from Soda Creek to Quesnel and when the *Enterprise* went farther north it ran to Cottonwood Canyon. In 1879 *The Victoria* was bought by Robert McLeese of Soda Creek and Captain John Irving. It remained in service until 1886 when it was retired from service at Alexandria. Meanwhile the *Enterprise* in 1871 attempted to go direct to the new goldfields. It went up the Nechako to Takla Landing by way of the Stuart and Tachie Rivers and Trembleur Lake, and there it remained. The journey had taken too long to be practicable, and the necessary equipment was by then travelling overland.

The Omineca gold rush was followed in 1874 by the Cassiar rush and that also brought business to Quesnel. When Cassiar was played out there was renewed activity on Lightning Creek. Thus right into the seventies Quesnel held its own and remained a gateway to the goldfields, though never again filled with such excitement and confidence as in the sixties when Dr. Cheadle and Lord Milton made their trip up river from Soda Creek on the *Enterprise*.

106

CHAPTER SEVEN

Williams Creek in 1863

In October 1863 when Dr. Cheadle and Viscount Milton visited the goldfields the three towns of Richfield, Barkerville (or Middle Town) and Cameronton formed an almost continuous street along Williams Creek. Byron Johnson, whose book *Very Far West Indeed*, was published in 1872, described the scene in detail:

For two or three miles down Williams Creek all the available ground appeared to be taken up, and the place bore a wonderful resemblance to an ant's nest. The unfortunate little stream had been treated in the most ignominious manner. A little above the town it flowed along silvery and clear as it had been wont to do; but soon inroads were made upon its volume in the shape of ditches cut from it, and continued along the sides of the hills, to feed the huge over-shot water-wheels that appeared in all directions. Then its course became diverted into five or six different channels, which were varied every now and then as the miners sought to work the surface formerly covered by them. At intervals dirty streams were poured forth by the sluices, in which the earth dug from beneath was being washed by the water; and here and there the stream was insulted by being shut up for a few hundred yards in a huge wooden trough called a "flume".

Across the breadth of the little valley was a strange heterogenous gathering of smaller flumes, carrying water to the different diggings and supported at various heights from the ground by props, windlasses at the mouths of shafts, water-wheels, banks of 'tailings' (the refuse earth washed through the sluices), and miners' log huts.

On the sides of the hills the primeval forests had been cleared for a short distance upwards, to provide timber for mining purposes, and logs for the huts. These abodes were more numerous on the hill sides than in the bottom of the valley, as being more safe from removal.

The town comprised the ordinary series of rough wooden shanties, stores, restaurants, grog shops, and gambling saloons; and, on a little eminence, the official residence, tenanted by the Gold Commissioner and his assistants and one policeman, with the British flag permanently displayed in front of it, looked over the whole.

In and out of this nest the human ants poured all day and night, for in wet-sinking the labour must be kept up without ceasing all through the twenty-four hours, Sundays included. It was a curious sight to look down the creek at night, and see each shaft with its little fire, and its lantern, and the dim ghostly figures gliding about from darkness into light, like the demons at a Drury Lane pantomime, while an occasional hut was illuminated by some weary labourer returning from his nightly toil.

The word here seemed to be WORK, and nothing else; only round the bar-rooms and gambling tables were a few loafers and gamblers to be seen. Idling was too expensive a luxury in a place where wages were from two to three pounds per day, and flour sold at six shillings a pound.

The mingling of noises was as curious as that of objects. From the hills came the perpetual cracking and thudding of axes, intermingling with the crash of falling trees, and the grating undertone of the saws, as they fashioned the logs into planks and boards. From the bottom of the valley rose the splashing and creaking of water-wheels, the grating of shovels, the din of the blacksmith's hammer sharpening pickaxes, and the shouts passed from the tops of numerous shafts to the men below, as the emptied bucket was returned by the windlass.

Byron Johnson had a good eye for the drama of the scene. Dr. Cheadle was more interested in the personalities, and in the social attitudes of the people, and the account he gives of his visit to the goldfields is worth reprinting in full.

Walter Butler Cheadle was born on October 15, 1835 in Colne, Lancashire, the son of the Reverend James Cheadle. He was educated first at Bingley Grammar School in Yorkshire, where his father had become vicar in 1841, and then at Gonville and Caius College, Cambridge. He studied at Cambridge from 1855 to 1859 when he gained his B.A. and was only prevented by a family bereavement from gaining his Rowing Blue and participating in the Oxford and Cambridge boat race of that year. While at Cambridge he had begun studying medicine, and he completed his medical training at St. George's Hospital, London, in 1861. In 1862, aged 27, he accompanied his friend William Fitzwilliam, the Viscount Milton, then 23 years old on a visit to Canada. He kept a journal of the trip, which occupied almost two years, and this was later used as the basis for a book *The North-West Passage by Land. Being the Narrative of an Expedition from the Atlantic to the Pacific, Undertaken with the View of Exploring a Route Across the Continent to British Columbia Through British Territory by one of the Northern Passes of the Rocky Mountains*. This book appeared in 1865 and the authors were given as William Fitzwilliam, Viscount Milton and Dr. Walter Butler Cheadle. The actual diary which was written entirely by Cheadle was not published until 1931.

Cheadle was an interesting man. After returning to England he was appointed physician to the Westminster General Dispensary in London in 1865 and became a Fellow of the Royal College of

108

Surgeons the same year. He was a highly successful member of his profession and particularly noted for his work for sick children and his support of the rights of women to enter the medical profession. He became a Fellow of the Royal College of Physicians in 1870, and was Dean of St. Mary's Medical School from 1869 to 1873, where he arranged the foundation of many scholarships and was a strong supporter of the various athletic activities of the school. He died in 1910.

Of his companion less is known. From various references in the journal it seems he was not as robust as Cheadle, who was both tall and of athletic build. He died in 1877 aged only 38.

We take up Cheadle's Journal at the entry for October 19, 1863, the day on which he and his companion left Quesnel Mouth for the goldfields.

Monday, October 19th. — On foot to Smith's, 2 miles beyond the Cottonwood. Awful trail, nothing but stumps, roots & mud up to the ankles. Saw 6 horses lying dead in the road, hundreds probably a little way off in bush. Thro' nothing but small pines & poplars. Tall 'Maine' man killed 2 martens which crossed the road & we treed, and 2 partridges with his revolver. Very tired and footsore tho' only 20 miles. Milton got thro' famously, walking in moccasins!

Tuesday, October 20th. — Sharp frost. Mudholes frozen. Big boots excruciating. Milton & I, each picked up a pair of cast away gumboots on the road & left our own at houses till return; 14 miles to dinner & 6 more after to Beaver Pass where we found the Gold Escort & 40 miners; 12 dead horses & mules on the road. I had an awful cold, sore heels & pack of 30 lbs which I found too heavy before dinner. Awful night last night; wind blowing thro' cracks in walls & floor; only one blanket apiece; 20 men in room; one afflicted with cramp in his leg which brought him on his feet swearing every 1/2 hour. Milton & another talking in their sleep; rest snoring; my nose running; little sleep.

Wednesday, October 21st. — In the morning passed along Lightning Creek to Van Winkle; past Welsh Company's claim which is stopped as wheel is broken. Milton walked very well; my heels very sore; snow getting deeper up to 3 inches. Called at Irishwoman's named Edwards, 3 miles short of Van Winkle, & had a cup of coffee for which she charged us 1/2 dollar each. Passed Welsh Company's claim which had stopped working on account of ice having broken wheel. At Van Winkle about a dozen houses (Lightning Creek). Passed on 2 miles further to a house where we got a capital dinner, beefsteak pie & beefsteak & onions & pancakes! a long weary walk winding along hill sides past the Bald mountain into William's Creek. Milton held out well walking like a man, carrying his hat slung like a pack although there was frost. At dusk we arrived at Richfield, the first part where gold was struck on this creek, & it was quite dark before we reached Cameron Town below, passing thro' Barkerville or Middle town. The whole 3 towns extending almost continuously down the creek for a mile, & containing about 60 or 70 houses apiece. This spring were only 3 or 4 houses at Cameron Town! Our path was a difficult one over endless sluices, flumes & ditches, across icy planks & logs, all getting tumbles, gumboots being very treacherous. Putnam the "Maine man", took us to his home & treated us, recommending Mr. Cusheon's as a good place to stay at. They gave us a good supper & plenty of blankets.

Thursday, October 22nd. — Got up very late, being very stiff & sore. In afternoon, Cusheon took us to Cameron Co's hut & introduced us to Steele & the other 3 partners of the Cameron Co. except Cameron & Stevenson who had gone down; they treated us to brandy & water & then took us down to view the operations below. The shaft about 30 feet down thro' gravel & clay to bedrock of slate. Numerous shafts all supported by timber & very closely roofed in with flat crosspieces. Wet, damp, dark & gloomy; the shafts being in many parts very low, the "pay dirt" not being extensive perpendicularly. At the bottom shaft the pay dirt was best high up; at the upper end, down close to the bedrock; they kindly helped us to wash out two pans which yielded some beautiful gold to the value of $21, nearly 1 1/3 oz; we could see the nuggets lying in the gravel before loosened out by the pick! The claim was bought for a mere nothing, & the thing quite a fluke. Steele showed me about $1000 of gold in a bag, & the Company's books, showing weekly expenses averaging 7000 dollars, the yield being generally from 40 to 112 oz per shaft (of which there were 3) per day or $29. on to $29,000 per week! over 100 feet of claim yet quite untouched. Steele very kind & intelligent.

Friday, October 23rd. — Got up very late, & towards noon walked up the mile to Richfield to see Mr. Cox, a capital fellow. Fat, tall, thick set fellow with very short coat, large features, retiring forehead, no whiskers & large moustache very German; but not in manner. Delicately polite, gentlemanly & jolly. Captain FitzStubbs came in. What a name! had been in army, came out with Barrett Lennard, now speculating in claims. Stayed there until 1/2 past 4 & on getting back to Cusheon's we found they had eaten our dinner. We had however a very nice one in adjacent house of mother-in-law & daughter who treated us hospitably. Steele invited us to Miner's cabin to have a pipe & we got much information from him.

Saturday, October 24th. — FitzStubbs took us to visit the Caledonian claim; did not go down himself for fear of dirtying his coat! Two or three proprietors took us round & helped Milton to wash a pan of dirt which produced nearly an ounce of very coarse gold. The shafts in this mine were very low & wet, the pay dirt being not of great depth. Then had lunch in miners' hut & smoked pipes with them. A large portion of this mine yet unworked. On return were introduced to Mr. Raby, a Cornishman & proprietor of the Raby claim. Also Mr. Courtney, a lawyer from Dublin; wonderful number of Irishmen. Raby took us down the "Raby claim" & showed us some rich pockets of gold. The dirt visibly full of it & we could see the 'plums', the bits of gold in the face of the cutting. The place where we found this "pocket" was under a large boulder & this is where they are

110

usually met with. And it is easy to understand how, when the boulder was lying in what was then the bed of the creek, & the water rippling past it, the gold would lodge in the crevices under the stone. Mr. Raby picked out a few lumps of the rich dirt, as much as would fill a quart pot perhaps, & Milton washed it. There was about an ounce. The Raby claim is very extensive, 1,000 feet, the pay dirt very extensive, being found high above the bed rock as well as on it, the claim being already worked on drifts 12 feet high in some places; gold has also been found plentifully in the gravel above the drifts & Mr. Raby expects to work this from the surface after the drifts are worked out. Enough to last & pay highly for 3 years. The gold seems evidently to have been washed down the old bed of the stream. The difficulty is to find out where the bed of the creek originally was, & the only way seems to be by following the lead. Claims are sometimes taken up & worked on the present bed, & it is found that the "lead" is not there; it passes right into the hill perhaps on one side or the other of the narrow valley; some slide, or volcanic erruption having changed the course of the stream.

We heard of the Dillon & Currie claim where 102 lbs. of gold were taken out as result of 8 hours work! The Wattie shaft where out of 100 feet of which it consisted $120,000 were taken, leaving over $70,000 clear profit.

Talking to one of the miners, he remarked "Well, Doctor, I've the greatest respect for both the professions of law & medicine; but its a curious fact that in this creek last year we had neither lawyers nor doctors, & we lived without litigation & free from illness. This year there has been a large influx of both lawyers & doctors, & there has been nothing but lawsuits & deaths in the place!" The appearance of William's Creek (so named from William Dietz, a Prussian the discoverer) is merely a narrow valley shut in by pine clad hills, the edges & bottom partially cleared & covered with wooden huts, flumes, waterwheels, windlasses, shafts, ditches & tunnels. In the evening went with Stuart, the Cameron Co's. foreman, to see a Scotchwoman who possessed the most beautiful specimen of native gold I have yet seen. Not more than 2 or 3 oz, but like the most perfectly frosted jeweler's gold & of fantastic shape.

Sunday, October 25th. — Did but little till afternoon, when Mr. Greer called & took us up to Richfield to call at his cabin to view some 'specimens'. I am already beginning to hate the name. But these were very fine, one nearly 6 oz. the other 7 oz. Both from Loughea; frosted looking bright gold with quartz. He kindly gave us several nice nuggets from the Greer claim on this creek. Introduced to Dr. Black practising here & who promised to go over to Loughea tomorrow with us, 3 miles from this. Dined with "Judge" Cox who was exceedingly pleasant. Present Courtney, a young Canadian, & an Englishman whose names I did not catch. A jolly evening, & home by bright moonlight in the snow.

Monday, October 26th. — Went over with Black to Loughea. He was very pleasant, having seen a great deal of mining in Australia. Loughea very like William's Creek, only smaller scale; 4 claims working. "Sage Miller", Vaughan, Crane's & another. Pays well, & beautifully fine gold; all done by tunnelling. Milton bought $37 worth of gold from Miller, I contented myself with $10. Miller had been all over the world, California, Australia & up the Amazon which he describes as a magnificent country; found gold (flower) in pan. Had pleasant walk over the hill back to William's Creek 3 miles. The great wants here are capital & steam power. Waterwheels freeze up early. Currie & another are now bringing up engines by the first sleighs. "Mr. Dixie", a nigger barber from Tennessee, was introduced to Milton, & as he said he should die happy if he could only shave a real live lord, he is to operate on Milton tommorrow.

Tuesday, October 27th. — Went to Bowling Alley with Cusheon, & he & I each licked Milton. Thence to see Mr. Raby of whom Milton bought 2 oz gold & 1 $10 of specimens. Witnessed washing up of one shaft Raby claim, shift & a half, (15 hours) over $4,000! A preserved meat tin case full.

At 6 went up to the Hospital the other side of the creek on the top of the hill. Found there Courtney, Mr. Blenkinsopp, an old H.B. Chief Trader now mining, Mr. Cocker, manager of Macdonald's bank here, Dr. Bell, a G. P. Brown, a young Irishman assisting Dr. Black, & Billy Farren, a successful miner in the Caledonia Claim, a rough boisterous Irishman who had been a sailor. Also Janet Morris a Scotchwoman, fair, fat & forty, the wife of a man who keeps a store, & who came to make the plum-pudding &c, & of course sat down & dined with us. Champagne ad-lib, & Dr. Bell rapidly became maudlin. He was a little smooth-faced man in dress coat, with large mouth & white teeth always smiling, under some obligation to the Fitz-William family under whom his father is tenant in Northamptonshire. He rose after the first glass before we had got to pudding & proposed in the most fulsome & absurd manner Milton's health & the Aristocracy of England. "Gentlemen, Dr. Black invited me here to meet a noble scion of the noblest house in England. I don't exaggerate when I say so. I can't exaggerate. I feel grateful to Dr. Black, deeply grateful for asking me here to meet the "noble scion" of one of the noblest houses England ever produced. It is a proud day for all of us & for this creek; it is the commencement of a new era," &c &c, quite nauseous, & he continued to propose toasts. Interlude, "He's a jolly good fellow" & sentiments, all full of the "Noble Scion". Then Dr. Black overflowing with loyalty, laying his hand upon his heart & willing to die at once for his Queen & country, proposing the health of Her Majesty. Interlude "God save the Queen". My health. Interlude "He's a jolly good fellow" &c. We then adjourned to the kitchen & had more healths; songs. And then Janet presented Milton very prettily with a handsome nugget (25 dollars) for him to give his mother from her. After which in a "gushing" speech Black presented Milton with a large gold ring made on the Creek out of "never sweat" gold worth some $50. Billy Farren then gave me a nice gold & quartz specimen, & Janet another. After all which Dr. Bell essayed several speeches but was sung down by the company in Auld Lang Syne, & after sitting half asleep for some time made a bolt for the door which he thought was next the chimney, & was led off to bed by Mr. Brown. He rolled off with a crash twice during the evening, cutting his head against the stove. The dinner was held in the Hospital ward, the only patient a poor devil with anasarca being covered up with a piece of baize hanging from the wall. We had whist & 7 up pitch, after which supper & hot grog with numerous arguments about the mining laws until two o'clock when I persuaded Milton to come home. Both quite sober.

Wednesday, October 28th. — Milton went down another shaft of the Caledonia, & I, sick of going down in buckets, & crouching along drifts, walked on to Richfield & had pipe with the Judge where Milton joined me shortly; we entered into negotiations to borrow $500 from Cox, who was very kind & lent it to us gladly; we were already out of cash, having spent $2000 since leaving Victoria, & Cox said that was very moderate indeed! ($200 of this went towards Milton's purchase of land at New Westminster.) To call next day for the money.

Thursday, October 29th. — Went with Black to call on "Janet" & bade her an affectionate goodbye. Introduced to Mr. Stenhouse, who had been a man of property in England, ruined by a 'Derby', afterwards made a large fortune as stage coach proprietor in Australia which he again lost, & is now living on speculations & his wits here; a very coarse vulgar but amusing man withal. Face purple-red like Bardolph's. Volunteers to go down with us tomorrow. Called at the Judge's for cash. Snowstorm; now nearly a foot of snow here, but not cold except at night when it is down to 5. In evening Black called & took us into Jem O'B's of the Caledonia to drink whiskey punch.

Friday, October 30th. — Bade goodbye to Cusheon & Cameron Town, called & bid adieu to Cox. Our bill for 8 days was 78 dollars each, & very moderate for the place. An Irishman caught us up & walked in company as far as the Edwards 4 miles from Van Winkle. He amused me keeping a constant talk all the way. He was a cattle driver & said he knew the whole country well. Had hunted cattle nearly up to the head of the Fraser & round to Fort George, starting from Antler Creek! a few nights ago in danger from a pack of wolves at Cottonwood. Out on horseback. Climbed into a tree & set fire to the gum &c. & they eventually cleared off. At Edwards we found Stuart (Cameron foreman) & Mathieson (partner in Victoria firm & in claims here); they were on their way to look at two men prospecting the 'Ayrshire Lass' claim on Lightning above on the hill; & we accompanied them down the creek, leaving the trail to the left. Our path lay along the top of the bank above the creek, & in a hollow of what appeared to be the old bed of a stream; at the further end was the 'Ayrshire Lass'; here we found 2 men working at a tunnel into the side of the mountain. Not yet struck the bedrock. They gave up work & led the way down the hill-side into the valley to their cabin. Invited us to stay with them all night as it was already nearly dark, & too late to see the famous Hill diggings that night. We agreed, & they cooked us bacon & beans & with a small bottle of real 'H.B. Rum' given us by John Ducie Cusheon at parting, we spent a very pleasant evening. Adam Ross one of the two, had been a very extensive explorer along Vancouver Island & this coast. Told us 24,000 of one tribe of Indians died last year of small-pox. Turned out into the bush when attacked by the disease, & the men shot themselves & the women hanged themselves; might be seen dead by hundreds; a continual fusillade; awful cold night & only one blanket apiece.

Saturday, October 31st. — Bade adieu to our miner friends & went on with Mathieson to view the Butcher & Discovery Claims on the hill; we found men at work on the Butcher, & some sinking a tunnel, others working out from the surface. Could pick out gold from the dirt about a yard below the surface; beautifully fine without quartz & deep yellow. Had all been worked by "hydraulicking", but now too cold, & sluicing used; 200 feet above creek. Old bed of a creek going at right angles into mountain; to be the great excitement next season. Lightning so terms from the Yankee expression, it being very difficult to work, & very uncertain. The lead is lost at every turn of the creek, where it passes round a point. Many claims thus found nothing. It is now supposed that the lead runs thro' the hill at these points, there having been slides which have covered over the original bed. The Hill diggings discovered by their being at a claim below in the bed of present creek, & finding that the lead evidently did not come down the creek, but from the hill. They tunnelled into the hill to no purpose, but one day one of the boys went on to the top & scratching the earth with his knife saw gold, & on further investigating, it was found in plenty, sometimes 3 or 4 feet only below. Never more than 15 or 16; in Discovery Claim less. Went to Van Winkle for dinner, & then to Welsh Co., 2 miles on. Evans the manager not at home. His son very civil; if there is gold in the creek, they must have it, for they will prospect the whole bottom. Wheel burst with frost, stopping working of shaft; great drawback to Lightning is bed of quicksand which bursts in the timbers from its water; 25 Welshmen employed; backed by Manchester Capitalists.

Sunday, November 1st. — Bade goodbye to Mr. MacCaffrey & walked on to the Welsh Company's claim. Found Evans Senior at home keeping Sunday. A contrast to William's Creek. He told us that they were now prospecting in the mountains all round & had come upon what he expected would prove a valuable silver/lead; no gold; expected to drop upon the "Last Chance" lead with their shaft. Provisions alone had cost $12,000, in 4 months. Had 4 pumps & were completely master of the water in the shaft, which he considered was the main point & which had been the great stumbling block to miners hereto. Had taken up that claim on Lightning because as the mining laws at present stand the Government cannot grant a lease for a claim over 100 feet unless of ground already worked & abandoned by other miners, therefore he must either take up this large piece of abandoned ground or put himself in the hands of his men by taking up 100 feet in the name of each. But it appears there was enough vacant ground in William's Creek if the law had allowed him to lease it. We passed forward to Beaver Pass for Dinner, 10 miles from Van Winkle & from there 6 miles forward to Edward's. He has been a mate on board a merchant-man for 8 or 9 years, after that mining in Australia, came over here in '58. He is a thorough-going Englishman & gave us several amusing stories of the state of things on the first rush to this country. How he was quite alone amongst the Yankees at Boston Bar (or one of the Fraser River Bars); how they bullied him & he gave them tit for tat, they at last rolling him in a ditch & covering him with sand to make an American Citizen of him. We also heard the stories (I forget from whom) of Abbott, the successful Cariboo miner, who shied a handful of 20 dollar pieces at a large pier-glass at Victoria worth some $200, and another who, having treated all the Company in the bar room & finding no more, had all the glasses of the Establishment filled up on the counter, & swept them off with his fist! Another who in the same way being unable to find enough people to treat opened a hamper of champagne & jumped into it, thereby cutting his shins considerable. Major Downie, formerly of Downie-ville, California, now on William's Creek, at the Christening of Downieville, set up champagne bottles in the ten pin alley & bowled at them! Most of these in fact all are in low water now. Edwards said altho' he hated Yankees, he had the greatest admiration of their energy; they opened out this country in '58 or '59, mostly southerners, at Boston Bar some of the Yankees got up an excitement, which was agitated by the steamboat proprietor who brought such a report down to Victoria that the Governor sent up Col. Moody & a company of the Engineers in the steamer at once. Steamer stuck on the rapids & was detained a day or two, the owner drawing pay all the time: when they arrived at the place there was a great laugh at the expense of the soldiers, the only disturbance which had occurred being between the notorious Ned McGowan & another, in which the former had blackened the eyes of the other. McGowan was fined $25, & the Officers went & had a champagne lunch with him afterwards! 2 Justices of the Peace, one at Yale & the other at Hope, each decided the cases according as he was paid & constant appeals from one to the other.

Monday, November 2nd. — A rough walk from Edward's to Cottonwood, 16 miles. Marten tracks every few yards. Milton & I treed one & fired 6 shots at him with our revolvers without effect. Dined at Smith & Ryder's, & then walked on in heavy snowstorm, to Ramsay's (Cottonwood) for the night. About 20 men there. Got plenty of blankets tho' not very clean. The same amount of snow as at William's Creek.

Tuesday, November 3rd. — Very muddy trail to 8-mile house, an Irishman's who gave us a very nice dinner. Chinaman cook. Trapping martens hard; had killed a dozen with a few wretched traps near the house. From there a long 12 miles in to Quesnel Mouth; where we arrived after dark; put up at Brown's where they made us very comfortable & gave us whiskey toddy as a nightcap. Milton not a bit knocked up.[30]

Cheadle and Milton saw the Barkerville area at a high point of excitement. The miners, convinced that they had come upon endless riches, were free with nuggets and drink and loud with prophecies. The three towns were on their way to becoming the biggest Western city north of San Francisco; new groups of miners from California and from Europe, as well as other parts of what was (in 1867) to become the confederation of Canada, were continually arriving and there was still land to spare. Williams Creek was riding high and the future prosperity of the country seemed assured.[30]

[30] *Cheadle's Journey of Trip Across Canada 1862-63*, 1931, pp. 247-48.

CHAPTER EIGHT

Barkerville's Heyday

Although there was a great deal of social life along Williams Creek during the early sixties it was somewhat limited in kind. In the beginning there were no pack trains to bring in supplies, everything having to be brought to Williams Creek by the miners themselves or by porters they had hired. The first pack train, that of A. G. Norris, arrived in August 1861, and around the same time J. C. Beedy began plans for setting up a store there. Saloons of various kinds and degrees of comfort had already begun to do business. By the spring of 1862 twenty concerns were working on buildings. These buildings were set out in a long line a little way back from the creek itself and raised well above the ground so that the frequent floods from the creek in run-off time and the additional floods caused by the constant piling up of tailings would not damage them. Indeed, when the buildings had all been completed they were linked together by a sidewalk some feet above the road level. This sidewalk was built on many different levels and was therefore something of a hazard to the unwary and the intoxicated. In 1862 the Victoria *Colonist* reported

An unknown man fell from a platform on Sunday evening in front of Smith's store. This was on August 16th. He fell twelve feet and died of a broken neck.

Naturally enough, once mines were in full swing and the saloons doing immense business, the ladies of pleasure came to town, setting up their establishments behind the main street, on the creek side of the valley in what came to be known as Back Street. Their accommodations were less than luxurious, often consisting of only one room just big enough to contain a bed and a dressing table and a closet. The girls of the mining towns were not always very feminine; there are reports of them smoking, swearing, and gambling riotously in the saloons, and many adopted clothing which was more practical than attractive. It was therefore something to take note of when wives first came to the Creek, and in 1862 the Victoria *Colonist* announced breathlessly "There are two respectable married ladies on the creek." In the same paragraph it also reported "Two billiard tables have been brought up to the creek and set up in a saloon at $1 a game."

This rapid increase in population led to difficulties. There were no drainage systems on the Creek, and the latrines were simply holes in the ground. Consequently, the heavy rains, the frequent floods, and the constant disturbance of the running waters in the area of mining activities, caused an intensification of the normal amount of seepage and in the spring of 1863 typhoid came to the creek, causing a number of deaths. The miners appear to have called the disease "Mountain Fever" though this term may also have been used to describe scurvy and other illnesses born of malnutrition. The miners, at a meeting, petitioned the government for a hospital. The government, in July, voted a small amount of money towards the project and the miners themselves provided the rest. The building—three rooms, log structure—was begun on August 24 and officially opened for business in October in Marysville on bench land across the creek from Cameronton. The Royal Cariboo Hospital remained there until 1891 though Marysville itself was gradually deserted, the nearby Forest Rose and Caledonia claims having dwindled in importance and the hotel, the Bowden, having closed, and the settlement itself was occupied first by Chinese and then by Indians. A new hospital south of Cameronton was built in 1891.

The Chinese population of Williams Creek organized their system of social services more quickly than the occidentals, for they opened the first Chinese Masonic Temple to be built in what was to become Canada, in Barkerville in 1862. This temple was the community centre for all the Chinese in the area. Not only did it serve as a Buddhist temple, incense being kept burning at all times before a picture of the Buddha, but also as an employment bureau, a funeral home, and a medical clinic. All disputes between Chinese were settled at a court in this building which formed the centre of the Chinatown, behind which, on the hillside, they created terraces in which they grew vegetables. Indeed the Chinese were the market gardeners for much of Cariboo; the remainder of the populations seemed to lack the required qualities of patience and industry to make the stony ground give an adequate yield of mixed garden crops. Although the Chinese were clearly among the most hard working and valuable members of the community they were not universally popular. It cannot be said that they were victimized in any way; respect was paid to their needs. A cemetery for them was created in

117

1866 alongside the Roman Catholic cemetery in Richfield, the first burial taking place in July 1866, and the Chinese stores and mining companies prospered as much or better than others. Nevertheless on August 7, 1869, the *Cariboo Sentinel*, conscious of the splendours of a new Barkerville rebuilt after the fire of the previous year reported rancorously,

> Chinatown is universally voted a nuisance in Barkerville in every shape, sense or manner. Pigs are fed in the streets in front of the buildings; there is no regular sidewalk, the drainage is corrupted with animal and every kind of filth; in short every inconvenience and disagreeableness characteristic of a semi-barbarous race is present in Chinatown. Let the Grand Jury take this subject into consideration with a review to removing or modifying these evils. Pig-feeding in the streets ought to be stopped forthwith. A great many Chinamen have been sick lately, and no wonder. Let us compel them, however, for our own safety, to pay some attention to sanitary conditions. We have now a neat, clean-looking town, but its neatness is marred by the causes above referred to.

In 1869 Barkerville may well have been neat and clean-looking, but it certainly was not that way originally. The *Sentinel* chose, however, not to think back to a previous year, and not to consider the possibility that the Chinese community had been unable to command as many resources as the occidental when rebuilding their part of the town. It chose rather to stick to its almost invariable tone of sardonic condescension, and to speak with the accents of bourgeois respectability.

The *Cariboo Sentinel* was founded in the early sixties by George Wallace and published in Barkerville. It was printed on a French press, and not the Ruggles used by Amor De Cosmos when he founded the *Colonist* in Victoria, as has been said. It was first used by a Catholic mission in California, and then brought to British Columbia by Bishop Demers and the Comte de Garro where it was used by the Catholic authorities. Wallace acquired the press and took it to Barkerville. He edited the paper himself until 1866 when Alex Allen became editor. In 1880, after the *Sentinel* had ceased operations the press was moved to Yale, and then to Kamloops, where it was among the equipment of the *Inland Sentinel* when Mark S. Wade took over the paper in 1904. Shortly after this it was given to the Convent of St. Ann in Victoria. The *Cariboo Sentinel* was a very small newspaper. It consisted of only four pages, each 11″ × 18″. However, it made up for the smallness of its stature by the loudness and authority of its voice.

In 1866 another amenity was added to the life of Williams Creek. James Loring, of the Diller, Loring and Hard Curry Company bought an upright piano in Victoria and invited a group of dancing girls up from California to perform in one of the saloons. These girls were known as "Hurdy Gurdy Girls" because they usually danced to the hurdy gurdy rather than the piano; they had been brought from Europe to the Californian mining camps, and they were German and Dutch in origin. They were stalwart rather than pretty girls, and their dancing was more energetic than elegant, consisting largely of a good deal of "knees-up," and of being hoisted as high as possible, feet kicking up to the ceiling, by their rumbustious partners. They wore red blouses, cotton print skirts, and what appears to be, from early accounts, a kind of peasant scarf. Shortly after their arrival the troupe were placed under the direction of Madame Fannie Bendixon, a sometime hotel keeper of Victoria, who had packed her possessions to Williams Creek from Antler on her own back, and set up the Bella Union Saloon there. She was, according to Fred Ludditt,[31] "a figure of dignity and composure," "a good looking woman of imposing build" and wore her "dark hair piled high on her head." The Hurdy Gurdy Girls, Fred Luddit, tells us "were vivacious girls, many of them pretty, eager to please, with pleasant personalities. Many tributes to their high moral character are to be found in records of the time." The Cariboo *Sentinel* was less flattering and recorded

... they are unsophisticated maidens of Dutch extraction, from 'poor but honest parents' and morally speaking, they are really not what they are generally put down for. They are generally brought to America by some speculating, conscienceless scoundrel of a being commonly called a "Boss Hurdy". This man binds them in his service until he has received about a thousand percent for his outlay. The girls receive a few lessons in the terpsichorean art, are put into a kind of uniform, generally consisting of a red waist, cotton print skirts and a half-mourning head-dress resembling in shape the top-knot of a male turkey; this uniform gives them quite a grotesque appearance. Few of them speak English but they soon pick up some popular vulgarisms, and like so many parrots they use them indiscriminately on all occasions; if you bid one of them good morning your answer will likely be 'itsh sphlaid out' or 'you bet your life'.

The Hurdy style of dancing differs from all other schools. If you ever saw a ring of bells in motion, you have the exact position these young ladies are put through during the dance; the more muscular the partner, the nearer the approximation of the ladies pedal extremeties to the ceiling, and the gent who can hoist his 'gal' the highest is considered the best dancer; the poor girls as a general thing earn their money very hardly.

The *Sentinel* also commented upon the accompaniment to the girls dances and described it as consisting of an "orchestra" "which

[31] Fred W. Ludditt, *op. cit.*, p. 83.

seldom consists of more than two violins—more properly 'fiddlers' in this case." As usual in everything to do with Cariboo, testimonies conflict. Did the Hurdies dance to an upright piano, a hurdy gurdy, or two fiddles? We cannot be certain, but we do know that each dance cost the miner a dollar, and that he was incited to buy drinks for the girls, who would turn up at the saloon the following morning for a rake-off on every drink.

Another description of the Hurdy Girls was given by James Anderson, the "Laureate of the Cariboo." He arrived from Scotland in 1863, and soon became a leading figure in Cariboo society. He had a pleasant singing voice and a talent for making verse in a style frequently reminiscent of Burns but with a content anticipatory of Robert Service. His *Sawney's Letters* (1868) was a popular success and the first book to be published in Cariboo. An enlarged edition entitled *Sawney's Letters and Cariboo Rhymes* was published in the spring of 1869. In March 1866, he wrote:

> Last summer we had lassies here
>   Frae Germany — the hurdies, O!
> And troth I wot, as I'm a Scot,
>   They were the bonnie hurdies, O!
>
> There was Kate and Mary, blithe and airy,
>   And dumpy little Lizzie, O!
> And ane they ca'd the Kangaroo,
>   A strappin' rattlin' hizzy, O!
>
> They danced at nicht in dresses light,
>   Frae late until the early, O!
> But oh! their hearts were hard as flint,
>   Which vexed the laddies sairly, O!
>
> The dollar was their only love,
>   And that they lo'ed fu' dearly, O!
> They dinna care a flea for men,
>   Let them coort hooe'er sincerely, O!
>
> They left the creek wi' lots o' gold,
>   Danced frae orr lads sae clever, O!
> My blessin's on their "sour krout" heads,
>   Gif they stay awa for ever, O!
>
> *Chorus* - Bonnie are the hurdies, O!
>   The German hurdy-gurdies, O!
>   The daftest hour that ere I spent,
>   Was dancin' wi' the hurdies, O!

What think ye, Sawney, o' my sang?
A good thing, it's no very lang;
The name I've gied's "The German Lasses."
The air's the same's "Green grows the Rashes,"
Maun, Sawney, ye wad like to see
The way they dance in this kintre
They left the lassies aff their feet
In sic a way that's no discreet—
That a' at aince they let them drap;

Syne ilka lad begins to clap,
An thro' the din, an' fun, an' stoure,
Ye'll hear a voice say "sock it to her!'
They whirl them round in waltz and galop,
Wi' a real Glengary walop;
They strike their hands, and beat their feet,
Then turn aboot, and sune they'll meet;
An' after every dance, just think,
They walk up to the bar and drink!
They'll jingle glasses left an' right,
Their dollar gane — then "Gesund act,"
Gif I get hame, I'll put Meg thro'
The way they do in Cariboo!

This suggests that the Hurdy Gurdies had been in Cariboo earlier than 1866 which is the date most usually given for their arrival, and that those who give 1863 as the date might well be correct.

Whatever the case may be, they proved to be a most popular institution, and on March 16, 1867 a further group of, according to the *Sentinel*, "German damsels" arrived "direct from the Bay City." They were "under an engagement with Messrs. Barry & Adler of the Fashion Saloon of this place. We believe they will be introduced to the 'boys' next Saturday night when the ball will open for the season."

The opening of the "season" on Williams Creek in 1867 bore little resemblance to the opening of the season in other cities. The *Sentinel* reported, with its usual sardonic glee,

Messrs. Adler & Barry's large saloon was crowded on Saturday night with the 'boys' who had collected from every corner of the creek, to have a peep at the 'hurdies' who made their debut on that occasion. As a matter of course, many of the 'boys' were unable to resist the temptation of indulging in the 'mazy' dance while their 'chums' crowded around them in a circle and applauded their efforts in a most demonstrative manner. So great was the noise at times that it was next to impossible for the leader of the orchestra to keep anything like regularity in the management of the dance and the consequence was an occasional 'break down' in the figure which was always hailed with an uproarious burst of approbation on the part of the spectators, much to the evident discomfort of the ladies, who were doubtless unaccustomed to such noisy scenes, or still more to the peculiar fashion adopted by the 'boys' of throwing them up a foot or two from the floor at the end of every figure.

Not all the social activities of Cariboo were as rumbustious as this, and the *Sentinel* was not alone in being concerned to improve the "cultural tone" of Williams Creek. John Bowron, one of the overlanders who had arrived in Quesnel in 1862, persuaded the government to provide land upon which to build a public library and reading room, and this was established in Cameronton in 1864, moving to Barkerville in 1867. Bowron was also a leading figure in the Cariboo Amateur Dramatic Association which gave regular performances in the town's Theatre Royal which opened in May 1868, having been built by public subscription. The theatre not only presented performances by such popular travelling groups as Taylor's Nigger Minstrels, but also concerts and recitals, one of the most popular performers being James Anderson, who sang both currently popular songs and songs of his own composition, and who recited his own verses, in many of which he commented upon the local scene. Indeed his verse comments are just as illuminating as those of Dr. Cheadle, and being written from the viewpoint of the poor working miner, a good deal more earthy and even passionate. In the first of his *Sawney's Letters*, written in February 1864, he says:

Dear Sawney, — I sit doon to write
A screed to you by candle light,
In answer to your friendly letter —
I ne'er had ane that pleased me better.
Your letter cam by the Express,
Eight shillings carriage — naethin' less.
You'll think this awfu' — 'tis, nae doot —
(A dram's two shillins here about);
I'm sure if Tamie Ha' — the buddy
Was here wi' his three-legged cuddy
He hauls ahent him wi' a tether,
He'd beat the Express, faith a'thegither —
To speak o't i' the truest way,
"Tis Barnard's Cariboo Delay.

You'd maybe like to ken what pay
Miners get here for ilka day.
Jist two pound sterling, sure as death —
It should be four — atween us baith.
For gin ye count the cost o' livin'

There's naething left to gang and come on;
And should you bide the winter here,
The shoppy-buddies'll grab your gear.
And little wark ane finds to do
A' the lang dreary winter thro'.

Sawney — had ye your tatties here,
And neeps and carrots — dinna speer
What price — tho' I could tell ye weel,
Ye might think me a leein' chiel;
Nae, lad, ye ken I never lee,
Ye a'believe that fra's frae me;
Neeps, tatties, carrots — by the pun'
Jist two for a penny — try for fun
How muckle 'twad be for a ton.
Aitmeal four skillins, flour is twa,
And milk's no to be had ava.
For at this season o' the year
There's naething for a coo up here
To chaw her cud on — sae ye see
Ye are far better aff then me —

For while you're sittin' warm at hame,
And suppin' parritch drooned in crame,
The deil a drop o'milk hae I,
But gobble up my parritch dry.
Of course, I can get butter here,
Twal shillin' a pund - it's far oure dear.
Aye — a'thing sells at a lang price,
Tea, coffee, sugar, bacon, rice,
Four shillins a pund, and something mair,
And e'en the weights are rather bare —
Sae much for prices.

Noo for claims:
And first a word about their names.
Some folks were sae oppressed wi' wit,
They cad' their claim by name "Coo — — —,"
And tho' they struck the dirt by name,
They ne'er struck pay dirt in their claim.
Some ithers made a gae fine joke
And christen'd their bit ground "Dead
    Broke."
While some, to fix their fate at once,
Ca'd their location "The Last Chance";
There's "Tinker," "Grizzly," — losh, what
    names —
There's "Prince o'Wales" — the best o'claims,
There's "Beauregard" and "Never Sweat,"
And scores o'ithers I forget —

The "Richfield" and the "Montreal,"
They say they struck the pay last fall —
But will they strike it in the spring,
Aye, Sawney, that's anither thing'
But by-an'-bye they'll ken, nae doot,
If they can pump their water oot.
Some strike the bed-rock pitchin' in,
And some the bed-rock canna win,
But ne'er a color can they see,
Until they saut it first a wee;
And syne they tell to ilka man,
They struck two dollars to the pan.
You'll see't in the Victoria Press
As twenty dollars — naething less.
Aye, Sawney, here, a wee bit story,
Gin aince it travels to Victoria,
Is magnified a hundred fold.
The bed-rock here, doon there is gold;
Some folks would manufacture lees
To mak' a bawbee on a cheese.
Shame on the man who salts a claim,
A man he is — but just in name —
NO MANHOOD'S IN HIM, HE'S A CHEAT,
A SMOOTH DISSEMBLING HYPOCRITE,
WHO, IF HE COULD BUT GAIN HIS END,
WOULD E'EN DECEIVE HIS DEAREST FRIEND.

There is a set o' men up here,
Wha never work thro' a' the year,
A kind o' serpents, crawlin' snakes,
That fleece the miner o' his stakes;
They're gamblers — honest men some say,
Tho' its quite fair to cheat in play —
IF IT'S NO KENT O' — I ne'er met
An honest man a gambler yet!
O, were I Judge in Cariboo,
I'd see the laws were carried thro',
I'd hae the cairds o' every pack
tied up into a gunny sack
Wi' a' the gamblers chained thegither,
And banished frae the creek forever.
But, Sawney, there's anither clan,
They ca' them "jumpers" — my belief
Is — "jumper" simply means a thief;
They jump folks' claims, and jump their lots,
They jump the very pans and pots;
But wait a wee — for a' this evil —
Their friend 'll jump them,
                    He's the deevil!

He comments upon the women in the creek also:

> There are some women on this creek,
> Sae modest, and sae mild and meek!
> The deep red blush aye pents their cheek,
> They never swear but when they speak.
> Each ane's a mistress, too, ye'll find,
> To mak guid folks think that she's joined
> In honest wedlock unto one;
> "She's yours or any other man's!"
> But dinna fear, for me at least,
> I'll never mak mysel' a beast!
> But let this drap — "to err is human,"
> An' "Frailty, thy name is woman."

In his second letter he gives Sawney an account of his own life and of the dismal state of affairs on the Creek in March 1866 when the letter was written.

> But first o' a 'anent mysel'
> A word or two I'm gaun to tell;
> Ye nae doubt think my pouch is lined
> Wi' gowden dust, in Geordies coin'd,
> That I'm rich as any Jew
> That swindles aff auld claes for new;
> Noo, just that ye may ken my story,
> I'll set my doin's a' before ye.

> In '63 I left my hame,
> In that same year I bought a claim
> Frae Cameron Jock o' Canada —
> As smart a lad's ye ever saw,
> Wha's greatest faut was nane uncommon,
> A gae strong likin' for a woman'
> An ill loon wi' some men was Johnny,
> Because he had sae muckle money!
> But I hae travel'd near and far,
> And aften hae I met wi' waur;
> The claim he sell't me was nae bad,
> An 'ere three months I siller had.

> Gin next year's spring I tried my luck
> At prospeckin', but I got "stuck,"
> An' Red Gulch eased me o' my cash;
> (I wish I hadna been sae rash!)
> Weel, I began the warld again,
> An' warked for months wi' might an' main,
> An' whan 'twas drawin' towards the fa'
> I wasna that ill aff ava;
> The "Cameron" was my auld stay bye,

125

To feed my pouch when pumped dry.
In '63 I gaed to seek
My fortune upon Lighning Creek;
I fell in love — noo dinna start.
Dear Sawney, I ne'er lost my heart
But aince — "the theft I have lang forgive,
Forget the thief — ne'er while I live."
But to my tale; I fell in love,
O'er head and lugs and hand and glove,
An' thocht that name could e'er surpass
The tocher o' the "Ayrshire Lass";
I tried my best to catch her tin,
But ah! the jade, she took me in;
For four lang months I ran her drift,
Then wearied oot, ga' 'er in a gift!
Syne back to Williams I did ca'
As puir a chiel 's ye ever saw;
A' summer then I staid at hame,
An' warked awa at my auld claim,
O' luck I had a real guid streak,
Whiles makin' thirty punds a week;
And yet I wasna half content.
On prospeckin' I still was bent'
Had shares in a' the kintra side,
In shafts gaun' doon thro' slum and slide;
Thocht ilka day I'd strike it big,
Sae didna mind the costs a fig.
O! had I kent what I ken noo,
I'd sent my siller hame to you;
For long afore the winter's snaw,
My cash took wings and flew awa',
And left me e'en withoot a groat,
But still an independent Scot.
And sae I maun begin anew
To fecht the ills o' Cariboo;
"But freedom's battle once begun,
Tho' baffled oft, is ever won."

Such, Sawney, is a mining life,
Cases like mine are unco rife —
In fac' there's dozens livin' here
Hae seen hard times for mony a year;
Yet still they wrestle on thro' a',
Tho' sometimes they do rin awa'.
For when a man can do nae better,
He has to leave the creek a debtor —
Altho' I think it is a flicht
That's no just a'thegither richt;
HOOE'ER SAE PUIR A MAN MAY BE,

126

HIS MOTTO SHOULD BE HONESTY.
Still, here the miner on the whole
Is a straight gaun' honest soul,
Wha pays his debts baith fair and free,
If he's the cash to pay it wi'!

James Anderson's poems first made their appearance in the pages of the *Cariboo Sentinel*, which commenced publication on June 6, 1865.

The *Sentinel*, as previous quotations from its columns have already shown, took its title seriously and not only served as an advertising medium for the town businesses but also, not infrequently, as the Voice of Conscience and as the Advocate of Social Order. It also, very obviously, regarded a part of its duty to be to write reports which should interest and advise the government authorities in Victoria. For later readers, however, its fascination lies largely in the picture it gives of the life on Williams Creek, frequently by means of its advertisements. Advertisements often indicate more clearly than straight journalism the nature and the prejudices of the society to which they make their appeal. One such advertisement reads:

HALLO! OLD JACK'S ALIVE!
JUST RETURNED FROM BEING ON A BENDER!
Fully prepared to Repair all BOOTS and SHOES
CHEAP FOR CASH. He kindly invites one and all,
great and small, to give him a call.
BARKERVILLE — next door to J. H. Todd's.

This contrasts with the advertisements of Washington Delaney Moses, the Barkerville barber, who had the distinction, before coming to Cariboo, of providing the city of Victoria with its first bathtub in his Pioneer Shaving Saloon with its "Private entrance for ladies." He advertised a "Hair Invigorator" which received a tribute in the *Sentinel* from three miners who, under the heading, "To whom it may concern" wrote:

This is to certify that from some cause or complaint of the head our hair commenced falling out so rapidly that we feared we should lose the whole. In this condition we went to W. D. MOSES and strange to relate in THREE applications of his wonderful Hair Restorative our hair became as strong as ever and is now soft and lively.

Another prominent citizen of Barkerville was the photographer, Frederick Dally, whose studio advertised itself as being able to provide all the most modern types of photograph. Frank Laumeister, of camel fame, opened a store in Barkerville in 1867, and Roderick Finlayson, who had been with James Douglas when the Hudson's

Bay Company founded Victoria, opened a Hudson's Bay store there in June of the same year. Messrs. Chantceller and Nicole established a Lager Beer Brewery in Barkerville. The first post office for the region was opened by John Bowron in Cameronton in 1866, though postal services had previously been supplied by the Express companies, both Barnard's Express and Wells Fargo. It moved later to Barkerville. The first bank in Barkerville was that of A. D. Macdonald; it was a branch of his main Victoria bank and the manager was a Mr. Crocker. Unfortunately the business failed before a year was out, and its customers moved to the branch of the Bank of British Columbia which opened at Richfield in 1863, and moved first to Cameronton, and then to Barkerville, the manager's name being Russell. In 1865 the Bank of British North America opened a branch in Richfield and moved to Barkerville the next year. This pattern of movement was one followed by many businesses and shows how Barkerville, the middle town of the three strung out along Williams Creek became established by 1866 as the centre of the goldfields.

These three were not the only places with pretensions in those years, however. The miners of Mosquito Gulch and Red Gulch had a public meeting on October 4, 1867 and decided to found Centreville on Mosquito Gulch; there were 100 houses there by May 1868. At around the same time Felixville sprang up on Conklin Gulch as the town for the Felix Company, and later in the 70's Gladstoneville and Carnarvontown were created. Barkerville, however, once founded, never lost its leadership in the goldfields. Though in 1865 the claims were not as prodigiously productive as in the previous two years, they still provided a good return, and the *Sentinel* in 1866, even while complaining of the government's restrictive regulations, expressed confidence in the future of the minefields, commenting in an editorial:

A little over two months have elapsed since the miners arrived, and already over one million dollars has been taken out in gold. There are now approximately two thousand miners in the district. If this territory were under a government that would foster and encourage the mining population instead of grinding men down by exceptional taxes so as to force them to leave the colony there would be four or five million dollars instead of one million in two months. It is well known that within a very few miles of Williams Creek there are innumerable gulches and creeks capable of sustaining an immense population and yielding easily $5 to $6 to the hand, but they are completely neglected and unworked, simply because miners will not stay where the government seeks to drag the last cent out of their hard earned money for taxes to support its iniquitous extravagances. The population of the Cariboo this year is not a half of last year, yet there is an increase of nearly half a million dollars over the same period of last year.

These claims of prosperity, and these accounts of the establishment of business and banks in such profusion in the Barkerville of the middle sixties should not be allowed to give the impression that the goldfields were rapidly producing a city similar to cities elsewhere, and with the same air of bourgeois stability and the same conventional society. Barkerville in 1866 was still one long muddy, rutted track between wooden buildings built upon piles each with a platform sidewalk in front of it, linked to the sidewalk of the next building by steps up or down or by bridges over the mud, so that the pedestrian was always climbing or descending from one level to another. The word "bank" suggests a certain solidity, a certain impassive grandeur even; the Bank of British Columbia at Cameronton, however, was simply a two-room shack, its board walls covered with paper and cotton; its strong room was an iron box measuring two feet by three foot and standing two and a half feet high, secured by one simple lock. The first pane of glass to be used in a Cariboo building is supposedly that provided for the Richfield Courthouse when it was built in 1862. Nevertheless on the 15th of April 1867 the *Sentinel* boasted

The appearance of this town is improving steadily and there is not a building site left unoccupied. The town has extended right up to the China buildings at the upper end and cannot be extended further unless by building on piles on account of the street being so high above the creek. The principal buildings of Cameronton have been moved to Barkerville.

In 1867 the town was certainly in celebratory mood. The Theatre Royal opened in May of that year, and Barry & Adlers Saloon was having a great success with its Hurdies, and the *Sentinel* tells us that at this time the town contained "12 saloons, 2 stores, 3 shoemakers, 3 restaurants, 3 lodging houses, 2 bank agencies, 1 printing office, 1 paint shop, 1 butchers stall, 2 drug stores, 2 watch-makers, 2 breweries, 1 express office, 2 carpenters shops, 1 post office, 1 public library, 1 clothing store and 1 public stable." Oddly, it fails to record the business of Frederick Dally, the photographer; more explicably it ignores the commercial enterprises of the young ladies.

It was certainly a vigorous town, full of itself, and also a town of many races and peoples. Sometimes somebody, with a sudden burst of enthusiasm for his native land would attempt a public gesture of patriotism. Harry Jones, one of Captain Evans' Welsh Company,

129

tells in his diary how on the 4th of July 1867 the Americans asked "old Jack," the shoemaker, to read the Declaration of Independence on the Streets of Barkerville. Old Jack, however, got far too drunk to attempt the reading and so it was read instead by a Mrs. Parsons. Harry Jones reported one of the other Americans as saying that "Old Jack figured it was less of a disgrace to get drunk than to read the Declaration of Independence in another man's country."

CHAPTER NINE

Fire in Cariboo

Barkerville was a proud place in the middle sixties, but its pride was soon to suffer a fall.

The catastrophe began, we are told, when a miner, intent on kissing a hurdy girl in the backroom of Barry and Adlers saloon while she was pressing her dress, knocked over a stovepipe. It was 2:30 in the afternoon of September 16, 1868; the day was cold and dry and the stovepipe was hot; it immediately set fire to the canvas ceiling and then the roof. Frederick Dally, the photographer, who had arrived from Victoria on July 21 that year, and had only recently set himself up in new premises, wrote an account of the fire, which Gordon R. Elliot gives in his book on Quesnel.

By the number of stove-pipes very close together coming through the wooden roofs of the buildings at every height and in every direction, that were sending forth myriads of sparks and numbers of them were constantly alighting on the roofs where they would remain many seconds before going out, and from the dryness of the season, I came to the conclusion that unless we shortly had rain or snow to cover the roofs, for they remain covered with snow all winter, that the town was doomed. . . .

The morning of the fire was bright and clear and the sluice boxes. . .bore traces of a hard frost as the icicles that were depending from the flumes were two or three yards in length. . . . Although trade was somewhat dull, still it was steady and profitable . . . little did I think that in less than two hours, not a vestige of the town would remain but a burning mass of ruins . . .

I . . . seated myself in a chair and again meditated on the probability of a fire when I heard one exclaim, "Good God! What is up!" I ran instantly to see the cause of the alarm and to my astonishment beheld a column of smoke rising from the roof of the saloon adjoining the steward's house. I saw the fire had a firm hold of the building and, as there was no water to be had, I felt certain that the town would be destroyed. So I collected as much of my . . . goods as possible together, and hastened with them to the middle of the creek, and left them there whilst I made several journeys after other goods. The fire originated in a small room adjoining Barry & Adler's saloon. One of the dancing girls was ironing and by some means or other, the heat of the stove-pipes set the canvas ceiling on fire, which instantly communicated with the roof and in less than two minutes the whole saloon was in flames which quickly set the opposite building, the Bank of British North America, in flames.

So the fire travelled at the same time up and down both sides of the street . . . and although my building was nearly fifty yards away from where the fire originated, in less than twenty minutes it, together with the whole of the lower part of the town, was a sheet of fire, hissing, crackling, and roaring furiously. There was, in a store not far from my place, fifty kegs of blasting powder and had that not been removed at the commencement of the fire, and put down a dry shaft, most likely not a soul would have been left alive of the number that was then present. Blankets and bedding were seen to be sent at least 200 feet high when a number of coal oil tins, 5 gallons, exploded, and the top of one of the tins was sent five miles and dropped at the saw-mill on Grouse Creek.

Every person was thinking of his own property and using desperate efforts to save it, and some not placing it sufficiently far out of reach of the element had all consumed, and others again had it taken so far that during the time they were away trying to save more property, Chinamen and others were stealing from them as fast as they could carry it away. One stout Chinaman showing too many creases about him that did not look quite natural, the police made him strip, and off came six shirts, two pairs of draws, three pairs of trousers, etc. Another, two coats, three shirts, and two pairs of trousers. Another had hidden away behind the false canvas wall of his house, over one thousand dollars worth of flour, rice, boots, etc., and every useful article usually sold by storekeepers in the mines.

The town was divided by the "Barker" flume, crossing it at a height of about fifty feet, and as it was carrying all the water that was near, it kept the fire at bay for a short time from the upper part of the town. But the hot wind soon drove those that were standing on it away. The fire then quickly caught the other half of the buildings, also the forest on the mountain ridge at the back. And as the sun set behind the mountain, the grandeur of the scene will not be quickly forgotten by those who noticed it.

And then the cold, frosty wind came sweeping down the canon (canyon), blowing without sympathy on the houseless and distressed sufferers, causing the iron-hearted men to mechanically raise the small collars of their coats (if they had been so fortunate as to save one) as protection against it. Household furniture of every description was piled up along the side of the creek, and the people were preparing to make themselves as comfortable for the night, under the canopy of heaven, as circumstances would allow. And in the early morning, as I passed down the creek, I saw strong men rise from their hard beds on the cold stones, having slept wrapped up in a pair of blankets, cramped with cold and in great pain, until a little exercise brought renewed life into their systems.

At a quarter to three p.m. the fire commenced; at half past four p.m. the whole town was in flames, and at 10 o'clock the next morning signs of rebuilding had commenced, and lumber was fast arriving from the saw mill and was selling at one hundred and twenty-five dollars per thousand feet. The number of houses destroyed was one hundred and sixteen. After the fire I found I had the key of my house in my pocket which reminded me of a circumstance that occurred two years before at a town a mile from Barkerville when a certain Barrister who was in the habit of drinking more than was good for him, when informed that his house was on fire, left the saloon he was in and went and stood on the opposite side of the street to his house and exclaimed, "Never mind boys; never mind! I don't care, let it burn, I've got the key in my pocket." (And so had I.)

The fire was caused by a miner trying to kiss one of the girls that was ironing and knocking against the stove displaced the pipe that went through the canvas ceiling, and through the roof, which at once took fire. This information I got from an eye-witness who never made it generally known, thinking that it might result in a lynching scene.[32]

Though the majority of accounts tell us with more drama than accuracy that the whole of Barkerville was destroyed, in fact it seems that about a quarter of the contents of the buildings not at the very centre of the fire were saved. Some goods were rescued, and retained, by others than their owners; those who carried their possessions away from the fire and left them to get more sometimes found items missing. Some buildings escaped entirely. Scott's Saloon stood next to the Barker Companies workings and the water from the flume was used to dampen the building so thoroughly that the flames could not take hold. McInnes' saloon, and the warehouses of J. Weill and Hudson's Bay were situated at the lower end of the town and the fire stopped short of them. When the fire had expended its rage, less than two hours after it had begun, the citizens of Barkerville sought shelter for themselves and their families and goods wherever they could, some even travelling as far as Conklins Gulch to make use of the deserted cabins there. Fred W. Ludditt gives the total loss in the fire as "close to a million dollars" and says

The greatest single loss was that suffered by Strouss' Store. This was estimated as being $100,000. The losses ranged from $1500 up to this figure. Some were as follows: Hudson's Bay Company, $65,000; Lecuger & Brun Hotel, $20,000; Cohen & Huffman Store, $32,000; N. Cunio, Brewery, $40,000; B.N.A. Bank, $10,000; Masonic Lodge, $4,000; Kwong Lee Store, $40,000; F. Castagnetto Store, $33,000.[33]

Great though the disaster was, the citizens of Barkerville were not to be defeated. On the morning following the fire they began to rebuild their town, and on the 22nd of September 1868, less than a week after the fire, the *Sentinel* (whose offices must also, obviously, have survived to some extent) reported

Already are there over thirty houses standing in symmetrical order on the old site, and the foundation of several others laid; and many more would yet

[32] Gordon R. Elliot, *op. cit.*, pp. 35-37.
[33] Fred W. Ludditt, *op. cit.*, p. 83.

have been in the course of erection were it possible to obtain carpenters and tools. .... The town when rebuilt will present a much more uniform and pleasant appearance. By the regulations of the local authorities, in concurrence with the people, the main street has been increased in width fifteen feet and the sidewalks fixed at a regular and uniform grade. Vacancies which were originally intended for cross streets but occupied by sufferance, are now to be left open, and altogether the new town will be much more convenient for business, and will be a decided improvement on the old; and we would not much wonder if in the course of a few years time many who are now heavy losers will cease to regret the conflagration of 1868.

Among the businesses and buildings burned to the ground were W. D. Moses' barbershop, the Theatre Royal, Madam Bendixon's Hotel, Dr. Carrall's home, J. C. Beedy's store, and Barnard's Express office, as well as Barry & Adler's Saloon where it all started.

The Barkerville that rose from the ashes was a less haphazard affair than its predecessor, but it still fell short of being a planned town. Nevertheless the sidewalks of the buildings while not being exactly on the same level had less dramatic differences, and some thought was given to the design of at least some of the buildings. Johnnie Knott (or Not) the town carpenter was kept extremely busy. He not only helped build many of the new stores and houses, but also constructed for himself the Barkerville Hotel which he operated in 1869. By the end of 1869, indeed, the town was almost completed. The Masonic Cariboo Lodge, which, first opened on June 24, 1868, had been destroyed in the fire, had been replaced by a larger one. The new Theatre Royal opened its doors to the public on January 16, 1869. On June 16, 1869 D. Lewis opened a bathhouse and in the *Sentinel* of that day begged

leave to inform the ladies and gentlemen of Barkerville and vicinity that he has spared no pains in fitting up a Bathing Room for their accommodation, next door to Taylor's Drugstore, and hopes to merit a share of their patronage. He is also prepared to fill Teeth with Gold, Silver or Tin Foil, set in Teeth on pivots, repair Plates and extract Teeth. Having considerable experience in that line, Mr. Lewis feels assured of giving satisfaction.

In spite of the confidence felt by Mr. Lewis and others in the growing prosperity of the new Barkerville, the losses suffered in the fire combined with a decreasing return from many of the mines, to reduce the population of the area. Some small businessmen left. Some buildings were not replaced.

Fire was a great a hazard and as powerful a destroyer in the Cariboo of the early years as it was in the seventeenth century in Britain. The houses and buildings of most settlements were as crowded together as were the houses of Charles II's London, and, being made entirely of wood, were highly combustible. The great Barkerville fire did more than destroy the livelihood and the homes and businesses of many people; it reminded them of the insecurity of their communities to such an extent that the collective optimism characteristic of Cariboo suffered severe damage. This sense of insecurity was increased in the summer of 1869 for on July 17th or 18th another fire broke out in the area. While it did not reach Barkerville it caused a black pall to hang over the town. A diarist quoted by F. W. Lindsay wrote:

I was working in the Hapvale claim when about half past three o'clock in the afternoon the men working on the surface called us up to the top of the main shaft to see the darkness. It was as black as any night we had ever seen in our lives. At the McDowell claim there was a man by the name of Edward Cyrs. He was a very religious man and maybe a little superstitious too. He was so frightened by the darkness that he dropped on his knees and prayed to the Lord for mercy as he thought the end of the world had come. Doc Holloway who was one of the men working underground who had come to the surface to see the darkness... made a joke of the whole thing. He said that he'd spent thirty years of his life mining and now the first time he had a chance to make a stake the whole damn world came to an end. I should say that Ned Cyrs wasn't the only one praying that day and old Doc Holloway's remarks spurred Cyr's prayers to greater strength. He prayed like a son-of-a-gun — loud enough so that God would be sure to hear him. But about six o'clock a wind sprang up which lifted the clouds and the ashes fell on the ground around us and was quite thick. However an hour or two later the clouds had gone and daylight came back and remained with us until the darkness of night.[34]

This fire, the Great Cariboo Fire of 1869, burnt through a great deal of the country. It burnt out Cedar City completely. At Quesnel Forks it only destroyed the jail, the rest of the town being protected in the angle between Quesnel and Cariboo rivers, though 18 Chinese miners were caught working in the river and were killed. According to some sources the black cloud did not lift in one afternoon but lasted for four whole days. The great cedars at Cedar Point were saved by the placer miners, and by being situated in the centre of a triangle made up of the 1200 foot flume of the Aurora Company on one side, huge piles of tailings on another, and Quesnel Lake on the third. The miners also saved the huge cedar known as the Cornish Miner's Prayer Tree. This was a tree around which the Cornish miners would hold their Sunday prayer meetings. While the fire was at its height it is said that a number of caribou that had been swimming in the lake came up on to the shore and stood among the miners. The miners

[34] F. W. Lindsay, *Cariboo Yarns*, 1862, p. 30.

took heart from this as also from the presence of a little brown wren, for miners regarded Jenny Wrens as lucky and were delighted whenever one chose to build a nest in a shafthouse or on the windlass beside the workings.

In spite of this good omen the miners in Cariboo must have been more than troubled at the way things were going. Just a little while before the fire, on July 14, 1869, the *Sentinel* printed a report which testified less to the increasing respectability of Barkerville than to its decreasing prosperity.

One of the popular institutions of Barkerville is about to disappear. Sterling's Terpsichorean academy will shortly lose its principal attraction by the departure of its lady professors, who contemplate returning to their wonted homes and these are not in British Columbia. Cariboo toes are not so light and fantastic as they used to be, neither are there quite so many of them. The filthy lucre becomes more precious with its scarcity, and the dance now most appreciated is that which is induced by the monotonous music of the water as it runs over a glittering dump-box. The temples of Apollo and Terpsichore are losing their devotees, who now evince an increasing disposition to frequent those of Mammon. In the meantime, subscriptions for the proposed building of a church are small and few. Whither are we driftin?

This particular saloon, Sterling's El Dorado, closed in 1873 and was sold at auction on September 1 of that year. The Wake-Up Jake Restaurant and Bakery closed on June 30 of the same year.

For all this, the community did not abandon its dream of a rich and prosperous city, and took steps to protect it from further fires. The first fire brigade had been organized under Mr. McHenanie in April 1867, but as its only equipment was a collection of buckets it was not able to do much to help the town when the fire began. The new Williams Creek Fire Brigade was organized by Isaac Oppenheimer, and it mounted its first full scale fire drill on May 24, 1869. The drill showed the team to be somewhat disorganized still, but when, on June 4, a bush fire erupted beside Van Volkenburgh's slaughterhouse in the Richfield area, it went resolutely into action. The following day the *Sentinel* contained a message of thanks to the WCFB from the owners of the slaughterhouse, thanking them for their "heroic and persistent efforts in subduing the fire in the forest immediately adjacent to our Slaughter house and corrals, thereby saving our property, valued at $5,000 from imminent destruction." A more sceptical Richfield reader stated in the *Sentinel* of the following week that "the hand of Providence was with us, not the Barkerville Fire Brigade." Isaac Oppenheimer was not discouraged. Through the good offices of his brother he arranged for fire fighting equipment to be sent up from San Francisco. Until it arrived the Brigade used buckets, as before, and locally constructed ladders. The long leather hose arrived from San Francisco in July 1869; the carriage for it arrived in October 1871. Barkerville would never burn again.

Other towns of Cariboo were not to be so fortunate. In 1916 the town of Quesnel, which had grown in size and importance as Barkerville had dwindled over the years, suffered its first major fire. It began in the early morning of January 16 in the Strand Theatre which was housed in the same building as John Strand's New Cariboo Hotel. Although J. Allen, whose hotel room was situated over the theatre gave the alarm very quickly, and Mr. Strand was able to wake his guests and get them all out of the hotel, the fire could not easily be stopped. The flames spread rapidly to the north, destroying Strand's other enterprise, the meat market, and Collins' and Foots' haberdashery which shared the building. Here it was halted by a force of forty or fifty Chinese. To the south it was more destructive still. It took hold of the north annex of the Occidental Hotel, spread to the main building, and then to the south annex and the store belonging to John A. Fraser. In an attempt to stop the holocaust the Bank of British North America was blown up with gunpowder, but the fire continued to spread and destroyed Fraser's number one warehouse and the Reid Estates Building which contained the stock of the Cowan Supply Company. The Fraser Company building which was the next to be threatened was rapidly torn down, and a bucket brigade put out the last of the fire with snow.

Little was saved from the fire. The bank was totally destroyed as were Lamb's Barber Shop and Vaughan's Realty. The Occidental Hotel had been insured for $15,000, exactly a sixth of its true value by its owner, E. L. Kepner, and all that Kepner had managed to save from the flames was a little furniture and bedding. Kepner also owned some houses on Carson Avenue, and these, though not destroyed, were badly damaged. John A. Fraser had also under-insured his property; the property destroyed was valued at $20,000, and he had insured it only for $12,000.

Cariboo folk are resilient. It was not long before the various businesses found new accommodations. The bank moved into the old Express Office; Strand set up his meat market in the old Broughton House; Fraser found a smaller warehouse on McLean Street; Cowan relocated in a billiard hall; and Lamb, the barber, set up shop again next to Marion's store. *The Cariboo Observer* observed:

For years this town has enjoyed immunity from serious fire which was wonderful, when we consider the natural disadvantages the people have to contend with. Our fire fighting applicances were utterly inadequate to cope with the situation, and it was also apparent in the early stage of the fire that leadership in the fight was lacking. .... Perhaps our immunity in the past has made us more or less careless. If so, we have received a lesson — costly but necessary if we are to avoid similar experiences in the future.

The Fire Brigade was quickly reorganized under J. F. Brady, H. V. Harris and D. R. McLean. New ladders and buckets were bought, and the towns firebell was moved to a more strategic location. Unfortunately, however, the town had suffered so great a financial loss that it was hard to raise money for more advanced and expensive equipment. This shortsightedness was brought home to the citizens in the summer of 1925 when, on June 25, another fire broke out. It began in the Good Eats Cafe, spread rapidly through most of Chinatown, and destroyed the government liquor store. Many small businesses and two unoccupied cabins were destroyed and two men, in whose bedroom over the Good Eats Cafe the fire had started, lost their lives.

The citizens of Quesnel were neither numerous nor wealthy enough to protect themselves adequately. There was no water supply other than the river, and it was four years before, in 1929, the first water mains were laid. It was not until after the depression of the thirties, in 1940, that the town managed to purchase a truck and a fire fighting hose, and the town's first real fire-fighting truck arrived in 1946.

One would have imagined that the Barkerville Fire of 1868, the Cariboo Fire of 1869, and the great Quesnel Fire of 1916 would have alerted everyone in the area to the need to plan the layout of their villages in such a way as to prevent the rapid spread of any fire that should occur. This was not, however, the case. In 1921 the new and rapidly growing settlement of Williams Lake looked much like early Barkerville and was just as vulnerable to fire. The houses and businesses were linked together by boardwalks some feet above the mud, and in July of that year a rapidly spreading fire destroyed Fraser and Mackenzie's Store, the Lakeview Hotel, a new partially constructed dance hall that Herb Spencer was building, and Jack Elliott's meat market, and killed both Bernard Weelman and Johnny Salmon.

Williams Lake rose again from the ashes, as had Barkerville and Quesnel. Fire might damage Cariboo and slow it down, but it could not destroy it.

CHAPTER TEN

The Keepers of the Law

It had taken the miners on Williams Creek eight years to perceive the necessity of establishing some efficient way of protecting their property from fire. They had, however, been more fortunate with regards to other forms of protection. The low incidence of crime in the Cariboo during the first gold rush years must be attributed partly to the great difficulty any miscreant would have, first in remaining undetected in such close-knit communities where, for all the flood of new gold seekers, everyone was soon known to everyone else, and, second, in getting out of the area, flanked as it was on the one side by the country of the not altogether friendly Chilcotins, and on the other by almost impassable mountains, with only one road running its length, this road being necessarily furnished with stopping places where every visitor was scrutinized and noted. It was also, however, due to the nervous alacrity with which the government, recalling the anarchy of the Californian rush, set about creating a police force and a workable legal system, as soon as the first miners reached the lower Fraser.

In 1859, six months after the first gold had been found on the Fraser, New Caledonia became the Colony of British Columbia, under the Hudson's Bay Factor of Victoria, and Governor of Vancouver Island, James Douglas. Douglas had as yet no other government-appointed officials to help him and so when there were disturbances in the lower Fraser, he took emergency measures on his own authority. Margaret Ormsby says that he

decided not only to show them that he represented British authority, but that criminal acts would be punished. To bring a murderer to trial he set up a temporary court at Fort Hope. George Pearkes, the Crown Solicitor of Vancouver Island, presided over it, American miners gave testimony, and in the absence of a gaol, the murderer was sentenced to transportation. Douglas then organized a police force, appointed special constables to be stationed at Yale and also set up there a temporary court for trying offences. The miners themselves spoke of the necessity of the appointment of additional magistrates, and he was much gratified to learn that "the general feeling is in favour of English rule of Fraser's River, the people having a degree of confidence in the sterling uprightness and integrity of Englishmen which they do not entertain for their own countrymen".[35]

In fact, of course, the American miners had many of them experienced the lawlessness of the California Rush, and the majority realized that there was little point in attempting to make a fortune if there was no likelihood of retaining it. They also understood that, in order to give each miner a fair chance, there must be some means of regulating the size of claims and of settling territorial disputes. At the miners' request, therefore, Justices of the Peace were appointed for the communities on the lower Fraser and these men were the effective governors of the settlements. They not only settled minor disputes over claims, ordered public work to be done, caused buildings to be erected, allocated land for business purposes or for the raising of produce, but could also stop mining activities altogether when the weather was considered too bad for work to be done safely or when mining supplies were so short as to cause difficulties. They also tried civil court cases involving less than $250; other matters they referred to the Supreme Court.

The organization of these matters became easier after the fall of 1859. In April of that year the British government had selected the chief officials of the government of the new colony of British Columbia. These included James Douglas as Governor, Matthew Baillie Begbie as Judge, and Chartres Brew as Inspector of Police. Begbie arrived in Victoria on November 19, a cold rainy day, and James Douglas promptly administered the oath of office to him, whereupon he, in his turn, read Her Majesties commission which created James Douglas Governor of British Columbia.

Like Alexander Mackenzie, Simon Fraser, and Sir James Douglas himself, Matthew Baillie Begbie was a lowland Scot, though actually born either in Mauritius or at the Cape of Good Hope in 1819, his father being a Captain in the British Army. His birthday was either May 9th or September 13th. As is usual with anything to do with the Cariboo, there are conflicting testimonies. After his father left the army in 1832 and went on half pay as a Major the family settled in Guernsey, where young Matthew learned to speak French with the fluency for which he was later renowned, and which enabled him to act as his own interpreter whenever neccessary in later years. At Elizabeth College he studied Latin and Greek, and developed a

[35] Margaret A. Ormsby, *British Columbia, A History*, 1958, pp. 160-61.

140

talent for drawing and for the making of maps. He was a brilliant student in all these subjects as well as in Mathematics, and went up to Trinity College, Cambridge in 1836, moving to Peterhouse in 1838. He graduated in 1841 in both Classics and Mathematics, and enrolled in Lincolns Inn. He was called to the Bar in November 1844, and soon became an experienced lawyer in the Chancery Courts. He also worked as a law reporter for *The Times*. It is said that one day the Lord Chancellor enquired "Who is the reporter who so faithfully does my remarks?" and that soon afterwards the two men became acquainted, which led to the Lord Chancellor's appointing Begbie to be the Judge of British Columbia.

In March 1859 Judge Begbie left Victoria to visit the mainland and the mining settlements, taking Arthur Bushby with him as his Registrar. This was the first of many circuits that he made. David R. Williams in his admirable book *"The Man for a New Country..." Sir Matthew Baillie Begbie* describes the main purpose of these circuits as "to 'deliver' the gaols, that is, to hold trials, thus delivering or emptying the gaols, of accused persons; if convicted, a man might return to the same gaol but in a different category, as a prisoner. The system was founded on the notion that persons accused of crime should be tried by their peers in the locality where the crime allegedly occurred. Such criminal trials were referred to as 'Assizes'."[36]

Begbie's reputation for justice was established on this very first circuit, for he freed two Indians accused at Yale of murdering an American, making it clear that suspicion was not enough and that hard evidence was required. From Yale he travelled up to the edge of southern Cariboo. David Williams describes his journey:

Travelling on foot, the party went up-river from Yale to Spuzzum, crossed the Fraser at Chapman's Bar to the east bank, and followed the Hudson's Bay Company brigade route over the hills to the Anderson River, which they then descended to the present-day town of Boston Bar. They then followed an Indian trail around dangerous Jackass Mountain to Lytton, and walked over the upland plateau to present-day Lillooet, crossing the Thompson and Fraser Rivers en route. From there they went south to Port Douglas, along the chain of lakes from Lillooet, walking eight to ten hours daily, but canoeing on the lakes. There was considerable danger, as Bushby records:

"We first had to cross a tremendous snowy gorge and hard work it was — came to the Four Mile House and had a cup of coffee — this was a rum way for a judge to go on circuit — after passing Four Mile hut, we commenced the descent and very good fun we had, Indians and all, sprawling and

[36] David Williams, ... *The Man for a New Country, Sir Matthew Baillie Begbie*, 1977, pp. 44-45.

141

scrambling right and left — sliding, tumbling and rolling — and by no means safe — as had we slid off the trail we must have gone ... goodness knows where. We then came in sight of the Fraser, winding its way through immense rocks and precipices — a superb sight it was from the height we were at. ... Awfully dangerous, and had the foot once slipped, we must have been dashed to pieces. ... Two or three places we descended, although almost perpendicular, by the aid of one or two trees which had been partially cut so as to hang down — deuced dangerous — another pass I caught hold of a piece of rock to save myself. It gave way and I saw it bound down an immense height into the river."[37]

On this as on later circuits Begbie lived largely off the land, providing his own food by fishing and shooting. He was a powerful man, over six feet tall, and full bearded, with an imposing presence. He carried himself with pride, and, when in court, even if the court was taking place in the open air beneath a tree, or in a clearing, he wore his judge's robes. While he became quickly attuned to the way of life in the country, and as handy with a gun or in a canoe as anybody, he never forgot that he was a man of law, and the representative of Justice. His reputation grew rapidly. Even on this first circuit David Williams tells us, he received a deputation of Indian chiefs, who came to complain of the attitudes and the downright thievery of the Americans, the "Boston Men," though they, perhaps tactfully, praised the ways of "King George's Men."

Begbie made a second circuit in September 1859, and reported many things about the country to Sir James Douglas, as he had done after his earlier journey, making a number of important recommendations. In September 1860 he visited Cariboo proper for the first time, travelling as far as the north fork of the Quesnel River, by way of Clinton, Green Lake, Bridge Creek, Lac La Hache, Williams Lake and McLeese Lake. He held no courts on this journey, but made copious notes about the country, and drew maps of the terrain and of the trails for the information of later travellers. It may seem odd that he was not required to perform his duties as a judge on this occasion. The explanation may be that earlier in 1860 it had become so obvious that the mining activities to the north made additional officials necessary that a Justice of the Peace had been provided for the area. Philip Nind was sworn in as Justice of the Peace for the District of Alexandria on July 17, 1860, and he travelled north accompanied by William Pinchbeck as his constable. He made his headquarters at Williams Lake and travelled immediately up to Fort Alexander and then to Fergusons Bar where many miners were active. He wrote back to his superiors,

[37] *Ibid.*, p. 46.

Immediately my presence became known on the Bar great satisfaction was expressed by the most respectable of the community at the arrival of a Peace Officer amongst them as they had hereto felt beyond the pale of the law and protection and completely at the mercy of a few drunken desperadoes.

Nind was fortunate, in some ways, to be faced immediately with a serious crime. The local Indians were in a state of ferment because an Indian boy had been shot by a miner called Moses Anderson. Nind calmed the Indians, and appointed the first special constable in Cariboo, Isaac Holden, to arrest Anderson. He also, in response, to the miners' anxieties, took up again a plan he had suggested earlier of providing an armed escort for the gold from the mines to ensure its safe transport to Victoria. In 1861 the Gold Escort of twelve uniformed, armed, and well-mounted men, took its first shipment from Quesnel Forks at a charge of one shilling an ounce. Unfortunately the government refused to guarantee safe delivery and so the miners preferred to continue in their old ways, carrying their own gold from the fields, either singly or in groups, concealing the treasure upon their persons. Robberies still occurred, however, and after a particularly savage murder for profit at Quesnel Forks in 1862 the Gold Escort was instituted again; this time it numbered fifteen men and was in the personal charge of Thomas Elwyn while Nind oversaw the whole procedure. Nevertheless only the banks made much use of the service, and the miners stayed with their old ways, being the more inclined to do so because of talk of lost receipts and because details of the amounts carried which were supposed to be confidential not infrequently found their way into the columns of the press. From 1859 right into the 1870's many of the miners made use of the Mitchell Trail or the Berry Trail as it is sometimes called. This was created by "Captain" J. E. Mitchell and, until the wagon roads were built, it was the easiest trail for foot travellers and for horses from what became 108 Mile House a little southeast of Lac La Hache to the goldfields and back again. It appears to follow the route that Dunleavy took, running through many little valleys and by seventeen small lakes to the mouth of the Horsefly River where Mitchell had provided an old single-wheel paddle steamer to take the miners the ten or twelve miles up Quesnel Lake to the old camping ground at Cedar Point. From Cedar Point the miners could travel onwards either by way of the Cariboo River, crossing it some way below Cariboo Lake where Mitchell had a toll bridge, or by way of Quesnel Forks. From then the trail led by Cataline's pasture to Keithley Creek and up over French Snowshoe, a plateau so called because the snow lay longer there than elsewhere and showshoes were needed for most of the year, and by Yanks Peak and then down to Antler Creek, Antler, Cunningham Pass, and so to Williams Creek. This last part of the trail was hard going. Judge Begbie commented on a map he made of the trails in 1861 that he estimated the town of Antler to be 3500 feet above sea level and the trail to it 3000 feet higher. His map marks Mitchell's bridge very clearly, and also shows how the Mitchell trail ran through areas where grass was abundant and then through "Cranberry Valley" before it reached Lake Quesnel, thus providing satisfactory subsistence for both man and pack horse. Lieutenant Spencer Palmer knew the trail but rejected it as the basis for a road because of the difficulty of making a road over Snowshoe Plateau and Yanks Peak. Although the Mitchell trail was a private concern he did receive some government assistance in making it. In 1865 he wrote a letter to the *Sentinel* which read:

I came to this country in 1861 with $200 and tried mining for one year. In the winter of 1862 I put a bridge across the North Forks.

North Fork was the name then given to that stretch of the Cariboo River between Cariboo Lake and Quesnel Forks.

In 1863 I commenced cutting trails, one to Keithley Creek a distance of 14 miles. In September of 1863 I started on a grand expedition of cutting a trail from the 108 mile post, Wright's wagon road, to Quesnel Lake, a distance of 55 miles for $3000 from the government. The job was completed in 1864. I then put boats on the lake and last year (1864) 180 persons crossed over the lake. Because I lost a dollar a head I cut a trail around the lake a distance of 12 miles at a cost of $100 a mile. I have now applied to Judge Cox, as government agent, for a loan of $200, which was refused as he has no authority, but offered to sign a subscription list if I would get it up.

It is to be hoped that Mitchell got his money but there seems to be no record of whether he did or not. The trail, however, was certainly popular. It was not only the relative convenience of the route for foot travellers and pack animals that made the miners use the Mitchell trail; it was Mitchell's curious ability to make the trail absolutely safe from fear of robbers and other marauders. Nobody seems quite sure how he managed it, though it seems that some kind of protection must have been bought from someone or other, and that Mitchell himself must have been somewhat feared. The miners would rent packhorses from Mitchell to carry both their gold and their equipment. He would weigh the equipment and the gold together, not separately as did the official organization; thus there was no indication to anybody of how much gold a man was carrying, and he

144

did not have to declare the amount to anyone. Nor was he required to pay any insurance. Mitchell did charge for the use of the trail, but the charge was apparently very small and it is said that he made little money out of it. In all the years it was used there was only one robbery and murder recorded. This took place just beside Mitchell's toll bridge across the Cariboo River, where a Chinaman provided food for travellers and collected the toll. The victim was a gold buyer. He was robbed and killed by two men, who were later caught and hung. The gold was never found and it is popularly supposed that the robbers found it too heavy to carry out of the country and that therefore it is still hidden somewhere in the area. The place was thereafter called, inevitably, Murderer's Gulch. The interesting thing about this crime is that the murdered man was one who had not rented pack animals from Mitchell or paid any dues for using the trail. It seems as if he had, in this way, deprived himself of the protection that Mitchell somehow contrived for all his other clients.

While the miners themselves, and especially those unconnected with the larger companies, used the Mitchell trail, the bigger concerns and the banks continued to make use of Nind's gold escort. In 1862 Nind went on leave and was replaced by Thomas Elwyn who rented an office at Quesnel Forks to supplement the one at Williams Lake. Quickly realizing that the Williams Creek area needed permanent officials he set about planning the building of a court-house and office at Richfield, and suggested that two magistrates were needed in the main mining area. This was agreed. He established himself at Richfield; Peter O'Reilly took the western half and made his headquarters at Quesnel. Elwyn stopped all the mining that winter and went south, leaving a constable behind him. Because he himself owned a claim and because the *Colonist*, on October 21, 1862, objected to government officials owning claims in the mines they were administering, he resigned his post, and Peter O'Reilly took over the Cariboo East area and William G. Cox replaced O'Reilly in Cariboo West. O'Reilly was extremely willing to take advice from the miners and an elected Mining Board was created to help him with amending existing regulations. When O'Reilly left for Wild Horse Creek in the Kootenays Cox took over the whole of the Cariboo until H. M. Ball arrived as Judge in Quesnel and became Gold Commissioner. Cox returned to Cariboo after a year (1865-66) as Acting Colonial Secretary. A year later, when Vancouver Island and British Columbia achieved union, Henry M. Ball became County Court Judge of Cariboo.

The majority of the work done by judges and gold commissioners in the sixties concerned disputes over claims and workings between the miners; criminal matters were attended to by the travelling court of Judge Begbie, who had a residence in Richfield, and who, more than any other single person was responsible for the relative peacefulness of the Cariboo scene. The *Colonist* reported on August 17, 1863:

Everything is very quiet and orderly on the creek owing in great measure to Mr. O'Reilly's efficiency and the wholesome appearance of Judge Begbie who seems to be a terror to evil doers and a sworn enemy to the use of the knife and revolver. Crime in Cariboo has been vigorously checked in its infancy by a firm hand, and seems to have sought some soil more congenial to its growth. The most prejudiced of foreigners on the Creek allow that a security of life and property exists which twelve months ago it would have appeared as useless to expect.

O'Reilly and Begbie worked well together and remained fast friends all their days, O'Reilly being at Begbie's bedside during his last hours in Victoria in 1894.

Begbie clearly recognized that niceties of law were less important than immediately intelligible justice, and that as long as justice was seen to be done, regulations might well be treated a little cavalierly. He was also aware of the importance of presenting himself and his authority dramatically, and of allowing nobody the opportunity to undermine his effectiveness by hinting at corruption. It is said that though he never married he had a fondness for the ladies and, rather than patronize the Barkerville establishments, would meet a girl in the hills beyond Richfield from time to time. He was very interested in theology; he would often, in later years, have theological arguments with his clerical friends in Victoria. Although he became known as "The Hanging Judge" he did not really earn the title, for in every case where we have records the death penalty appears to have been unavoidable. He was certainly no Justice Jeffries. Nevertheless we might suspect that he was not altogether unhappy at having a reputation for ruthlessness; judicial mercy would look uncommonly like weakness to many of the miners in the Cariboo of the last quarter of the nineteenth century. He seems, indeed to have gone out of his way to present an image of severity; on one occasion when a jury brought in a verdict of manslaughter, he said to the prisoner in open court:

Had the jury performed their duty I might now have the painful satisfaction of condemning you to death, and you, gentlemen of the jury, you are a pack of Dalles horse thieves, and permit me to say, it would give me

146

great pleasure to see you hanged, each and every one of you, for declaring a murderer guilty of only manslaughter.

On another occasion he told a man accused of a hold-up:

The jurymen say you are not guilty, but with this I cannot agree. It is now my duty to set you free, and I warn you not to pursue your evil ways. But if you ever again should be so inclined, I hope you select your victim from the men who have acquitted you.

On the other hand, during one of his 1865 sessions he simply said to a man who had pleaded guilty, "Go, and sin no more." Though his administration of justice was often harsh and usually idiosyncratic, it was based upon a code that the society he worked for could easily understand. He believed in flogging and told Chartres Brew, "if a man insist on behaving like a brute, after fair warning, and won't quit the Colony; treat him like a brute and flog him." On the other hand, in later years, when an admiring man in Salt Lake City said to him "You certainly did some hanging, Judge" he replied

Excuse me, my friend, I never hanged any man. I simply swore in American citizens like yourself, and it was you that hanged your own fellow countrymen.

This was strictly true, for Begbie in order to prevent trouble between the various nationalities, would always swear in a jury of the same race or country of origin as the prisoner. Judge Begbie endeared himself to the mining community as much by the straightforwardness of his speech and actions as by his demonstrable fairness in dealing out justice. He was passionately concerned that the law should be respected. On one occasion, while standing on a veranda he over-heard two men below him making rude remarks about the main-tenance of law in Cariboo, and, angered, picked up a pail of slops and threw it over them.

Acts such as these would have been more than fool-hardy had the judge not provided himself with a travelling companion and body-guard. According to legend, this bodyguard was none other than Long Baptiste who still preferred to wear his usual clothing, or lack of it, and who still covered himself regularly in grease, and used a bow and arrow in preference to a gun. They must have made an astonishing, even awe inspiring sight — the tall elegant Judge in his decent lawyer's black, and the equally tall near naked Indian with his hunting knife and bow. Begbie himself was proud of the low crime rate in Cariboo. On April 1, 1860, when the mines were still dominated by the Californians, who were more troublesome by far than the Canadians and British, Begbie wrote to James Douglas:

147

There have been but three murders committed since I first began to hold courts in British Columbia. They were all committed by Indians; in every case, the Indians were drunk.

He was proud of the efficiency of Chartres Brew and the police. In 1861 he told Douglas that there was very little crime in the colony and that most of the criminals had been caught,

the exceptions where criminals have evaded Justice during the past year are, I think, only 3 in number, one accused of murder which from what I learnt, would probably amount to no more than manslaughter, another for shooting with intent to murder; the third for larceny.

Judge Begbie, Philip Nind, Thomas Elwyn, William G. Cox, Peter O'Reilly, and Captain J. E. Mitchell: these were the men who kept Cariboo safe for the miners and for the settlers in the early days. Without their work and their deep understanding of the country and its peoples Cariboo could have become a social chaos, and the heartland of what was to become British Columbia might never have fully recovered from the tumult of its beginnings.

CHAPTER ELEVEN

The Law Breakers

For all the efforts of Judge Begbie and his fellow officers of the law, Cariboo still had its share of crime and disorder. The two main causes of crime were, predictably, drink and gambling. Both gave rise to quarrels in which knives or revolvers were drawn, and while many of the disputants in these cases were simply thrown into jail to cool off if no actual serious bodily harm had been done, and then released without trial when they had dried out, there was concern about the situation. Commissioner Elwyn decided that, while there would be a riot if he closed the saloons, he might get away with prohibiting gambling. The *Colonist* reported on September 10, 1862,

> A notice prohibiting gambling under a penalty of $100 was stuck up by Commissioner Elwyn, but the games go on openly as before.

There were, of course, a number of serious criminal cases in these years in Cariboo. The one which perhaps more than any other caused Begbie to be called the Hanging Judge was the so called Chilcotin War. It began in April 1864 when Chilcotin Indians murdered a ferryman 30 miles up river from a settlement being established at the head of Bute Inlet by Alfred Waddington, who was engaged in a project to drive a road through the Homathco Canyon from Bute Inlet to the mouth of the Quesnel. There were several explanations as to the cause of the trouble. Some believed that the smallpox epidemic of 1862 which reduced the Bella Coola tribe from 500 to 15 was the real cause. It was said that the disease had been spread by traders who robbed the graves of smallpox victims and sold the blankets they found there to the Indians, and that the Indians, discovering this, had become steadily more and more intent upon driving out the white intruders. Some said that Waddington's men brought the trouble on themselves by trading their guns to the Indians for native clothing, buckskin jackets, mocassins and the like, and thus leaving themselves practically defenceless. Yet others, including Judge Begbie, believed that the Indians, with whom no treaty had been made, objected to the white men stealing their land.

The murder of the ferryman, Timothy Smith, seems to have been unpremeditated. He is supposed to have insulted a Chilcotin warrior called Klattasine who had come down the Homathco Canyon to visit his friend, Chief Tellot, who was, together with others of his tribe, employed by Waddington, and to have refused him food. The Indians thereabouts were not far from starving according to some reports, and so it is not altogether surprising that anger and hunger caused Klattasine to kill Smith and take as much food as he and his companions could carry. The night of the murder is given variously as April 28 and April 29.

That night Klattasine joined Chief Tellot and his men, and it is said that they danced their war dance only a little distance away from Waddington's encampment. If this is the case it is hard to understand why Waddington's men posted no sentries on the night of the 30th and were thus caught entirely by surprise, the Indians cutting down their tents as they slept and stabbing and shooting them through the enveloping folds of the canvas. Of the twelve men in the party nine were killed. One was knocked unconscious by a falling tent pole and remained unnoticed as the Indians killed the other two occupants of the tent, and was able to escape when the attack was over. Another man, an Irishman called Buckley, managed to get away into the woods and travelled upstream through the darkness to give his news to the road superintendent, Brewster, who, with three other men, was camped four miles upstream in order to clear the trail ahead. He found all four men dead, Brewster's body having been savagely mutilated. Buckley, desperate, managed to make his way to the ferry crossing; here he found the two other men who had survived the attack on the main camp. The ferry had been cut loose, but Buckley contrived a sling on the single remaining ferry cable across the river and the three men managed to get to the other bank and set out for the head of Bute Inlet.

Meanwhile the Indians travelled inland to gather more recruits to the cause. At Punze (or Punzi) Lake they killed a settler, and then, on the Bella Coola trail, they ambushed a pack train of forty-two horses that was taking supplies down to the roadbuilders' camp. The packer, Alexander MacDonald, and his seven companions, defended themselves strenuously, and, by digging trenches and creating earthworks, held off the attack for several days, after which the Indians, led by Chief Tellot, withdrew. MacDonald and his party left

150

their defences and began to move off in the direction of Waddington's Camp, whereupon Chief Tellot's war party rushed from hiding and again attacked, killing MacDonald and two of his men, but failing to catch up with the other five who carried news of the uprising down the Bella Coola Valley.

The settlers in the region were now thoroughly alarmed and Chartres Brew set sail, with a group of volunteers, to Bute Inlet in H.M.S. *Forward*, commanded by Lieutenant the Hon. Douglas Lascelles, and attempted to follow the Indians' trail inland. The nature of the country made this venture quite impractical and he had to send for reinforcements from New Westminster. This second group is variously reported as consisting of the New Westminster Volunteer Rifle Corps with the Hyack Fire Brigade, and as a body of Marines and Sailors under the command of Rear Admiral John Kingcome in H.M.S. *Sutlej*. Whoever they were, they sailed up Bentinck Arm and landed at New Aberdeen (Bella Coola) which provided them with a much better route into the interior than Bute Inlet and the Homathco River. As this group travelled along the Bella Coola Valley towards Punze (or Punzi, or Punzee) Lake, another party set out in the same direction from Cariboo. There are, inevitably, several versions of what followed. According to some the group from Alexandria was led by William G. Fox, a Cariboo miner, and according to others its leader was William G. Cox, the Gold Commissioner. Some versions state that Chartres Brew, in charge of yet a third party, was involved. In any case it seems clear that all the groups met at Punzee (or Punzi or Punze) Lake and set up a base of operations there. The party under Cox (or Fox) was despatched in the direction of Bute Inlet. Governor Seymour himself, having accompanied the party from Bella Coola, remained behind at the Lake with ten men in the log fort that had been constructed, and persuaded Alexis, a powerful Chilcotin chief to help in the suppression of what had clearly become a rebellion. At least that is one version of the story. Another is that Fox (or Cox) persuaded Chief Alexis to act as intermediary in offering the Indians amnesty if they would give themselves up, and that the Indians agreed to meet the white men at an old Hudson's Bay Fort (some say at Chelamko Forks) where they were, in defiance of all promises, promptly surrounded and five of the war party, including Chief Tellot, were captured, to be tried at Quesnel with Judge Begbie presiding, and to be sentenced to death. The day of their hanging at Quesnel was made the occasion for a great celebratory party by the miners of the area. Two of the partygoers were William and Lizette Boucher, who regarded the trip from Williams Lake to Quesnel to see the hanging as their honeymoon.

The only other "war" which disturbed Cariboo in the sixties and caused Chartres Brew once again to travel north was the "Grouse Creek War" of 1867. This began when the Heron Company working on Grouse Creek, got a franchise from the Gold Commissioner's Court, the Gold Commissioner being at that time Judge Henry M. Ball, to enable them to build a long flume alongside the creek through which the creek itself could be largely diverted, so as to keep their workings as dry as possible. By this means they managed to get right into the gutter of the creek itself and very soon they were taking out between fifty and a hundred ounces of gold each day. Not surprisingly, this caused a good deal of interest in the creek and the whole length of it was rapidly restaked by hopeful miners, the Canadian Company being particularly cunning, by not only staking part of the creek that the Heron Company's flume had made easy of access, but also, in case of difficulties, getting Judge Begbie to agree to accept any judgment made by the Gold Commissioner's Court, should a dispute occur. A dispute did, of course, occur. The Heron Company felt that the Canadian Company had occupied territory which was theirs by franchise, even though they were not working it, and the Gold Commissioner agreed that this was the case and ordered the Canadian Company off. The Canadian Company was hoist with its own petard. They had already ensured that there could be no appeal against a ruling of the Gold Commissioner's Court on this particular matter. Still, they refused to budge, and when the Gold Commissioner ordered their arrest they resisted the officers. Ball, incensed, swore in between twenty and thirty special constables and sent them to the Creek to effect the arrests. The Canadian Company, however, did better. They gathered together what amounted to an army of four hundred men to defend their claims and the constables retired discomfitted. On July 19, 1867 the situation worsened. The Canadian Company, presumably gleeful at their victory, hurled their army of four hundred at the Heron Company miners and took possession of their workings, and began to take out gold in huge quantities, some say as much as a thousand ounces a day. The Heron Company could do nothing. They waited. They knew that Governor Seymour, who had been appointed Governor of British Columbia in succession to Sir James Douglas in April, had been appealed to for help. After they had waited three days, however, their claims lapsed and the Canadian Company instantaneously created a subsidiary company, the Sparrowhawk, to take over all the Heron Company's ground. Governor Seymour reached Richfield with a company of the Royal Engineers on August 7, 1867. Although the engineers were not called into action, they did suffer some casualties, for the warehouse containing their equipment mysteriously burned to the ground. Governor Seymour at last prevailed upon the Canadian Company to give up the disputed ground to the government and to turn the leaders of their army over to the police. Eight men were given up and they received three months' imprisonment, which, after other members of the Canadian Company had created a series of petitions, was reduced to two days. Governor Seymour returned to New Westminster among loud murmurs of discontent, for it was felt that he had taken the side of the rebels and encouraged the use of force in the mines. The Governor, after talking the whole matter over with Chief Justice Needham, who had claimed the title of Chief Justice from Begbie when Vancouver Island and British Columbia were united in 1866, gave him a special commission to investigate the whole affiar. The Chief Justice, together with his son, and Chartres Brew (who replaced Henry M. Ball) started hearings in Richfield on September 16, 1867. The hearings continued for ten days of lively and often acrimonious disputation. The ground was at last returned to the Heron Company as well as the gold held by the court.

In both these wars the forces of justice finally asserted their power, though in neither case does absolute justice appear to have been done, for the Chilcotins who were hung were quite possibly convinced that they were protected by an amnesty, and the thugs of the Canadian Company received no punishment at all. In both these cases, however, what was at stake was the fabric of society itself, and in both cases the settlements of the dispute and the court judgments made involved political expediency. It would have been quite possibly as dangerous to have let the Chilcotins go free and unscathed as it would have been to arouse the fury of the Canadian Company's army of four hundred.

In addition to these uprisings the police force had to deal with a number of murders and holdups. From time to time a lone miner on his way down the road would be robbed of his gold and sometimes killed. In 1866 (or 1865) a man called Morgan was found killed not far from Soda Creek. He had left the diggings with a heavy poke of gold and had been sporting a gold watch. Both the watch and the poke were missing. Some time later two Indians offered Mrs. Ritchie of Canoe Creek a gold watch and chain for sale. She suspected nothing for Indians were often paid for their services by gifts of this kind. After some bargaining, she bought the watch. Later, she realized that the watch might well have been Morgan's, and the two Indians, one from Lillooet and one from Nicomen were traced, questioned, and jailed in Quesnel to await trial. One day, however, the Nicomen Indian, who had until that moment been entirely peaceable, attacked his gaoler, Constable Sullivan, with a knife and nearly killed him before making his escape. The Lillooet Indian chose to stay where he was. The Nicomen crossed the border into the United States and Constable Richard Lowe of Osoyoos discovered that he had a girl friend on the Canadian side whom he often visited. He bribed other Indians to steal the Nicomen's rifle when he next called on the girl, and they did so. Lowe surprised the Indian with his girl and captured him; placing him on a horse and handcuffing his ankles together under the horse's belly, he led his prisoner to Lytton, by way of Princeton, Coultee's, the Nicomen trail to the Thompson River, and, at last, the Wagon Road, arriving in the middle of the night. From Lillooet his prisoner was sent to New Westminster where he joined his sometime companion of Lillooet. At the trial, held in Richfield, the Lillooet Indian turned state's evidence and was given a life sentence. The Nicomen Indian was sentenced to death. Although the watch had been recovered the poke of gold was never recovered, and it became a part of local legend that somewhere along Morgan Creek, (for the creek was inevitably named after the murdered man) that poke of gold is still hidden. Sceptics, however, maintain that miners travelling south often left their pokes for safekeeping in Dunleavy's safe at Soda Creek and that maybe Dunleavy had "forgotten" about it after the murder. Some even suggested at the time that Dunleavy had organized the killing.

The first holdup of the stage in Cariboo did not take place until twenty years after Morgan's murder, in 1886 at the 82 mile post. The stage contained only one passenger, a Chinaman, and was driven by Ned Tate. Two bandits took the big steel treasure box containing either four or eight thousand dollars in gold. It is said that the Chinaman, on being questioned about the incident and asked to describe what had happened, held up his hands to form a circle representing the muzzle of the bandit's gun and said, with some intensity "allee same stovepipe!" Another robbery occurred a few years later when a brother of Ned Tate's was driving the stage. This took place on the road between Quesnel and Soda Creek, and the amount stolen, and never recovered was estimated as between two and three thousand dollars.

It would seem that gold would be easy to dispose of at that time, for not only was it commonly accepted as currency, but because of the many varieties of it in the area, and because many miners moved from creek to creek and collected many different kinds of gold in their pokes, it was difficult to establish that a man had not acquired the gold himself, however many kinds he possessed. Nevertheless it was the gold itself which betrayed a miner known as Sam (or Jack) Rowlands who started a minor gold rush on Scotty's Creek near Ashcroft in the fall of 1891 (some say 1892). Many local people were dubious, for the Chinamen had already given up work on the creek and that usually meant that there was nothing left worth having. Others were more optimistic. All were very irritated at the brusque and cantankerous behaviour of Rowlands, however. He did not seem inclined to conversation and invited nobody to look over his diggings. Indeed he sent the curious packing, though all noted that he was working with very poor equipment, leaky sluice boxes and almost worn out riffles. His helpers were three Chinese, and he trusted them so little that he only cleaned up the sluices when they had left the workings to have their meals. After a while everybody but Rowlands left the creek; he however continued to find gold and to bank it regularly in Ashcroft. Eyebrows were raised all over the territory, for nobody had ever previously come across a creek that only paid off in one place.

This is one version of the Scotty Creek strike. There is, inevitably, another, in which the lone miner's name is given as Martin Van Buren Rowland, and in which Rowland was never actually observed working the Creek, but simply turned up in Ashcroft announcing his discovery, and buying drinks all round. He was, he said, going down to New Westminster to see if he could raise some additional capital for exploiting the Creek further. This caused surprise in his auditors, for whoever heard tell of a man with a rich new strike informing everybody where he had made it, at least not until he had established a company and gained control over as much of the area as the law would permit.

The next stage in the story is generally agreed upon. Chief Constable Hussey of Kamloops came into Ashcroft and Rowland's discovery became the subject of a discussion between him and Constable Burr, an ex-stage driver, who had become one of the finest trackers and most respected law officers in the country. Hussey was convinced that Rowland's gold had originated elsewhere than Scotty Creek, and most probably in the strong box that had been taken from the stage in a holdup at Bridge Creek, near 98 Mile in July of that year. It is said that there was only one passenger in the stage that day and that the driver, Steve Tingley (some say Billy Parker, some Rawlins) had stopped to rest the horses and was just filling his pipe when a small bearded man, with a red bandana covering the lower part of his face and a stetson pulled down over his eyes, suddenly appeared, levelling a Winchester, and commanded the driver to "stick 'em up" and to kick the strong box down into the road. Some say that the man emerged from behind a tree stump; others that he rode out of the bush. The driver did as he was ordered, whereupon the bandit either waved the stage on and proceeded to hammer and chisel the strong box open in the ditch beside the road, or heaved the strong box onto his horse's back and disappeared into the bush. In the first version the strong box was discovered in the ditch as soon as the search parties began their work; in the second we are told that a downpour of rain made tracking so difficult that all the eager reward-hunters were frustrated, and that it was not until some weeks later that the empty strong box was discovered in the bush. In both stories the man who found the strong box was Constable Burr.

Hussey and Burr, remembering this holdup, decided that Rowland would stand investigating. Hussey, indeed, decided that he should be arrested straightaway. They got a warrant from a magistrate and went to Rowland's hotel room and charged him with the Bridge Creek holdup, at which he expressed outraged astonishment. In some versions Hussey discovered a loaded .45 revolver under the miner's pillow, which supported his suspicions, and then he and Burr got Rowlands to write a full account of his mining career and witnessed his signature, before taking him to gaol for the night. In this version Hussey, on reading through Rowland's story, felt even more certain that he had got the right man, for the account showed that Rowland knew very little indeed about mining. Other versions say nothing of this, but all are agreed that Hussey examined the "Scotty Creek Gold" which Rowland had left for safe-keeping in Foster's Store, and discovered that it could not possibly have all come from the same place, for it was not all of one kind. Moreover, the characteristics of the different golds being so clearly defined, it was possible to see that the gold had originated in many different creeks and all of them in the Barkerville area. Hussey produced the gold in evidence at the trial at the Clinton assizes with S. P. Mills prosecuting and the stage driver said that he recognized Rowland's voice as that of the bandit. Martin Van Buren (or Sam or Jack) Rowlands was sentenced to five years. He was sixty years old, and one might well have thought him at the end of his career. He contrived, however, to escape from the prison in two years and was never recaptured. Only $3000 of the gold had been recovered from the Scotty Creek hoard and the strong box, according to the BX company, had contained around $15,000. Some Cariboo folk maintain that Rowlands had only taken part of his loot to Scotty Creek, just in case he might be caught and that, on his escape from prison he recovered the remainder and spent the rest of his days in comfortable retirement well away from the suspicious looks and the long memories of Cariboo. Others, predictably, suggest that Rowland's gold remains buried somewhere in the Clinton-Ashcroft or even the Bridge Creek area and that one of these days a man might have the luck to find it.

Rowland was by no means the only holdup artist in Cariboo, but his story has become a legend because of the boldness of his Scotty Creek subterfuge, and because Cariboo dearly loves an entertaining scoundrel and an ingenious rogue. Other holdups were less celebrated. A stage coach holdup occurred some years later about twenty-six miles from Quesnel on the road south. The driver was Jack Tate, and there were no passengers, and the single bandit got away with $2000. Neither the bandit nor the money were ever heard of again and some suspect that it was a put-up job and that Tate himself took the gold, for he retired from stage driving shortly afterwards. Another rather odd holdup was less successful; the bandit was quickly captured but turned out to be a woman in man's clothing. An even less successful holdup attempt was made by a man who fired several warning shots at the stage and found them absolutely ignored. He continued to blaze away as it passed him, but nothing he could do had any effect. He had, unfortunately for him, picked a coach driven by Charlie Restahy who was stone deaf and who had not heard the gunfire.

In order to make life difficult for the holdup men some of the gold was sent out in the form of ingots, each one weighing 350 pounds avoirdupois. On one occasion after a holdup at a dry gulch near 150 Mile the posse arrived to find the ingot still there. The robbers had simply been unable to carry it away.

Some of the Cariboo lawbreakers were not without a sense of humour. Isaac Ogden, the fur buyer and storekeeper at Lac La Hache in the 1870's was, like many Cariboo folk, a devotee of horse racing, and horse races were held regularly at Lac La Hache at the time. He was so keen indeed that he smuggled in a horse from south of the border which he called "Duty Free." He picked as his jockey a man called Billy Dunn, a little man from south of the border who was generally liked in the area, having worked for the McIntoshes and others, and who was easily recognizable because of the red and black bandana that he wore. Billy Dunn rode Isaac Ogden's horse — whether it was Duty Free or not we do not know — and won the race handsomely. Ogden was overjoyed and bore off the prize, a magnificent decorated saddle, with great glee. He did not, however, reward Billy Dunn for his part in winning the race. That night therefore little Billy Dunn broke into Ogden's store, stole the prize saddle, placed it on the horse he had taken to victory, and rode off. Neither horse nor saddle was heard of again, though the MacIntosh family for whom Dunn had worked and whose children had adored him received a letter from a United States prison some time later. Billy Dunn, the kindly little man, and the owner of Billy Dunn's Meadow near Lac La Hache had been holding up stages south of the border quite regularly before deciding to make his home in Cariboo.

The holdups occurred almost invariably when the stage carried very few passengers, and at a period when the mines were producing less gold than before, so that armed guards were no longer considered worth their hire. Moreover in the late eighties, the robbers had an easier and quicker means of leaving the area than before, for the railway reached Ashcroft in 1887, and they could travel anonymously in the crowd, no longer subjected to scrutiny by everyone they met on the road through the Fraser Canyon or on the Lillooet road. Certainly more miscreants evaded the arm of the law in Cariboo in the eighties and nineties than in the sixties and seventies, at least after the initial confusions of the rush were over.

One particular manhunt, and the murder which caused it, has become a classic Cariboo legend, and, like all Cariboo legends, it comes in a number of different versions. Whatever the version, however, the hero of the story is Washington Delaney Moses, the black barber of Barkerville.

In May 1866, Moses, on his way up to Barkerville fell in with a thirty-three year old American called Morgan Blessing the first night out from Yale. Blessing was a member of a rich Boston family who had travelled west to make his fortune in the Californian goldfields, and who was now on his way up to Williams Creek to try his luck there. California had been good to him. He had plenty of money and sported a stick-pin made of a big gold nugget in the shape of a man's head which the jeweller had mounted upside down. (Some say it was in the shape of an angel.) On the road the two men were joined by a third, a tall, handsome young fellow called James Barry. It is not quite clear where the three came together; some say at a road house on the way, and some say at Quesnel, where they arrived on May 28, 1866. According to one version Blessing liked Barry and offered to stake him on his journey, and did indeed pay for all his meals on the road, Barry professing gratitude and promising eventual repayment, writing down the cost of each meal in a small notebook. At Quesnel, Blessing complained of sore feet and Barry remained with him in Quesnel while Moses, in a hurry to get back to his barber shop, continued the journey to Barkerville. In another version, which has an air of precision about it which commands respect, Moses and Blessing arrived at Quesnel on the *Enterprise* at around seven o'clock in the evening of May 28, and settled down for the night, wrapped in their blankets, on the floor of Brown and Gillis' Saloon. It must be assumed that all the available rooms in Quesnel were occupied for Blessing and Moses were not without money. The following morning they met up with James Barry, who admitted to being a professional gambler, and they had a drink with him. Blessing paid for the drink with a $20 note, and made it clear that he had plenty of money. Blessing and Barry became very friendly and agreed to start off for Barkerville the next morning and, in order to avoid the discomforts of crowded Quesnel, to spend the night in a shack a little way along the road. Moses did not accompany them as he had to find a man in Quesnel who owed him money. He started off for Barkerville early the next morning, hoping to meet his friends at the shack, but when he got there an Indian who had been camping near at hand told him that the two had set off for Barkerville at dawn.

It is not clear exactly when Moses met Barry again. One version has it that he met him soon after getting into Barkerville and that Barry told him Blessing had given up the journey on account of bad feet and had returned south. Another version tells us that it was not until he had been in Barkerville a couple of weeks that he saw Barry, handsomely and indeed ostentatiously dressed in new clothes, and spending money very freely indeed. Moses may or may not have gone to the police at this time. Some say that he did so, and that the police were not particularly impressed either with his tale of Blessing's mysterious disappearance or that of Barry's sudden wealth. Many Barkerville citizens, and especially gamblers, made the transition from rags to riches, and from riches to rags, in a very short time indeed. There was nothing particularly unusual about Barry's sudden prosperity. Moses, however, remained anxious about Blessing and some say that he made enquiries of Sam Wilcox at whose boarding house Barry had stayed when he reached Barkerville, and discovered that on June 2 the man who had been unable to buy his own drinks on May 29, had paid in advance for his room with a $20 bill. In this version of the story Moses did not yet go to the police but became even more suspicious of Barry and worried about the fate of Blessing.

It was, in all versions of the story, the gold that brought about the denouement. Some say that Moses saw a Hurdy girl wearing that unmistakable nugget of Idaho gold shaped like a man's head (or like an angel) that Blessing had shown him. Some say she was wearing the actual stick-pin, and others that the nugget had been set into a necklace. Moses asked the girl where she got the nugget, and she told him Barry had given it to her, and that Barry was the son of a wealthy American plantation owner from the south who had managed to retain his wealth during the Civil War and who was now in the north looking for investments. In another version Moses was about to give Barry himself a haircut or shave when, while putting the sheet around him, he noticed that the stick-pin he was wearing boasted a nugget which looked like a man's profile; he saw this more easily because he was looking down on the pin from above, and the jeweller had set the nugget upside-down. Moses still did not go to the police but questioned one of his customers, a miner called Bill Fraser, about Barry. Fraser told him that from talking to Barry on the road up from New Westminster earlier in the year he had gathered that Barry had been in gaol, and had indeed been a member of the New Westminster chain gang. Moreover Barry always carried a gun and even slept with it under his pillow. He and Barry had parted company at Quesnel on May 28th or 29th. Moses told his story to Chief Constable W. H. Fitzgerald at Richfield.

Once again there are several versions of what happened next. According to some the police organized a search along the Quesnel-Barkerville road to see if they could find Blessing's body, and did indeed find a body at the foot of a bluff near Pine Grove two miles east of what was later to be called Wingdam, and Moses identified the body as that of Blessing. According to others Constable Sullivan came into the police station just as Moses had completed his story and reported the finding of a body near "Bloody" Edwards' place at

Beaver Pass. A grouse-shooting miner had found it in the brush forty feet off the road while he was looking for a wounded bird. There was a wallet on the body bearing the name Charles Morgan Blessing, and beside the body were a tin cup and a clasp knife scratched with the initials CMB. There was a bullet hole in the back of the man's head.

Whether Barry left town just before or just after the body was found is not clear. Some say that he had not only left town but had done it so unobstrusively and had travelled with such caution that nobody along the road had any news of him. A more interesting version tells how Constable Sullivan decided to catch up with Barry at Soda Creek, rather than Quesnel, presumably because he felt he could at least equal Barry's time to that point as Barry would have to suffer the usual delays involved in loading the *Enterprise* for its trip. He set off immediately on the 120-mile journey, riding hard, but when he reached Soda Creek he learned that Barry had beaten him by two days, and that he had, on his arrival, immediately taken the fast six-horse stage for Yale. Sullivan, exhausted from his long ride, was crestfallen, and then he realized that he could make use of the telegraph which linked Soda Creek with Yale and had been installed the previous fall. He promptly wired the police at Yale. It was the first such use of the telegraph in Cariboo.

Whether the police apprehended Barry the moment he stepped off the Yale coach, or whether they caught him on the Yale steamer in the very nick of time, just as the boat was being cast off, and while he was in the middle of telling stories of Cariboo to a circle of admirers on the deck, we do not know. He was however arrested, and though he protested his innocence, he was put into the gaol.

Here again the stories are in conflict. Some say that Sullivan, in answer to another wire, travelled down to Yale and identified Barry, and that Barry, while admitting his identity, maintained that he had left Blessing near Bloody Edwards' place, and had seen a group of Chinese on the road later, and that the Chinese were probably the culprits. Some say, too, that it is at this stage in the story that the nugget was found in the possession of the Hurdy girl, and that Barry admitted to having given it her but swore that he had bought it in Victoria some years before. Chief Constable Fitzgerald, who cross-questioned him, asked if there was anything odd about the nugget, but Barry could not come up with the correct answer, never having noticed the man's profile (or the angel).

Yet another version of the capture has Sullivan travelling day and night to get ahead of Barry and prevent him reaching the steamer at

Yale. On reaching the suspension bridge above Yale Sullivan asked the tollgate keeper if anyone answering to Barry's description had crossed the bridge. The keeper said no. Sullivan then said that as Barry would certainly try to cross by night, the keeper should not obey his request to open the gate but, on some pretext or other, leave him standing waiting there, and then call Sullivan. All went as planned, and Sullivan grabbed Barry and handcuffed him the moment he got through the gate.

However Barry came to be arrested, arrested he certainly was, and taken to Richfield and tried before Judge Begbie.

At the trial a witness, Patrick Gannon, said that he had seen Blessing and Barry at breakfast beside the road near "Bloody" Edwards' place not far from where the body was found. The case was clear, and the more so because Wellington Delaney Moses, the star witness, was able to prove that the nugget was unmistakeably that belonging to Blessing, because of its unique formation.

Even Barry's last moments are told in different versions. Some say he was hung from the projecting beam of the Richfield Courthouse. Others say that a special scaffold was built outside the courthouse on August 8, 1867, and that he was hanged at seven in the morning, very quickly, and that within the hour the scaffold was taken down. It was Richfield's first public execution, and some say that Barry shared the limelight with the Nicomen Indian who had been condemned to death for the murder at Morgan's Creek. Indeed, there is a story that, as there was no official hangman available, the Indian was asked to do the job in return for his life. The Indian is reported as replying proudly and dramatically, "No! Me no hang Barry! Big Indian me, big brave!" Constable Sullivan, who either arrested or did not arrest Barry, later became Gold Commissioner for the Cassiar area. He was lost in the wreck of the *Pacific* off Cape Flattery in November 1875.

That the murder of Charles Morgan Blessing should have become so much a part of the oral history of Cariboo and have developed so many rich variations over the years, indicates clearly how rare such murders were. Indeed the crime-rate in Cariboo during the early years compares most favourably with that in most other parts of British Columbia, even though the goldfields were the most densely populated area of the period. Some of this is certainly due, as I have said, to the difficulty of entering and leaving the area unnoticed, but perhaps the main cause is the efficiency of a police force which knew all the ins and outs of the country, and the shrewd commonsense of both police and judges who realized that if misdemeanours were largely ignored, and brawls treated leniently, the rough and vigorous people of Cariboo would realize that the law was not there to make them suffer for failing to behave like paragons of virtue or for sudden and unpremeditated outbursts of rumbustiousness, but to protect life and property and to ensure that Cariboo could progress steadily towards that era of splendid prosperity they all believed to be on its way.

CHAPTER TWELVE

Pioneers of the Churches

The first missionary to reach Cariboo was Father Modeste Demers. He was born on October 11, 1808 at St. Jean-Chrysostom, Quebec, and studied at the seminary in Quebec City, becoming ordained as a priest on February 7, 1836. The following year he travelled west to the Red River and then to Fort Vancouver, where Peter Skene Ogden, the Hudson's Bay factor, agreed to take him with him north to New Caledonia. He arrived at Fort Alexander in 1842, having travelled with Ogden along the trails of the fur brigade, and found himself appalled at what he considered to be the degenerate state of the Indians. Before he left for Fort George he baptized sixty-seven Indian children, and on his return he talked the Indians into building a church, which was the first church in that part of the country. He held the first Mass in it on December 4, 1842.

Feeling that the church must establish a permanent presence in this wild country he travelled south to Williams Lake where some authorities state that he bought land on which to build a mission house, though nothing seems to have come of the plan at this time. On November 30, 1847, Father Demers was consecrated Bishop of Vancouver Island.

There is very little information about the New Caledonian missionaries in the later forties and the fifties: the next person we hear of is Father Charles Grandidier who visited the goldfields and the Indians around Fort Alexander and Williams Lake in 1861.

Father Grandidier was a member of the Congregation of Missionary Oblates of Mary Immaculate, which was founded by Charles Joseph Eugene de Mazenod, the Bishop of Marseilles, and which came into being on February 17, 1826. The Oblate Fathers and Brothers took the three vows of poverty, chastity, and obedience, and the letters O.M.I. after their names signified their membership in the order. The motto of the congregation was *Evangelizare pauperibus misit me*, He hath sent me to preach the Gospel to the poor. Five Oblates came to the Pacific Northwest of America in 1847, travelling first by ship to New York, then by riverboat and stagecoach to St. Louis, by steamboat to Kansas, and then by wagon train to Oregon where they settled in Walla Walla. During the next few years there were frequent outbursts of violence, in the country inhabited by the Yakima and the Cayuse Indians, and in 1858, when the gold strike on the lower Fraser had changed the whole social situation in the region, and when it became clear that the violence and social instability south of the border were making true missionary work almost impossible in most areas, Father Louis D'Herbomez, O.M.I., the new Superior of the Oblates in the northwest, decided to concentrate his attention upon British Columbia. Father Grandidier was only the first of a number of Oblate Fathers to visit and to serve Cariboo. He it was who decided that a permanent mission should be created in the country and made copious notes on possible sites.

As the activity at the goldfields increased the interest of the various churches increased also. Two Anglican priests, the Rev. Lundin Brown and the Rev. C. Snipe arrived the same year as Father Grandidier; they were succeeded by the Rev. John Sheepshanks and Mr. Dundas. In 1862, when Van Winkle seemed likely to become the centre of the goldfields the Anglican Bishop of British Columbia preached there regularly during the mining season. In 1863 the first cemetery in the area was created by John A. "Cariboo" Cameron on a bench overlooking his mine, and the first man to be buried there on July 31, 1863 was one of his own men, Peter Gibson, aged 31. In 1865 Father Florimond Gendre, O.M.I., came to the fields and celebrated Mass every Sunday morning at Richfield. He left Cariboo at the onset of winter, and the next year his place was taken by Father James Marion (or Maria) McGuckin, O.M.I., whose name seems to have caused more difficulty to historians than any other name in Cariboo for it is spelt in different places as McGuikin, McGoggin, McGaggin, and MacGuckin. Father McGuckin bought a house in Richfield and established a permanent place for services for the Catholics. Two years later a church was built and dedicated by Bishop Louis D'Herbomez, O.M.I., D.D., who had been made Bishop of British Columbia in 1864, on July 19, 1868. That summer the new St. Patrick's Church was occupied by Father Jolivet and Father McGuckin, the first English-speaking Oblate Father in the province, and an Irishman.

Father McGuckin was born in 1835 in Cookstown, Co. Tyrone, and spent his early years travelling Ireland as a commercial traveller for his father's linen manufacturing business. In 1859 he decided to enter the priesthood and joined the Oblates as a novice at Sickinghall in England, after which he studied in Marseilles. He returned to Ireland in 1863, and left for British Columbia that summer. He was ordained in Victoria on November 1, 1863 and taught for three years at St. Louis College there. In 1866 the Oblate Fathers left Vancouver Island to work on the mainland and Bishop D'Herbomez picked Father McGuckin as the man to work in the goldfields and to establish a permanent mission and school in Cariboo.

St. Patrick's was not quite the first permanent place of worship in Cariboo, for "Captain" John Evans of the Welsh Company built the Cambrian Hall "for literary and religious purposes" in 1866. The Anglicans' progress is less easy to chart. It is said by some authorities that they selected a site for a church in 1863 but did not build on it. Others say they did indeed build a small church in 1863 with $12,000 raised from subscriptions but after the Rev. Sheepshanks left the area this fell vacant, though it housed a library of 250 books which Sheepshanks had provided. In 1868 the Reverend James M. Reynard arrived and bought Penfold's Saloon which he used as a place of worship until it was destroyed by fire in 1868. The Wesleyan Methodists apparently only had two representatives in the area in 1863 the Reverends Ephriah Evans and Arthur Browning, who stayed only four months. It was not until 1869, after the fire, that the Reverend Thomas Derrick built a Wesleyan Chapel which was dedicated on June 20, 1869. Most of these ministers left Cariboo during the winter, the only known exceptions being the Reverend James Reynard who almost perished of cold and malnutrition during the winter of 1868-69, and the Reverend D. Duff who gave Church of Scotland services in the morning at Cameronton and in the afternoons at Richfield in the period before 1871. James Anderson confuses the picture further for us by stating in a poem written in March 1866:

> We've three toom kirks upon the creek —
> Oor ministers are a' sae meek —
> They canna live a year up here,
> But gang below for warmer cheer;
> But maybe this is just as weel,
> When they're awa' so is the deil.
> He'll think he has us a' his ain,
> And for that reason let's alane.

Which were the three churches in 1866? In a poem written in 1867 the situation is further confused:

> There's neither kirk nor Sunday here,
> Altho' there's mony a sinner'
> An' if we're steep'd in a' that's bad
> Think we there's muckle win'er?
> There is a little meetin' house
> That's ca'd the Cambrian Ha',
> Its members few — but these I view
> As saut preservin' a' —

The Welsh certainly seem not only to have been the first off the mark but also to have been the most impressive religious influence on the creek at this time.

There were some other churches and buildings used as churches in other parts of Cariboo, of course. Father Pierre Fouquet built a Catholic Church in Quesnellemouth in 1864, and it remained in operation until 1871 when it burned down. The priests who built churches in Cariboo at this period did so frequently against heavy odds. Perhaps no one worked harder or deserves remembrance more than Father James M. Reynard who arrived in Barkerville only two weeks before the great fire of 1868, intent upon gathering subscriptions for the building in Barkerville of a really handsome Anglican church. He spent a hard winter, unable to begin his campaign, not only because the winter population of Barkerville was always smaller than the summer one, but also because everyone was far too busy replacing and renewing established buildings to think seriously about the creation of a new one. In early 1869 Reynard told a correspondent, "We live as cheaply as possible; potatoes on Sunday by way of marking the Christian feast and cabbage on Christmas as a very special luxury."

Weakened by this diet, he found himself losing his memory and growing afraid of meeting people. Nevertheless he gathered together every penny he could, himself made the designs for his church, to be named St. Saviour's, and launched his appeal for community support in June 1869. It was not a good time to ask for subscriptions. Barkerville citizens were no longer as free with their money and their gold and even as the Rev. James Reynard was building his church the community it was planned to serve had begun to dwindle. Nevertheless he continued his efforts, working himself as one of the labourers. It is said that he also made many of the furnishings, including a chair constructed entirely without the use of nails. He is

167

also said to have helped saw the lumber for the building, and to have assisted the blacksmith in making nails. He confessed to coveting the church of St. Patrick's at Richfield whenever he heard Father McGuckin tolling its bell. In 1869 the *Cariboo Sentinel* reported

The new church now building promises to be an elegant structure. It is built from design by the Rev. J. Reynard, which are being ably carried out by Messrs. Bruce & Mann. The style is 'Early English' in which architectural effect is attained by due proportion of parts, bold and simple forms, rather than by elaborate ornament. The church will consist of nave, 30 ft. x 20 ft. and apsidal chancel, 16 ft. x 12 ft. Height of walls 18 feet; of ceiling, from floor 23 feet. A schoolroom and vestry complete the building.

The building began in November 1869. Reynard himself wrote of the occasion:

At length we opened ground for the new church — St. Saviour's. I had secured a suitable lot in the spring, paying for it $200, and balks and props for the foundation cost me $150. At last the two best workmen in the place began to build. Their wages, $10 a day each, timber costing 10 cents a foot, and nails (very cheap) 25 cents a pound. My means, consisting of subscriptions, balance of church fund grant, and my Christmas quarter's stipend, just covered the first amount for labour done. I was compelled to stop work when the building was a mere shell, not quite roofed in. I was resolute to have service on Christmas Day in the schoolroom, and therefore set to work myself, with my two lads for assistants. They are only little fellows: but they could hold one end of a board while I secured the other, and between us we finished the room in time... The Barkerville people at this time grieved me much. A little sympathy goes far with hopeful natures, and the lack of it, not to speak of open ridicule, is hard to bear. But I was not beaten. On Christmas Day three persons attended the service; on the following Sunday morning, two; that same evening, none. Now seemed the justification of all the condemners of my building at all, and my building a church as a still more foolish thing. I had one answer to all such: 'Do what you can to help cheerfully, or not at all.' For myself I am not afraid of poverty, or hand, or heart, or head labour; but I am afraid of doing less than my all, or of offering to God that which costs me as little as possible. I shall do my best unstintedly.

He did his best unstintedly. The church was completed and dedicated on 18 September 1870. It was used not only as a church but also in part as a school, for the Rev. Reynard gave classes in English Literature, Greek, Algebra, and the New Testament there. He also organized and conducted a military band and led a choral class. These projects were better attended than most of the services. The church itself, however, as a building was a notable success. Its design testifies to its designer's wish to provide the citizens of Barkerville with, in the words of the *Sentinel*, "a church, which in form, if not in material, will remind them of the village churches of the 'father-land'." It reminds one less of the English village church, however, than of the nineteenth-century Methodist chapel. Reynard had been brought up as a Methodist. The church had only been in existence for twelve months when the Rev. James Reynard worn out by his labours, left Barkerville for Nanaimo. He died in Saanich in 1875. He was 30 years old. He left behind him a beautifully proportioned church which compares favourably with many of the chapels that its design recalls. Made of the same materials as the rest of the town it seems more of an expression of the community spirit than do many religious and civic edifices whose stone and marble set them apart from the villages in which they stand.

St. Saviour's Church at Barkerville remains, and is perhaps the most attractive church in Cariboo. It was not, however, as influential as St. Joseph's Mission, which had first been planned by Father Demers in the early forties. It took some years for the plan to mature, however. In the winter of 1867-68 Father McGuckin travelled down to Williams Lake from Richfield and bought more land to accompany that already purchased in the beautiful San Jose Valley twelve miles from the lake, and the mission began to be built. The building of it was supervised by Father Blanchett, and it was opened in 1871, the superior being Father Grandidier. Father James Maria McGuckin, O.M.I., returned to the Mission in 1872 and took up with enthusiasm a discarded plan to start a boys' school there, and on December 2 that year the school opened with eight boarders and three day scholars. In order to help the mission support itself a ranch was also started, the cattle being branded OMI. In September 1872 Father McGuckin asked his bishop for some teaching Sisters so that the school could be expanded, and in October he called on the Superior of the Sisters of St. Ann in New Westminster to ask her to help him. A year later in October 1873 he was still without Sisters. He wrote to the bishop in something like despair,

I am very much annoyed about not having learned anything definite about the Sisters. If they are not coming I think I may clear out this part of the country, for it is almost unbearable the complaints the people are making about their not having come before this. Have the goodness to give me some information on this subject as soon as you possibly can...[38]

In August of the following year he wrote,

It is really too bad that the Sisters are not coming. Our wooden houses will be rotten before they are made use of and the children that we baptized will

[38] Kay Cronin, *Cross in the Wilderness*, 1960, p. 115.

169

become demoralized for the want of carrying out what has already begun with so many sacrifices. . . .[39]

On September 20, 1876 three Sisters of St. Ann arrived and by the end of the year there were 42 boys and 33 girls in the school. In 1877 Father McGuckin wrote to his bishop in a different mood.

I cannot praise the Sisters of St. Ann sufficiently for their work at the school. The good they do is truly wonderful. The transformation of the children, even within a year, is almost incredible. These children come to them destitute in every sense — many do not speak either English or French. They come without any knowledge of the principles of our religion. It could not be otherwise. Most of them have parents who are half-savage. The father often deserts them; if he does not, he does not care for the spiritual welfare of his children for he has no knowledge of Catholicity. The mother, too, is a savage who has to be trained in even the elementary principles of duty to God and her family.

What can you expect from youngsters who have spent from 8 to 15 years of their youth in such an environment? No constraint, exposed to so many dangers and temptations. Then they come to the school. The first days are days of boredom and sadness. The change is so radical. But little by little you see the change — from laziness, disobedience, etc., even vice — to a lovable child, industrious, obedient, polite, even pious. They love the Sisters.[40]

For all the success of the Sisters the going was still tough. Some years later he wrote to the bishop,

We are in a precarious position. Many parents send their children, promising to pay. Yet they cannot even pay a dollar. A father speculates — he hopes to find his fortune in the gold fields. No luck. Another dies. Another deserts and leaves behind him nothing but debts. One farmer is ruined by drought, another by flood, another by fire. And finally there are some who abandon their children. One owes us $600. He writes 'I have been disappointed in my mining. I cannot pay you this year'. He has three children at the school. Another owes us $1000. He has four children at the school. Illness struck him, so the money from his ranch must pay hospital bills. Perhaps the only thing I shall obtain from him is a fifth child whom I shall have to feed and instruct *gratis pro Deo*.[41]

Father McGuckin ran the Mission until 1882, when it was well established. In 1890 Indian children were admitted to residence. In 1892 Father Le Jacq took over the school, though already extremely ill with cancer of the intestine. He was a courageous man, completely able to handle knife-wielding rebellious children. One of his pupils, Mrs. Christine Rope of Alkali Lake, said of him later

[39] *Ibid.*, p. 116.
[40] *Ibid.*, pp. 116-17.
[41] *Ibid.*, p. 117.

He was so thin, and sick-looking, but he was sure kind to us children. He used to read us stories from the Bible all the time. And he could talk to all the Indians in their own language, no matter what tribe they belonged to.[42]

Father Le Jacq died of cancer in 1899, and in 1903, after saving the Oblate University in Ottawa from ruin by his expert administrative skill and determination, and after giving Vancouver its Gothic Cathedral, Father McGuckin also died.

The Sisters of St. Ann had eventually to give up running their part of the mission for financial reasons; once the gold rush was over money had become short in Cariboo. They were replaced by four Sisters of the Child Jesus who came to Cariboo from France in 1869.

The importance of The Mission, as it is popularly called, to the life on the Cariboo Road in the early years can hardly be underestimated. There were few schools in the region. The first school at 111 Mile was built in 1875 and this catered to the whole of Lac La Hache Valley, the first teacher being John Lane Phillips and the second William ⋅Abel from Ontario. In the 1880's the population dwindled and the school closed around 1885, whereupon Mr. Abel bought the 111 Mile House and turned farmer and hotelier, and the house became a staging post. When he left, the McLures had the property. Captain Watson bought it, as he also bought the 108 Mile House at the end of the century. There was a school at Clinton, of course, and, eventually a school at Soda Creek, but, especially during the winter, most of the children in Cariboo found schooling hard to come by for very many years. Schooling was therefore the more prized. Angelique Dessault, the daughter of Joseph Dessault, a voyageur, and his wife Helene, a Shuswap girl and the daughter and grand-daughter of Shuswap chiefs, spoke French and Shuswap as a child, but not much English. She worked in the kitchens at the Mission in order to pay for her schooling, and, when business among the pots and pans was slack, the little Sister of St. Ann who was working with her, would help her study. It seems that the pupils were made to study the English dictionary intensely, for, as an old lady, whenever asked the meaning of a word she always knew it, however abstruse the word might be. Schooling did not become a great deal easier over the years. In the early 1920's Angelique's grandchildren, Nellie, Allan, and Rose Robins lived at a ranch across the Fraser from Soda Creek and could not get to school there in the winter so their father, Will Robins bought the old gaol in Soda Creek which had been built originally by his father-in-law, Angelique's husband, Billy Lyne, and the children

[42] *Ibid.*, p. 134.

171

lived there during the winter, sleeping in the cells. The family has a tradition that Grandfather Billy Lyne not only built the gaol, (which still stands, sturdy as ever) but that he was its first inhabitant, having celebrated the completion of the job with disastrous thoroughness.

Many Cariboo families have mixed backgrounds, and both the Church and the Law took a broadminded view of marriages that were not always as formally celebrated and lasting as that of Joseph Dessault. Some of the early miners and settlers took common-law Indian wives and discarded them with very little difficulty or embarrassment when they had made their way in the world and proceeded to acquire legal wives of their own race. It is said that in these instances the first wives usually accepted the situation with equanimity. Peter Curran Dunleavy himself took as his common-law wife a Dené girl from the Fort Alexander area, and their daughter Isabella was married on May 28, 1881 at Soda Creek to Samuel Witherow, who was one of the first ranchers to take up land in the Chilcotin. A few years before her marriage, in 1877 to be exact, she had acted as sponsor at the Baptism by Father McGuckin, of "Canissa Rose Mary, born May 4, 1877, legitimate daughter of Peter C. Dunleavy of Pittsburgh, U.S. and of Jane Elizabeth Huston of Victoria, B.C. at this time residing at Soda Creek, B.C."; it looks therefore as if the two families remained on good terms. Another "legitimate daughter" — the register of births, marriages and deaths at St. Joseph's Mission makes the distinction between "daughter" and "legitimate daughter" — was born on December 2, 1882, the mother being, this time, recorded as Jennie Holstien, which was clearly a mistake. Peter Dunleavy, who can reasonably be called one of the founders of Cariboo, died on October 15, 1904, six days before his 70th birthday. His widow, a large buxom English lady, married the local doctor, who had a reputation for curing everything from a broken finger to a broken neck with a dose of salts, though he was also celebrated for saving a child from what everyone regarded as a fatal scarlet fever. His name was Samuel Edward Moyston Hoops and his new wife, neé Mary Jane Elizabeth Huston, insisted on being addressed as Mrs. Doctor S.E.M.M.J.E. Hoops, a name that will not be forgotten by the story tellers of Soda Creek, who relish human eccentricity.

During the early days of Cariboo, both marriage and education were treated somewhat informally and well into the twentieth century schools and churches were often created by making use of whatever empty building was available. From 1871 when Father

Fouquet's church burned down, to 1902, there was no Catholic Church in Quesnel, and visiting priests would celebrate mass in private houses. Father Reynard's St. Saviour's church was used as a school for many years, there being no other building available. There was no protestant church in Quesnel until 1895 when the Reverend Dr. A. D. McKinnon built the Union Church. This church was used by all protestant denominations until 1911 when the Anglicans built a mission. Fathers Fouquet's church was replaced by another Catholic church, St. Ann's, in 1902. It was built by Father Thomas of St. Joseph's Mission.

Religion and education were important to the people of Cariboo during the early years, but every church and every school that was built had to overcome many obstacles. The population was always a shifting one. A place with many worshippers or children of school age in one year might well be almost a ghost town the next. Perhaps the only people to realize that the solution to the problem might be the creation of a church and a school right in the geographical centre of Cariboo were the Catholics, and St. Joseph's Mission continued to serve Cariboo effectively throughout the years and serves it still today.

CHAPTER THIRTEEN

Ranches and Rails 1870-1920

Although, in the late sixties, Cariboo felt confident of having a glorious future, in fact, if we take Dunleavy's strike on Horsefly in 1859 as signalling the beginning of the gold rush and therefore of the settlement of Cariboo, we could maintain that after its first decade of life Cariboo began to lose a little of its original hectic vitality. The many stories of the goldfields and the accounts of the hundreds and thousands of miners travelling Cariboo in snowfree months not only during the sixties but also in subsequent years might well lead to a belief that the whole area was not only thriving, but that all the settlements along the road were growing in size as more and more people arrived to cater for the travellers and to raise crops and cattle to supply the mines. This was not, in fact, the case. While it is true that more farms were established, most of these were very simple affairs, and while their herds might be large, their buildings were few and small. When the British naturalist, Macoun, travelled through the region in 1872 he found Soda Creek a "stirring little place," but commented that Clinton was "the first village" they came to after leaving Quesnel on the road south and that it appeared to have only twenty houses. From one point of view Macoun was clearly correct, but from another entirely wrong, in that the whole of Cariboo from Clinton to Quesnel could be said to constitute one village, whose main street was the Cariboo Road. The area was certainly treated as if it were one village by its inhabitants. A horse race or a dance at Clinton would gather folk in from everywhere along the road, as would any festivity in Quesnel. Moreover, Cariboo folk all knew each other well and many of them moved their businesses and their homes up and down the road with a frequency that sometimes makes it hard to keep track of them, rather as if they were moving from one part of the village to another. The village was, of course, unified by its "main street" and by the way in which the stage drivers and other regular travellers passed on the news at every stop they made and, it seems,

174

also improved upon the news more than somewhat. The news they brought was of matters of obvious concern — the latest gold strike or the latest mine to be "played out," the fortunes and misfortunes of the ranchers and mile house keepers along the route, and, inevitably, the antics of some of the more entertaining Cariboo characters. When the rail reached Ashcroft in 1887 it brought some change in the pattern, for it made cattle ranching a much more feasible proposition.

Cattle ranching in Cariboo began as an attempt to provide meat for the Cariboo miners, and at first the cattle were imported. One of the first men of Cariboo to see the importance of cattle was Jerome Harper, who, with his brother Thaddeus, became involved in one way or another with almost all aspects of Cariboo life. The brothers arrived in Cariboo at the beginning of the sixties, and started buying land in 1861, in the area west of the "Main Street" of Cariboo, at Dog Creek on the Fraser River Trail; Dog Creek itself had been a packing station from the middle fifties. Raphael Valenzuela built Dog Creek House in 1856 as winter quarters. He was one of a number of Mexicans in the area at that period. A great many of the remainder, however, were French, and Dog Creek Valley in the sixties must have been one of the few places in Cariboo where French was more usually spoken than English. Pierre Colin got a licence to use water for domestic use and for irrigation in 1861. Le Conte de Versepeuch used the water for power also and built a splendid house with a real fireplace of adobe bricks, and, disliking the discomfort of whip-sawing, built a saw pit over the creek and powered the saw with a water wheel. This must have been the first sawmill in this area of West Cariboo. Charlie Brown settled there later and, using imported French Burr Stones, built a grist mill, much of the wheat being supplied by Moses Pigeon who raised wheat on his farm on the river bank. Pigeon later moved twelve miles farther up the valley and founded Grandview Ranch. Nels Gustafson took over his River Ranch and also developed hay meadows at the head of the creek and gave his name to the two lakes there, Nels Lake and Gustafson Lake. Similarly, British settlers took over and gave the name to Empire Valley; some of the early ones were Cal Boyle, Tom MacEwan, William Wycott, and Anthony and Jack Bishop. Canoe Creek was developed by the B.C. Cattle Company, and there were big spreads at Alkali Lake and Springhouse where the Boitanio Ranch was situated. Bill Wright attempted to defeat Indian prophecies that the area between Springhouse and Grandview Ranch was unlucky by taking up a ranch there. He was, and almost all his successors have been, unlucky. An American, he called his place U.S. Meadows and the name has remained. After he had lost his money he became ferryman at Soda Creek. Other ranches, however, prospered. In 1886 J. S. Place bought Raphael Valenzuela's place and established a new stopping place and bought a liquor license. In 1887 he married a girl from Huddersfield, Jane Beaumont, and while she was occupied in raising their family of five sons and a daughter he occupied himself in buying up his competitors. He gradually bought out all the other Dog Creek Stores and acquired the ranches of Pierre Colin, Tom Hutch, Le Conte de Versepeugh, and Nels Gustafson, consolidating everything into a 10,000 acre Dog Creek Ranch. He expanded the original stopping place until in 1912 it contained twenty-two rooms and a large basement. He lost most of his small empire after a time but the Place family retained a hold on the area for many years, running the postal service until the 1960's.

West Cariboo, though chiefly concerned with raising cattle, was not totally unaffected by gold fever. Some gold was found in Dog Creek in the early sixties and the Chinese miners came into the area, the wealthier ones importing coolies direct from the home country, paying a $200 head tax for each worker. These coolies made miles on miles of flumes to operate the sluice boxes and enough gold was taken out for a time to keep the place busy. There were four Chinese stores, each with some hotel rooms and a liquor license, at the height of the mining activity. The coolies, however, did not share in the prosperity of the merchants or their employers for they never earned enough money to pay back the $200 head tax which was set against their earnings, so that they were in a state of near serfdom. While mining continued until the end of the first world war, it was of little consequence after the 1890's and J. S. Place found the Chinese stores and hotels relatively easy to buy out, taking over the last one in 1909.

By 1909 the Harper Brothers who were among the first to see the value of the land in West Cariboo for ranching and for growing wheat had left their mark upon almost the whole of the territory. In 1863 Jerome Harper built a profitable sawmill at Quesnel, and a little later moved to the mouth of the Bonaparte River. Thaddeus Harper, in the eighties, owned most of the mining property around the China Company's claim at Horsefly, which was then generally known as Harper's Camp. It was the brothers' cattle ranching, however, which was most important to the development of Cariboo. In 1863 and for the remainder of the sixties Jerome Harper spent the winter months in Washington and Oregon buying cattle, and then in May, when the snows were leaving Cariboo, he would begin the long drive north to Barkerville, each drive consisting, usually, of 400 head of steers, 50 head of milk cows, and 50 horses. On arrival at Richfield the herd was settled down on Bald Mountain about two miles from the town, and cattle were driven down to the slaughterhouse as needed; about 1400 cattle were slaughtered each mining season. At the end of the sixties as the mines became less prosperous, the Harper lands, both in Cariboo and in the Kamloops area, began to produce sizeable herds. Jerome Harper died in 1870, but his brother Thaddeus continued to run the business and in 1876 decided that since there were now too few customers for his home-raised beef in Cariboo he would mount a cattle drive of 800 head to the Chicago stockyards, placing the herd on board the freight train at Salt Lake City, the nearest available railhead at that time. In May 1870 Thaddeus took his herd down the Cariboo Road, and added another 400 head to it before he crossed the border. He wintered his herd of 1200 in Washington, and still had 600 miles to go to Salt Lake City. He therefore altered his plan and spent the summer in the grasslands of Idaho. That summer California suffered a drought so severe that an enormous number of that state's herds of cattle died. Harper therefore changed his plans again as, after all, San Francisco was nearer to Idaho than Salt Lake City, and California clearly needed the beef. He sold his herd at $70 a head on the San Francisco Market. Had he sold them a year earlier he would only have got between $13 and $17 a head.

Harper's great cattle drive took over eighteen months to complete, and while it brought him a small fortune, it also proved that the exporting of cattle from Cariboo to the American market was no easy matter. Once the C.P.R. arrived at Ashcroft, however, the situation altered dramatically. The exporting of cattle, and of horses, from Cariboo became a practicable proposition. Now the herds could be loaded onto freight trains rather than driven down the killing Cariboo Road through the Canyon or by way of Lillooet. The new railhead also made it easier to ship out gold in bulk to the United States Mint, for Canadian gold was, in general, not sent to the Canadian mint until well into the next century.

It was not only gold that drew men to Cariboo after the opening of the C.P.R. railhead at Ashcroft, however. It was also the lure of a possible new life of pioneering in an unspoiled country. The C.P.R.'s achievement interested many and caused quite a number of people to contemplate settling in this area of British Columbia, which was rapidly arousing real interest in the rest of Canada and, more particularly in Britain. Some of this interest was caused by the reports reaching the east from the small but influential groups of tourists who visited the colony, and from those citizens of Cariboo who from time to time visited the "old country." One of these last was Charles George Cowan, known to some as Dead-eye Dick Cowan. The son of a protestant Irish Parson, Cowan first visited North America to assist in the work of the church, first in Minnesota and then in North Carolina. Finding this type of work was not exactly to his taste he joined the recently created North West Mounted Police and was stationed for some time in the Yellowknife area. He fell in love with the whole country and, on leaving the force, started up in business as a big-game hunter, collecting specimens for private collectors in England, including Lord Rothschild whose collection is now in the Natural History Museum in South Kensington. Both adventurous and silver-tongued, he was in great demand at house parties on his visits to England, where he would hold the table with his accounts of his solo canoe trip for two thousand miles down the Yukon River, and of his encounters with grizzlies. He was a resourceful man. On one occasion having killed a moose on a commission from Lord Rothschild, he turned in for the night at his camp, and in the morning discovered that a grizzly had taken off one of the beast's legs. The moose had a particularly fine head, so Cowan, rather than provide the good Lord with a less impressive trophy, shot another moose, and used one of its legs as a replacement for the one the grizzly had stolen, no doubt giving Rowland Wards of Piccadilly, who stuffed the animals for him and his clients, at least one moment of puzzlement. Cowan did not only collect grizzlies, moose, bighorn sheep, stone sheep, and mountain goat for his clients, he also collected land for them. He bought 100 Mile Ranch for Lord Burghley and 108 Mile for Lord Egerton, and ran them as the owners' agent. He himself later became owner of the Onward Ranch and of 150 Mile. He was busy also outside Cariboo; the Kamloops area was settled very largely by his clients.

It is hard to determine just how much effect on the future of Cariboo these activities of Cowan had, though it is obvious that had he not brought the Cecil family into the area the town of 100 Mile would in all probability not now exist. Cowan himself lived the life of Reilly, both on his visits to the aristocracy in England, and in Cariboo itself, where he created the equivalent of an English (or perhaps Irish) country house, complete with an expert cook and a chauffeur who had once been the second groom at Glamis.

Dick Cowan was not the only person to attempt to graft gracious living onto the Cariboo way of life. Captain Lionel Watson ended his service with the Yorks and Lancs Regiment in the first years of this century and came out to Cariboo where he bought 50,000 acres for $25 an acre, and built up a herd of 10,000 head of cattle, sending drives of 250 head regularly to Ashcroft. He had a good eye for horses and would buy half-wild horses from the Indians and ship them to Nanaimo where they sometimes fetched as much as $300 a head. He was not, however, inclined to give up the luxuries of his British background, and to the intense interest and pleasure of his hands and his neighbours would drive up and down Cariboo in the latest model Cadillac. He decided that he should build a house suitable for his English fiancée to live in when they were married, and in 1911 built, at 108 Mile, an elaborate architect-designed mansion, whose walls were clad in specially designed wallpaper, and whose rooms were glorified with imported Italian marble and enlivened by his collection of ivory carvings. He provided his ranch hands with a separate bunkhouse with its own kitchen, built an ice house with a thatched roof, and a stable capacious enough to hold a hundred horses, as well as several large barns. He was a practical man, however, as well as a pleasure-loving one. When, in the grouse-hunting season, the day's bag exceeded the amount required by himself and his guests he sent the extra birds off to Ashcroft for sale. He may have been the first person in Cariboo deliberately to make money out of tourists, for he arranged for his sister to send out jewellery, scarves, and gew-gaws from England as well as cheap penny novelties which he sold for a pleasing profit at 50 cents each. His fiancée, unfortunately, broke off the engagement, being, it is said, frightened at the prospect of living at close quarters with wild cowboys and wilder Indians, but Captain Watson remained happily in his mansion as a bachelor, his only companion his Chinese house-boy, until in 1915 he returned to his regiment and was killed in the first world war. Major "Dick" Cowan later bought the 108 Mile for the Marquis of Exeter in 1918 and managed it on his behalf, himself living in Captain Watson's mansion from 1928 to 1930 when the Marquis' son, Lord Egerton came to British Columbia.

Another instance of the way in which many Cariboo settlers attempted to remake the territory in the image of the old country is provided by the story of the Cornwall Ranch. Although this is at Ashcroft and therefore, strictly speaking, just outside Cariboo proper, the story of Ashcroft is important to the understanding of

179

Cariboo. In 1862 the English barrister, Clement Francis Cornwall, and his brother Henry built Ashcroft Manor, and, this being the period when the great Cariboo Road was in the making, soon were milling flour from their grain and selling it to the travellers and the workers on the road. Indefatigable devotees of horse racing and fox hunting, the brothers imported an Arabian stud, and initiated a series of highly popular horse races on Cornwall flats. They also bought a pack of English foxhounds, which after a long journey round the Horn, enabled them to found the Ashcroft hunt. In the absence of foxes the quarry was the coyote, and the brothers Cornwall invited the local cowboys to be members of the hunt, having first of all instructed them in the correct etiquette, and taught them the conventional hunting cries of "Tally Ho!" and "Gone away." The brothers opened the hunt in fine style, accoutred in the pink coats and peaked hats proper to the occasion and the hunt set out. It was not long before the hounds raised a coyote, whereupon the cowboys, forgetting all their lessons, yelled enthusiastically, "There goes the son of a bitch!", set their horses at full gallop, over-ran the pack of hounds and lassooed the coyote. It is said that after this the brothers never put on hunting pink again.

The Ashcroft Hunt may have failed to become an institution but Ashcroft itself flourished. In the sixties and seventies it was a very rich grain growing area. Thaddeus Harper moved his mill from Clinton Creek to the mouth of the Bonaparte River near Ashcroft in 1870, and in 1884 Bill Bose brought up a wagonload of liquor, furniture, and crockery and household goods and started a hotel for Mr. Barnes, one of the ranchers, who also began to sell lots in anticipation of the arrival of the Canadian Pacific Railway. Though the railhead was not truly established until 1887 the first train came through in 1884.

The Foster store was built in 1885 and the Tom Kirkpatrick store in 1886. The multitudes of Chinese working on the railways swelled the population hugely and soon there were many Chinese stores and restaurants. Wing Wong Chai opened his doors to customers in 1892 and Loy's General Store began operations ten years later. It was not until the P.G.E. arrived and provided Cariboo with other railheads that Ashcroft lost its position as Gateway to the Cariboo, just as Lillooet had lost its similar position earlier when the road through the Fraser Canyon had been completed. From 1885, however, when the railhead at Ashcroft was linked to the main Cariboo by another road, until the nineteen twenties, Ashcroft was of great importance. The B.C. Express Company moved its headquarters there, and cattle ranching became the area's main industry. The Chilcotin country across the Fraser became an area of huge cattle ranches. Among the ranches that were founded as a direct consequence of the creation of the railhead at Ashcroft and the opening up of the country were the Carson Ranch and the Grange Ranch at Pavilion, the Gang Ranch at Dog Creek, the Chilco Ranch across the Fraser, and other ranches sprang up at Canim Lake, Bridge Lake, Forest Grove, and, indeed, all over the southern Cariboo. What had begun as a means of providing the goldfields with food had become of more importance to Cariboo than the goldfields themselves.

CHAPTER FOURTEEN

Quesnel and Quesnel Lake 1870-1920

Though the increase in ranching affected Cariboo in general it had less effect in the northern part of the area than in some others, and Quesnel, even though close to the developing ranges of the Chilcotin country, and at the northern edge of the cattle country whose centre was to become Williams Lake, remained dependant upon the gold mines for its prosperity for many years. When the Omineca rush of 1869, and the Cassiar excitement of 1874 had finished, and Lightning Creek had lost some of its renewed vitality, however, Quesnel began to decline. Nevertheless the town retained its jovial and hospitable character. On February 12, 1875 the *Cariboo Sentinel* reported:

One of the pleasantest events that ever came off in Cariboo came off on the evening of the 10th at Quesnel. I refer to the ball held there and to which invitations were sent over the whole country, from Camerontown to Cache Creek. The Committee were evidently determined to make the affair a success, and it was a success in the fullest sense of the word. By Wednesday evening all had arrived including many from Barkerville, Lightning Creek and Lake La Hache and the ball opened at 9 o'clock p.m. Some sixteen ladies and about twice as many gentlemen were present. Among the former were Mesdames G. Elmore, Duhig, Green, Barlow, and the Misses Hyde, Byrnes, Parker, Felkers and Barlow. At 12 midnight the company sat down to a splendid supper and afterwards dancing was resumed and kept up until daylight made the lamp burn dim. On the following evening the ball was again reopened and kept up with even more spirit for by that time everybody knew everybody... dancing (was) kept up till 4 o'clock in the morning. On Friday the party broke up and nearly all went home.

Such balls as this were events of importance to all Cariboo and did much to alleviate the hardship of the long winters for those living outside the main centres.

From the middle seventies to the end of the century life in Quesnel altered very little. Though the rush itself was over there were still many mines in operation, and the farms supplied more and more of the needs of the settlements, so that, to a considerable extent, the northern Cariboo became self supporting. Luxuries still had to travel from the south by freight, as did any machinery that was needed, and the hotels were obliged to import their wines and spirits and cigars. The arrival of the C.P.R. lines at Ashcroft in 1887 provided another gateway to the Cariboo and made the provision of goods from the east easier. No new towns of consequence arose, and life took on a fairly steady rhythm only occasionally interrupted by rumours of new gold strikes. For the first time since the sixties Cariboo had become a sleepy place, and it seemed in the nineties, as if all the excitement was over for ever. Quesnel was, indeed beginning to decline.

As so often before in the story of Cariboo it was gold that came to the rescue, when a new and quite extraordinary mine opened up beside Lake Quesnel. This mine was the brainchild of one of the most original and interesting of the early miners in Cariboo, John Likely.

John Likely, a blue-eyed, broad-shouldered Irishman, with a short body but long legs and a most independent mind was born on March 17, 1842 at Saint John, New Brunswick, and at the age of seventeen, partly in order to escape an epidemic that was raging in Saint John at the time, partly because he had read of the gold strikes in the west, took a ship to Panama, walked across the isthmus, and took another ship to Victoria, joining the placer miners on the lower Fraser in 1859, and shortly afterwards moving on up to the Cariboo goldfield, where he located Likely Gulch and became a familiar figure at the Cedar Point camping ground. It was here that he earned his nickname of Plato John, for he carried the works of Plato with him wherever he went and when the miners grew weary of the fire and brimstone sermons of the usual preachers at their Sunday meetings he would speak to them of Plato and Greek philosophy, which they found a stimulating change. He was very much an enthusiast for education and placed copies of Plato in a tin box which he lodged in a hollow tree at Cedar Point so that anyone who wished to study could use the box as a lending library. He also conducted what we would now call seminars on Plato and Socrates on an island in Quesnel Lake which became known generally as Plato Island.

He was extremely knowledgeable about all aspects of gold mining, but rarely chose to mine for himself. He would freely give advice to others, however, and often helped prospectors to find paying claims. In 1872 he worked as an axeman on the C.P.R. survey to Bella Coola, and met a number of engineers from whom he learned a great deal. It was as a consequence of his writing a letter about the possibility of hydraulic mining to the C.P.R. directors that several directors put up their own money to bring another Irishman, the Dublin-born John Bogard Hobson up from Auburn County, California, and finance him to create what became the biggest hydraulic mining enterprise in the world some miles to the west of Likely Gulch. Hobson, with Likely as his right hand man, harnessed together a chain of lakes 18 miles long to produce the enormous amount of water required for the operation. He imported Chinese and Japanese labour, and a crew of his own from California. His water gunmen were Spanish. He used local men only for work on the dam and for ditch digging. The sluice box he built was six feet wide and over 2000 feet long and the riffles were made of steel rails in double rows. Before the end of the operation over 29 million yards of gravel were removed and the pit itself, once called the biggest man-made hole in the world, averaged 645 feet in depth, was a quarter of a mile long, and between 1000 and 1500 feet across. It is not known how much gold came out of this Bullion Mine, for the operation was a private one and therefore no records were given. Indeed what figures have been given are typical of Cariboo in their disparity. According to the *Williams Lake Tribune* Centennial Edition, two and a half million dollars were spent on working the mine and three million was removed from it. According to Captain Norman Evans-Atkinson, who had some sources of private information, between 30 and 40 million dollars worth must have been taken out. However, in its earliest days under Hobson it cannot have been consistently profitable for it was worked from 1897 to 1905 only and then closed down operations until 1927 when it was operated for a further 5 years until 1932. It opened up again in 1937 and closed in 1941. These dates are given by the B.C. government's *Coast-Chilcotin Survey* of 1971. Others in Cariboo state firmly that the mine did not close until 1952 and make no mention of its ever ceasing operation between 1897 and that year. It is more than likely that the government dates refer to a particular mining company, and Cariboo memory more simply, and perhaps accurately, to whatever men or companies were operating the mine. Be that as it may, Captain Evans-Atkinson is convinced of the mine's riches as are all other Cariboo people, and recalled seeing photographs of gold bricks awaiting shipment in piles three or four feet tall.

John Likely retired from active work in 1919, crippled by arthritis. He sold out his claim on Likely Gulch to a Chinaman and bought himself a small homestead on a beaver meadow flat in Beaver Valley twelve miles south of Guy's Roadhouse, where he spent the winters. He had always been a private man, and even something of a recluse, and during the twenties he retreated almost entirely from the world until ill health obliged him to take up residence in the Provincial Home in Kamloops. He died in 1929 and rests in an unmarked grave. The Bullion Mine is now a strange and haunting wilderness of overgrown bush in whose clearings buildings, half collapsed, lean and totter in strange geometric shapes. Under the largest building there are still scores of bottles of liniment which were manufactured by one of the last managers of the mine as a valuable sideline. The piles of tailing and gravel have a desolate air. The pit itself, however, remains, monstrous, incredible, and, in the summer, eye-dazzling. To stand at the edge of it and to look down is to be awed by yet another instance of the power of man's mind and of man's hunger for gold.

Bullion was the most interesting and ambitious of the mining operations that supported Quesnel at the end of the century, but it was not the only one. Many mines begun in the late sixties and early seventies were still in full operation. The Waverley, begun in 1868 in the Antler Creek area continued to produce gold for fifty years; gold was being taken from Walkers Gulch at Richfield until 1922, and the diggings at Forest Rose Gulch continued to operate until 1912. To these existing operations others were added. Lightning Creek, where slum and drainage problems had earlier defeated Captain Evans and his Welsh Company and other miners also, was attacked once more and successfully by Harry Jones, J. Price, and F. J. Tregillus at the century's end. In 1897 John Hunter decided to damn the western outlet of Quesnel Lake in order to get at the gold in the bed of the south fork of Quesnel River. He completed the dam in 1898, working with a force of 500 men, spending $76,000 on the operation and taking out almost three times as much in gold. The area around Quesnel Forks brought a good deal of gold during these years: between 1896 and 1900 it is recorded that 48,884 ounces of gold were taken out.

All this activity brought money into Quesnel, but did not swell its permanent population. In 1885 only fifty-one people were listed as getting mail at the post office, and in 1887 the number had risen only to fifty-eight. The population remained at around two hundred people, half of them Chinese, for many years.

The little town was, however, sturdily successful in its own way. In the eighties the flow of transients made the two hotels paying propositions. There was considerable demand for the services of the two blacksmiths, Alfred Carson and Robert Middleton. The three Chinese stores, Kwong Lee and Company, Wah Lee and Yan Wah were busy, and the fur trade provided a living for both "Twelve Foot" Davis and the brothers Elmore.

The small community had more problems in providing itself with social and educational amenities than in finding customers for its commercial enterprises. The School District of Quesnellemouth was created on April 14, 1881, but it was not until August 4, 1884 that Miss Alice Northcott, the first teacher arrived from Victoria, and taught a class of nineteen children. She was replaced by Miss N. Dockrill for a time, but returned in 1888 to teach in the new school which had been built in 1886, in which year the district had been renamed Quesnelle. She taught there until 1891 when she left to get married, and her post was taken by John A. Fraser who taught a class of nineteen children until 1893 when he gave up teaching to join James Reid in his business enterprises. In 1903 he became a school trustee. In 1900 Quesnelle became, at last, Quesnel. In 1906 a school opened at Soda Creek and the children from there, who had been living in Quesnel in order to attend school, returned home. A few years later, however, when the Grand Trunk Pacific Railway reached Fort George, the population rose sharply and a new school with two teachers was created. The railhead at Fort George caused a land boom in Cariboo and many new settlements came into being both in the Fort George area and between Quesnel and Williams Lake, and new schools were created at Alexandria, Barkerville, and Dragon Lake in 1912.

The land boom of 1911 to 1914 altered northern Cariboo considerably, and brought a rush of prosperity to the area. In 1911 the *Cariboo Observer*, which had commenced publication in 1908, with J. B. Daniell as editor and owner, was taken over by Albert Dollenmayer and John G. Hutchcroft as an important vehicle for real estate advertisements as well as a useful medium for local news. Unfortunately in that very year the government slowed down land sales in the area by reserving all the land, and Hutchcroft, in July, contemplated stopping publication. Fortunately, E. L. Kepner, who could afford it, being a hotel owner, took the paper over and kept Hutchcroft on as editor. The *Cariboo Observer* remained important to the town thereafter.

There was no hospital in Quesnel until 1910. Before that time the Royal Cariboo Hospital in Williams Creek, whose foundation stone — or, rather, foundation log — had been laid by Judge Begbie on August 24, 1863, was the only hospital in the area. This hospital, which moved to another site in 1891, remained in operation until

1925. It was hard for Quesnel folk to get to this hospital in the winter and so in 1909 a committee was formed to found another. In 1910 a small hospital consisting of one large ward, a private ward, a surgeon's room, and a room for his assistant, together with the necessary kitchen and outbuildings was built. There was some difficulty in finding staff. The first resident physician resigned at the moment the hospital opened and the first nurse even before that. In 1911 Miss Laura Mellefont took the nursing post and attended to her first patient, a horse. In 1912 Doctor G. R. Baker became the hospital's doctor, and was soon one of Cariboo's most beloved characters. "Doc" Baker did not spend all his time in residence but travelled the country on horseback, even in the worst weather, to wherever he was needed. He later acquired a model T Ford which became famous in the area.

The hospital was enlarged after the flu epidemic of 1918, and in 1924, to accommodate the sudden rise in population and prosperity caused by the arrival of the P.G.E. in 1921, a new hospital was built.

In 1896, when the Bullion mine was still in the making, river traffic had been at a standstill for some ten years. The *Enterprise* had stopped in 1871 and the *Victoria* in 1886. James Reid, Steve Tingley, the ex-stage driver, and Captain John Irving who had owned the *Victoria*, decided therefore to build another boat. They formed the Northern British Columbia Navigation Company, and the new ship, the *Charlotte* was so christened by Mrs. Reid on August 3, 1896. On the last trip of the year, however, the *Charlotte* became embedded in the ice at Alexandria on the trip north from Soda Creek and had to remain there during the remainder of the winter. Seeing the old *Victoria* lying there, the owners decided to buy the old boat and demolish it: in this way they provided a better berth for the *Charlotte*.

When the railway reached Fort George and construction was booming in that area it was decided that the *Charlotte* should make a run from Soda Creek to Fort George, but she came to grief in Cotton-wood Canyon, and was only narrowly saved from destruction upon the rocks.

In 1909 Telesphore Marion, a fur trader of Quesnel, decided another steamer was needed and got John Strand, a Quesnel hotel owner to build one. The *Quesnel* was launched later that year. In the same year the newly founded Fort George Lumber and Navigation Company built and launched the *Nechacco* at Quesnel. Later named the *Chilco*, the ship was wrecked in Cottonwood Canyon in 1910, despite the governments having, after many complaints, blasted out some of the rocky obstacles in the canyon. In February 1910 the British Columbia Express Company entered the steamboat business; and the *BX*, the "Queen of the Fraser" was built by a force of fifty men at Soda Creek, the foreman carpenter being Will Robins, and the designer Alexander Watson, the son of the designer of the *Charlotte*. The *BX* though at first regarded as a white elephant because of her size, was extremely successful. She was launched on May 23, 1910 and made several trips from Soda Creek to Quesnel before attempting the trip to Fort George on June 23rd. The *Cariboo Observer* commented:

Each stateroom has two berths with the exception of the beautiful bridal chamber. In each stateroom are stationery and washstands, electric push buttons and reading lights. In the after part of the vessel is a bathroom with a porcelain tub and nickel fittings. The steamer will be heated throughout with steam heat, including radiators in each separate stateroom, an excellent provision for the cold months; and electric fans will cool the vessel in the warm summer days.

The hangings of the staterooms and social halls are of a delicate green on this luxuriant steamer, and all upholstering of red car plush. The crockery, blankets and linens were all made especially for service on the "B.X." and are individually marked with the "B.X." monogram. Even the toilet soap is marked distinctly in the same manner. The house flag is of red and yellow, the company's colors, and the insignia is in the centre.

The Fort George Lumber and Navigation Company decided that the *BX* should have some competition and, in a shipyard just a little south of the one where the *BX* was being built, it produced the *Fort Fraser*, a small sternwheeler for use in prospecting, that was later renamed the *Doctor*, and the *Chilcotin*, a larger vessel for freight and passenger service.

Earlier in 1910 the *Charlotte* struck a reef, was badly damaged, and beached at Quesnel where eventually she was burned. In November of the same year the *Chilco* was beached and was not able to be salvaged. In 1912 Alexander Watson returned to ship building and created the *B.C. Express*, and under Captain Bucey, made the trip from Soda Creek to Fort George without disaster, arriving there on July 4th.

As soon as the railway arrived in Fort George the steamer traffic on the river increased. The *Quesnel*, under new ownership, was used and also the Fort George boat, the *Fort Fraser*, now renamed the *Doctor*. In 1919, the *BX*, carrying cement to Deep Creek, sank, and although salvaged never sailed again. In 1920-21 the *B.C. Express* was taken out of service. In April 1921 the *Quesnel*, the last of the great steamboats, crashed onto rocks in Fort George Canyon. There was an unsuccessful attempt to salvage her. She was the last of the Fraser steamboats. In the same year that she sank the P.G.E. reached Quesnel and the steamboat age had definitely given way to the age of rail.

The arrival of the P.G.E. in Quesnel meant that the heavy equipment needed for the hydraulic mining which was now in vogue in the mines could be brought easily into the area, and there was a considerable increase in mining activity and therefore also in the business activity of Quesnel. The twenties, indeed, began on yet another tide of optimism. Cariboo was still moving forward. The Cedar Creek Strike of 1921 arrived together with the railway and all was well in the best of all possible worlds.

While the story of Quesnel throughout the twenties was one of increasing prosperity, and of great changes brought about by the new railhead, the life in the countryside around did not change a great deal. For all the exciting strikes, the rushes, the thrills of riverboats and rail, there remained a mode of existence traditional to Cariboo which refused to be transformed. The trappers, who, along with the Indians, had provided furs to the Elmore Brothers and to Marion, were still in existence. The lonely prospectors were still exploring their chosen creeks, and these went on in the same old way, though the longest established ones who had come in with the first wave of prospectors and settlers were growing old. One such old-timer was Bob Winkler, who in his independence and deliberate solitude exemplified the typical loner of Cariboo. He worked mostly as a trapper, though he did do some gold mining from time to time. As was the habit of the old-timers he would take gold instead of dollar bills for his furs. Dollar bills wear out; gold does not. He had a cabin by Quesnel Lake near Likely, which he kept spotlessly clean. He told Evans-Atkinson one day, "When I get to the end of my poke," and he pulled it out and there was little left in it, "I'm going to arrange for my own departure." Evans-Atkinson says

I didn't take any notice of it because I never argue with anybody. I didn't want to be drawn into anything. Soon afterwards I heard he'd shot himself. What happened is this. He hadn't been for groceries for a little while and the storekeeper sent Bob Morton, his clerk, over with a letter; some mail had come for him. Bob went to his cabin and the door wasn't open. He looked through the window and there he was lying there on the bed. He'd been shot with a .22 rifle and beside him was a bottle of rum, but one drink only had gone, and there was a ten dollar bill and a note, saying "This is for the boys to bury me with" pinned to the ten dollars and the bottle of rum. His empty poke lay on the floor beside him and the letter was the announcement that

189

he had been awarded his old age pension and contained the first cheque. So that's how Winkler Creek, where he used to have a trap cabin, got its name.[43]

The way of life of the solitary trapper was not very much affected by the road building and the rail building that went on in the last years of the nineteenth century and the first quarter of the twentieth. He might get his mail a little more frequently and not have to travel quite so far for it, and he might find his supplies a little easier to obtain than in the eighteen-sixties but otherwise there was little change. The cabin would be still of logs, the window panes made of old flour bags soaked in grease to make them transparent enough to let in light, the bunks provided with "bed springs" made of willow rods and with mattresses of pine boughs. Outside the cabin there might be a sundial made of a couple of sticks. There would be no lamps, but tallow candles fixed on hand forged iron hooks set into the walls. The flies would be discouraged by a home-made smudge pot created from a lard pail full of holes filled with punk bark. Each fall one trapper would make a huge stack of flapjacks and put them into deep freeze for use through the winter, the deep freeze being simply a cage of wire mesh called a fly cage hung outside the door. When he came in from his trapping he had a dinner all prepared. It was a hard and lonely life, but one which seemed to appeal to many proud and independent men. Most of them, nevertheless, welcomed company. As soon as a figure was spotted approaching a cabin the owner would begin thinking of the meal he could offer the stranger, and the stranger would be considered insulting if he refused, however unpalatable the dish placed in front of him. It was also usual for a trapper never to lock his door, so that his cabin could always be used as a refuge by someone caught in a blizzard or simply lost.

There were, or course, exceptions to the rule. During the early days there were many trappers who had reason not to be sociable. They were fugitives from the law. Their numbers increased during the first world war when a considerable number of men thought it better to face the wilderness than the trenches. These men were suspicious of all strangers and quite likely to shoot anyone who came near their cabins. After the war was over they emerged from time to time to collect their mail from the nearest post office under an assumed name. This led eventually to difficulties when it became time for them to collect old age pensions and many cheques were sent to "the man living under the name of Y," at outlying districts. It was always

[43] From a Tape Recording in the Department of Aural History, the Provincial Archives of British Columbia.

considered unfriendly and rude to ask a man his name in the early years of Cariboo. It was judged that if he wanted you to know it he would tell you, and if he didn't tell you he probably had a good reason to keep it quiet.

Most of the loners in Cariboo were, however, quite free with information and happy to welcome strangers. In the twenties there was a trapper living at the eastern end of Quesnel Lake, 70 miles from what was to become Likely whose eccentricities were particularly endearing. He hailed originally from the Balkans and was known variously as either Franz or Fritz. From time to time he would row the whole length of the lake and make his way to the store twelve miles from Quesnel Forks which, originally owned by Long John McRae, now was owned by Al Campbell. There he would buy, in addition to the usual provisions, two packets of cigarette papers, each of which had to contain exactly ninety-nine papers. He would count them and recount them to make sure the number was exact. The length of the lake made these trips necessarily infrequent and he received few visitors, so was obliged to deal with the problem of solitude in his own fashion. On one occasion when Captain Evans-Atkinson approached his cabin he heard voices raised in argument and was somewhat surprised. He was even more surprised to find that Franz was alone. He was sitting at his table with a knife and fork in front of him and cheerfully asked his visitor to join him for a meal. He explained the argument quite simply. He said "I always have a good argument with myself every Friday night. If I didn't have an argument with myself once a week I'd go crazy, wouldn't I!" On another occasion during the summer Evans-Atkinson overheard a similar conversation, this time down beside the creek. Franz was calling out, "Hi, you men over there, do some more work now or you're fired. I'm going to send you out tomorrow!" On seeing his visitor he said, "Oh, I'm just having a little bit of fun with myself. I like to hire a crew once in a while and then I enjoy firing them."

Franz had been living alone in that cabin for thirty-two years when Evans-Atkinson knew him. He had not troubled to provide it with windows of any kind, not even of greased flour bags, but had remained content with a single hole in the roof. Under his bunk he hoarded all his worn out gumboots, for reasons which remain inexplicable. His originality occasionally got him into difficulties. Once, having killed and skinned a year old black bear he brought it into Al Campbell's store to trade, but Campbell would give him nothing for it. He had skinned the animal the way one skins a weasel,

191

by turning it inside out, and so the skin was absolutely complete. When he got back to his cabin with the skin he thought it might be interesting to put it on like a combination suit. It would be warm, he was sure, and he could think of no other use for it. He put it on and it fitted him nicely; in fact it fitted him so snugly that he couldn't get it off again. Unwilling to cut it open because he had taken such trouble over the skin in the first place he kept it on for three and a half weeks, looking exactly like a sasquatch, until finally he contrived to slide out of it. On another occasion when he visited the store a practical joker nailed a plank to the bottom of his boat so that he would find it absurdly difficult to row it home. Nevertheless row it home he did, the whole length of the lake, an almost incredible feat of strength and endurance. Like most trappers he panned a little gold now and then. Only once, however, did he find a nugget. He reported it as being "the shape of a baby's milk bottle and about the size of a pin's head," and said "I put it on a leaf on a boulder that I was working round in the sand bar and the wind blew it away, and, do you know, every spring for nine years I've looked for it. I'll find it again." He never did.

Most of the trappers in the Lake Quesnel area lived a long time but eventually found that arthritis forced them to give up and retire to the provincial home in Kamloops. Franz had a different ending. One spring they found his body lying by the creek near his cabin in his underclothes. He had been dead three or four months. He had apparently gone down to the creek to get water and had been unable to make it back to the cabin.

Franz's nine-year search for his nugget and his thirty-two years alone in one small cabin illustrate something of these loners' attitude to time. They were never in a hurry. Season followed season and year followed year in regular and deliberate fashion, and their way of life remained unaltered by the events in the outside world. Strange happenings or the visits of strangers were remembered and recalled clearly over many years. Generosity was never forgotten and grudges were held long, as is shown by the story of two men who lived in cabins on opposite sides of Quesnel Lake. One was a small wiry energetic man, and the other a rather strange individual whose face was almost entirely lost to sight within hair and whiskers. From a distance you could not tell the back of his head from the front. In the twenties and thirties men with full beards were a little suspect. Moustaches were totally acceptable but a full beard made one think that perhaps the wearer had something to hide. This particular hairy man was also odd in other respects. He lived almost entirely on porcupine stew. Porcupines were normally regarded as food for emergencies only, and were otherwise left alone. It was a kind of tacit form of preservation for practical reasons. His greatest crime, however, according to the smaller man on the other side of the lake, was that he had once borrowed a hunting knife and had failed to return it. This had occurred eighteen years before he met Evans-Atkinson who tells the story, and for eighteen years he and the man across the lake had never exchanged a word, though they were practically neighbours. Evans-Atkinson had occasion to visit the hairy one a little later and mentioned the hunting knife, and was told that it had been returned. "The cabin was empty," said the hairy one, and locked too, "so I put it outside on the window ledge." When Evans-Atkinson, weeks later, saw the affronted one he told him this, and they both went outside and scraped at the accumulation of dead leaves and debris on the window ledge and discovered the knife. An eighteen-year-old breach was mended.

These are the stories of the men who remained at the very heart of Cariboo — loners, like John Likely, who had chosen a way of life that suited them and who would not be persuaded away from it by any passing fancy or impulsive modernity. As the confident twenties gave way to the depressed thirties these men remained in Northern Cariboo, as they still remain, living out their lives in some of the wildest and most beautiful territory in the country and paying little heed to the changes taking place around them.

CHAPTER FIFTEEN

Soda Creek, Cedar Creek, and Williams Lake 1912-1930

Had the loners in their remote cabins ventured out onto the great Cariboo Road during the first years of the century they would have noticed many changes, for the stopping houses were busier than before. The new ranches and the increased size of many of the settlements around the mile houses had made Cariboo an attractive market for the businessmen to the south, and the railhead at Ashcroft had made it easier to deliver goods in the first decade of the twentieth century than it had been in the seventies and early eighties. To the pack trains and the stage coaches therefore were now added the "jerkies" of the commercial travellers, and by 1910 these were speeding up and down Cariboo at regular intervals. The jerkies were like stagecoaches in having bodies set on leather springs, but they had only two or three seats and no superstructure at all. They travelled much faster than the old coaches, and most commercial travellers would make one or two trips every year during the snowfree months. When the snows came it was necessary to use horse-drawn sleighs. These also were open to the weather, and they contained three or four rows of seats which could be taken out if necessary to make room for luggage or goods. The passengers used specially made footwarmers to keep from freezing. These were metal boxes twelve to fourteen inches long, about eight inches wide, and five inches thick, and into them would be placed a charcoal brick which had been heated until it glowed. The warmer itself would be covered with a strip of brussels carpet so that the metal would not scorch anyone who touched it, and there was a small sliding damper at one end so that the amount of heat it gave out could be controlled. These were placed beneath the feet of the passengers, two being used to each seat, and they kept them really quite warm, though, of course, the faces remained unprotected.

At 150 Mile, which was now the most important road junction in the area, the main traffic remained freight. Here the freight trains split up, one group going east to Horsefly and Bullion mine and Quesnel, and another travelling west into Chilcotin country by way of Soda Creek. There was a general store, a telegraph office managed by a Mr. Fred Hall generally known as Old Daddy Hall, a hotel, and a policeman, Fred Rose. The policeman was kept busy enough dealing with rowdyism and with exuberance rather than with major crimes, though theft of goods from the freight trains was always a problem. One particular kind of theft caused a good deal of irritation in the first decade of the century. Saloon keepers in Quesnel began complaining that the barrels of liquor they received were often short four or five or even ten gallons. As a consequence of these complaints the shippers began to stamp the weight of each barrel on the end of it, and then the barrels could be rolled on to the scales at the delivery point and the weight could be checked. This worked fairly well for a time, but then one of the freight drivers known as Old Hank had an inspiration. He discovered that he could take a hammer and cold chisel and knock the hoop on the end of the barrel down just a little way and then drill two holes, one to let air in and one to let whisky out. When he had done this he would take a big horse syringe and fill it with water and put in exactly as much water as he had removed whisky. At the end of the operation he would tap the hoop back over the holes he had made and no one was any the wiser. The weight, after all, had not altered. Only those with suspicious minds and palates experienced in neat whisky would be likely to find anything wrong. Unfortunately for Hank his method was discovered, and thereafter a good deal of attention was paid to the affixing of hoops to the barrels more firmly, and barrels were more closely scrutinized. Hank had been defeated by improved technology.

150 Mile itself was soon to suffer defeat also and at the same hands. While the establishment of the railhead at Ashcroft had affected Cariboo quite considerably, the arrival of the C.P.R. was as nothing, in terms of altering Cariboo society, to the arrival of the Pacific Great Eastern Railway Company. The P.G.E. was incorporated on February 27, 1912, but even before its incorporation surveying gangs had travelled Cariboo and laid out plans for the route the line should follow. The full story of the creation of the P.G.E. is too complicated and too tangled to be told here; the political and financial manoeuvring took place outside the boundaries of Cariboo, in any case, and it is the consequences of the railway building rather than its causes which should concern us in this book. Nevertheless a brief summary of the affair is worth giving.

The P.G.E. was not the first railway to be planned for the area. The first project was that of the Cariboo, Barkerville, and Willow Railway Company, which dreamed of a line running from the Grand Trunk Pacific at Eagle Lake to Barkerville along the Willow River, with side lines to Quesnel Forks, Horsefly (earlier known as Harpers Camp) and Cunningham Creek. This was eventually to extend cross country and meet up with the Thompson River. The plan came to nothing. The P.G.E. was planned to link the Peace River country with Vancouver, and also to link up with an Alaskan railroad due for construction by the United States. Foley, Welsh and Stewart formed a company to build the railway, and guaranteed to equip and operate it as well as build it, the completion day being set at July 1, 1915. Shares in the company were sold, but the venture was also subsidized by the government at the rate of, first $35,000 and later $42,000 a mile. The money proved inadequate. Though by the end of 1912 the whole route had been graded, a number of necessary bridges were not yet built. By 1915 the line, beginning at Squamish, had reached Lillooet only; Clinton received its railhead in 1916. Then, however, the whole operation collapsed. The Company money ($2,160,000 from the sale of bonds, $40,000 from the company itself) had been exhausted as also had the government trust fund which supplied the subsidy per mile. In 1918 a new government headed by John Oliver and a newly created Department of Railways gave the contract to complete the line to Northern Construction Company. The line reached Lone Butte in 1919, Williams Lake in 1920, and Quesnel in October 1921. The line was then continued along the Cottonwood River to join with track being laid from Prince George. Somehow or other the lines failed to meet and work ceased. The public was by now heartily sick of the P.G.E. It was variously nick-named Provincial Government Expense, Promoters Get Everything, Please Go Easy, and Past God's Endurance. The second world war saw the steel beyond Quesnel torn up for use in munitions in 1942; at the end of the war, however, an extension to go through Pine Pass to Dawson Creek was planned; work began in 1949. At last on October 31, 1952, Hallowe'en, the line reached Prince George, almost exactly forty years after the project had begun. The Vancouver-Squamish stretch was not, however, completed till 1956 and the railway did not reach Dawson Creek until 1958.

The creation of the P.G.E. was attended with numerous scandals, accusations of financial swindling, complaints of mismanagement, and John Oliver, the prime minister of British Columbia who took over the project in 1918, once confessed, not long before he left office "I don't know what to do with the dashed thing." Cariboo did, however, know what to do with "the dashed thing." It was determined to profit from it, and was the more excited about it because the completion of the Grand Trunk Pacific Railway link between Vancouver and Prince George in the first years of the century had shown how prosperity could follow the railway. Indeed Cariboo ranchers had profited enormously from the needs of the railway workers' camps in the Prince George area, and there had been a boom in the land prices around Quesnel. During the making of the P.G.E. which, as regards Cariboo proper, took place in the years 1912-16 and 1918-21, the population of the area was swollen by hordes of labourers, at first grading and building bridges, and then laying the track. Soda Creek, which had lapsed into relative sleepiness with the lessening of activity in the mines, became, in 1912-13, something like a metropolis overnight when the grading crews arrived. It slumped again afterwards but again in 1920-21 when steel was being laid it became as rumbustious and bustling as before. James W. Keefe, a rancher living in those parts at the time tells us,

There wasn't room to put up another building along there anywhere. There was little Chinese restaurants and gambling dumps and everything you could want and good big restaurants and two good stores. It was quite a place then.... Any place you could put up a shack there was one.[44]

The bootleggers were doing good business at that time. According to Mr. Keefe

There was five blind pigs there and bootleggers every place you'd go, and so the police were trying to catch these bootleggers, and they got a fellow named Riley to come up there to catch 'em.... So Riley, he throwed a party in his house one night and we all took in booze and that, and he had some, so the party was getting down on the booze and the party was kinda dying he give me a dollar bill and told me to go and buy a bottle from old Bill. He was the bootlegger they wanted to catch. So I went out and bought a bottle and took it down to the other end of town. A bunch of us drank it down there. So next morning when I met Riley he says "You never come back with that bottle last night" I said "Hell, they mobbed me soon as they seen me with a bottle." I never did go back with his bottle. I knew what he wanted. He was just making a stool pigeon out of me.[45]

Whisky was the favoured drink in Cariboo of the first years of the century. In some places it was still the custom, as it had been in the 60's and 70's, for a man to pay for a drink and then be given the bottle

[44] *Ibid.*
[45] *Ibid.*

so he could have as long a pull at it as he wished. On one occasion a man with a particularly large amount of whisky inside him caused a certain amount of confusion. The night stage had come in to Soda Creek and the horses had been stabled and the driver was just about to dowse the lantern at the back of the coach when he heard a man saying "Leave that alone. I'll put it out" and a shot rang out and the lamp was shattered. The happy gunman then went into the saloon of the first hotel waving his six-shooter and, as people ran for cover, shot out all the lights. He then, with admirable fair mindedness, went over to the competitor hotel and shot out all of their lights also.

Not all the practical jokers were as violent as this one. An old Scot once took a great deal of trouble to teach an Indian to write his name, and caused a lot of ill feeling among the Irish patriots in the area thereby, for the name he taught the Indian to write was Charles Stuart Parnell. The Indians were, in general, regarded as inferiors and sometimes even as objects of commerce. It is said that big Jim McKill once either gave or received an Indian girl in payment of a debt. When an Indian became a nuisance he was dealt with summarily and often brutally, even though until the time of his transgression, he might have been regarded as a friend and boon companion. On one occasion an Indian, Sandy Frank, visited Jack and Red O'Connor for an evening of festivity, and turned "mean," upon which one of the brothers shot and killed him. Nobody ever discovered which of the brothers actually pulled the trigger. The Chinese were equally insecure socially. Two drunken white men beat Jumbo, a well-known local Chinaman to death.

On the whole, however, there was very little racial violence in Soda Creek or in Cariboo generally at this time. Many of the Chinese worked as cooks though not always with a full understanding of the tastes of their employers. Angelique Lyne once was expecting important guests to dinner and the Chinese cook duly served up a roast chicken. Unfortunately, however, he did so with the explanation "Chicken come sick; we killum." Predictably, nobody ate the chicken. Some of the Chinese ran stores; one in Soda Creek was nicknamed "Ten Centie" because he ran a store whose goods always seemed to bear that price. Others were laundrymen as was another Soda Creek citizen who was known popularly as "Cheesy Clie" because in the very cold weather he would constantly exclaim "Cheezy Clie!—forty below!"

The Chinese were patient and hard working and many became wealthy. One of them, Louis Pang, had a store in Soda Creek in the twenties, and did well enough to sell it out to Louie Bow and return to China and to the two wives he had left there.

Soda Creek provided a good living for the industrious in the early twenties, and across the river in the Chilcotin country the ranchers also profited from the boom provided by the P.G.E. They were, however, troubled by the presence of huge herds of wild horses that were roaming the country. These herds had grown up from the large numbers of horses that the earliest miners had lost or let go free, and the studs that led the herds would often descend upon the ranches and lure away the mares. James W. Keefe, who had a ranch just across the river from Soda Creek tells how one day in 1922 he arrived home to find that his horses had all gone. As it was just on haying time he was understandably annoyed. He borrowed a pony from a little girl and set out to look for his horses but when he found them the bandit stud chased him off. He tells the rest of the story in this way:

So I come back and I got an Indian and we went out after him and I kept this little horse — I was riding it — and so I give the Indian the rifle and I told him "Shoot that stud!" and so we run on to him and he monkeyed around with the gun till the stud got away and he didn't get him so I got pretty huffy about it and I took the gun and we followed them again and I guess we were an hour and a half before we found them again and I got off and he was a beautiful horse. And this Indian says "Crease him! Crease him!" so I took about ten feet of rope with me and shot him high enough in the neck that it would knock him down and I run over and I was going to hogtie him and I looked at him and pulled his mouth open and looked at his teeth and they were that long and I called the Indian to come and he says "Tie him up! Tie him up!" I said "Come and look at his mouth" and the Indian he started over there and the stud jumped up and took after me and I started running backwards and shooting him with the 3030 and the rest and I shot him three or four times then I fell down and he fell down over a log and his feet were dangling around there. Anyway it knocked him out and so we go in to round the horses and got em headed out towards home. We got about four or five miles from where I shot this stud and I heard a little noise behind and I looked back and here come the stud. He was all bent over and he was still coming, blood running out of him and foam coming out of his mouth that was all pink, and I turned around and shot him in the neck and downed him. . . . He was an old-timer, but he looked like a four-year-old.[46]

In 1928 it was decided that the land had to be cleared of wild horses and in that year three thousand of them were shot, the remainder being killed in 1929.

It was not only the P.G.E. that brought sudden and temporary prosperity to Soda Creek in the early twenties. It was also the news of

[46] *Ibid.*

a new gold strike which, spreading rapidly south, brought many eager prospectors back into the country.

The strange thing about the new strike is that it took place in an area which had already been well surveyed. In fact it had been known for a long time that there was gold on Cedar Creek at the westernmost point of Quesnel Lake. Benjamin McDonald had found gold there in 1859, and a little to the east of the creek, near Cedar Point, in 1862, "Sailor" Jack Edwards sank a shaft that brought him a hundred dollars a day, and, beside him, Billy Barker was working his Aurora claim in the days before he struck it rich on Williams Creek. It was the pile of tailings that these two left behind them when they moved on over the mountains to Williams Creek that helped to save the Cedar Point cedar grove in the fire of 1869. The Chinese as usual, followed the white miners and in 1866 there were several hundred of them working the area, and they were still there in the eighteen-seventies. White miners had, however, dismissed the creek as played out until in 1920 old John Likely, who had retired from active mining in 1919, advised A. E. Platt and John (or Johnny) Lyne, a grandson of William Lyne, Pinchbeck's early partner, and the brother of Billy Lyne of the Nine Mile Ranch just south of Soda Creek, that the mother lode of the Cedar Creek gold had not been found and suggested that they should work higher up the canyon benches. The story of the actual strike is dramatic as is usual in Cariboo. The Centennial Edition of the *Williams Lake Tribune* 1969 tells it as follows:

For months the two prospectors laboriously worked their way along the canyon, panning as they went to find the elusive 'color'. In August of that year the find was made.

Like many gold strikes, it came by accident. The two men were on top of Warren Mountain and Platt stopped at a small, reed-choked water hole to get a drink. As he knelt down and scooped up the water in his cupped hands, he saw the unmistakeable color. He scooped up the gravel and to his amazement found he had more gold in his hands than rock. He leaped to his feet and shouted to Lyne, who thought his partner was having a fit as he mouthed almost incoherent words and pointed to the pond.

The two men set about staking their claim and making plans to go to Horsefly to get Bob Campbell to finance their expedition the following spring. But Platt made two mistakes, both of which were to cost the two discoverers a small fortune.

First he placed his staking lines in a half-moon along the top of a gulch. Then he wrote a note to a trapper friend advising him that they were pulling out for Horsefly but would be back to work a claim on the upper end of the trapper friend's trap line.

Before spring six trappers in the area had staked claims on the upper end of the creek.

But worst was yet to come. At that time a system of leases was in effect and claims were for a lease of a maximum of 80 acres. When the surveyor came to run the lease lines, he struck a straight line from Platt's starting post, and the land that followed Platt's original curved line was found to be included in one of the trapper's claims. It was, of course in this area that the gold lay in quantity.

The six trappers, Ed Stevenson, Mike Sheridan, two brothers, Mike and Daniel Grogan, Danny McCallum and Fred McMahon were luckier.

The next player on the scene was a promoter named Munson, who paid the trappers $40,000 each for their claims, unopened and unworked. The suspicion is that the trappers were paid off with their own gold though. The promoter borrowed a dollar to seal the original deal and then had the men work for him on the claim. The first payment on the purchase was made in gold. The claims yielded $7,000 in the first 10 days.

By this time the news was out, and the rush was on. At its height it is estimated that 7,000 people flocked to the area and the ground was staked for miles up the lake and down the river.

The newcomers arrived in Williams Lake first and then headed for Quesnel Forks. Many rode horseback in, and since there was no bridge across the Quesnel, there were a lot of stray horses on one side of the river as the rush progressed. Old-timers had crossed on the dam erected by the Gold Quesnel River Company in 1900 but this was blown up in 1921 to let the salmon up the river.

There was one policeman at the 'Forks' when the rush started and he left soon after. As a result a rough element soon drifted in and set up head-quarters on Goat Island, from where they dispensed bootleg liquor. In the spring of 1923, 12 provincial police under Greenwood arrived on the scene. They came on a Thursday and spent the following two days watching Goat Island from a distance. On Saturday night they made their raid and the next morning 82 men and women were manacled to trees on the island. They were shipped out immediately.

Except for the original find, nothing new was turned up by the rush. But lawyers had a field day as claims and counter claims were disputed.

And all was not going smoothly with the original claim. Hijacking was rife, and the promoter had 50 men working with 21 security guards watching them. He, in the meantime, was travelling the country selling "units" in the mine. Since there was something like a million printed, and no records kept, it is doubtful if the unit holders got anything.

Hi-jacking was carried out to such an extent that one laborer who was working on supporting timbers, and had nothing to do with the gold-bearing gravel, left after six weeks and sold 83 ounces of gold at Ashcroft. From the clay wedges in the heels of their boots, workmen could get 75¢ a shift.

About this time the government stepped in and took control to safeguard the 'unit' holders. The mine was turned over to a trust company and eventually bought by Otto Baer who in turn sold it to the Cariboo Mining Company for $4,000. This company brought in heavy equipment and worked the Canyon for 10 years, leaving in 1938.

Still working his leases on the creek is Captain Norman Evans-Atkinson, who was on the site before the big strike. He was in Vancouver during the winter of 1921 when he got a telegram from Chief Trillium saying "come back quick, lots of gold."

He arrived back in time to stake below the six trappers and later extended his lease to the mouth of the creek.

But what of the six trappers?

Stevenson went back to his former home in Maine and bought a farm with his $40,000. Sheridan left for California and came back broke. He later died of an overdose of sleeping pills and two people were involved in a manslaughter charge. One of the Grogan brothers, Mike, married Valentine Walters and moved to California. Daniel Grogan now resides in Maine. McMahon left for Vancouver where he married and presumably enjoyed his $40,000. McCallum left for Ashcroft and bought a big McLaughlin-Buick car. He couldn't drive it but started back to the 'forks', travelling in low gear all the way. He drove the car off the road near the 83, received a couple of cracked ribs in the accident. He later died.

And the original discoverers?

A year after the fabulous find, Platt died in a taxicab in Prince George of a heart attack. Lyne is still in Williams Lake and philosophically avers that it was just as well he didn't get all that money. He will be 90 years old this June.

The prosperity of the little town that grew up around the Cedar Creek area led to the post office being moved to the area from Quesnel Forks and to some discussion of what name should be given the town. It had previously been known as Quesnel Dam because of the dam that had been built across the river to enable placer mining to take place more comfortably on the river below it. It had also been called Cedar City. At a Free Miners Meeting Captain Norman Evans-Atkinson, who had himself hurried to Cedar Creek from Victoria on receiving the telegram from Chief Trillium, reading "Come back quick. Lots of gold," asked the question "Would any of us have been here if it hadn't been for old John Likely?" and suggested the name Likely. Until that moment most people had been in favour of Cedar City as the name for the place and, most importantly, for the new post office which was to serve Spanish Creek, Cancer City, and Likely Gulch, as well as Cedar Creek and its previous site of Quesnel Forks which had been the first townsite in all Cariboo. John Warren, the President of the Consolidated Mining Company, supported Evans-Atkinson and so Likely came into being.

The Cedar Creek gold rush was nothing like the earlier excitement and the town of Likely did not long remain a bustling and busy centre, but the effect of the strike was important. Not only did it bring some prosperity to Quesnel, for Quesnel was now the obvious gateway to the new mines, it also excited new interest in gold mining itself and brought prospectors fresh hope. Before the Cedar Creek operation was a year old there were miners working up and down the creeks as assiduously, if not in as large numbers, as in the eighteen sixties. James W. Keefe tells how in 1922 he saw no fewer than sixteen rockers on one little island in the Fraser six or seven miles above Soda Creek. They were mostly hand rockers and the miners were both white and Chinese. One fellow picked up an eight dollar nugget in the shape of a heart that he found just lying on the rock in plain view, and another took out over four hundred dollars. One big Swede displayed a poke ten inches long and full of nuggets.

The effect of the gold rush and of the P.G.E. on Soda Creek, however, did not last. As soon as the steel was laid the people left, prospectors, storekeepers, bootleggers, all of them, until all that was left was a few houses and Ah Wing's general store.

The railway caused more permanent changes elsewhere, for once the route of the line was known some people began to plan new businesses in strategic places. One of these perspicacious traders was Roderick McKenzie who left his business in Squamish and built, largely by himself, a hardware store at Williams Lake, completing it a year before the railway arrived, and to such good effect that before long he was taking business from the much longer established Harvey Bailey in Ashcroft. The renaissance of Williams Lake was perhaps the most obvious and dramatic consequence of the coming of the railway. Just as it had been prevented from growing into a centre for Cariboo in 1863 by Gus Wright's bypassing the land near the lake to take the road over the mountain, so now in 1920 the arrival of a steel road reasserted the strategic importance of the place as the geographical centre of Cariboo and caused 150 Mile to begin to lose importance. Nevertheless, because teamsters considered that there was more feed available on the Carpenter Mountain route than on any road nearer the lake it was not until 1932 that a main highway through Williams Lake was built, and Williams Lake came into its own at last. The original creation of the new Williams Lake, however, was attended with the same kind of confusion as the bypassing of the earlier one. Prime Minister Oliver, visiting the area, picked a townsite out, but because the owner of the land wanted $1,500 for it, changed the well-laid plans of Foley, Welsh and Stewart and selected, instead of the pleasant lakeside area, a bleak dusty hillside a mile further to the north, which added $15,000 to the construction costs. Nevertheless, the new town prospered. Mackenzie's store soon received a competitor of the name of Fraser; Mackenzie, however, bought him out. The Bank of Montreal, a branch office of the 150 Mile bank, set up business in a quickly built shack as did the Bank of Commerce. Bob Henderson operated the post office. In September 1919 the track around the lake was finished and a huge crowd gathered to hear the bell and whistle of the train as it came in from the Onward ranch. People had gathered from all over for the occasion. The population of Quesnel, Soda Creek, and 150 Mile and the ranchers and their people from the Chilcotin, together with Indians from all over the area were there in indescribable excitement and confusion as the train arrived. The confusion did not lessen in 1920. Workmen were busy constructing the stores for the contractors who were being urged on by even more impatient merchants. Every night seemed to be a night of celebration, ranchers, gold miners, cowboys, and construction workers all living it up with the help of quantities of bootleg liquor brought in from Alberta. The festivities were marred by no nice adherence to legality, for the town had as yet neither policeman nor jail, and wisely the authorities seem to have decided not to risk a riot by providing them too precipitously. The annual Stampede which was now inaugurated had the benefit of some shelter for its patrons in the partly built Lakeview Hotel, and it was regarded as a great success. Herb Spencer managed the whole affair with the eager assistance of Joe Flieger, Bill Smith, "Cyclone" Smith, Leonard Palmentier, and Antoine Boitano. The first stampede was held on land that was originally the grain fields of Pinchbeck and Lyne. This was a natural enough development for, even before the white man came, Williams Lake had been a meeting place for Indians and for games, it being at the northern limit of the Shuswap country, the southern limit of the Carriers, and on the eastern border of the Chilcotin. The first stampede was a get-together of cowboys from the ranches of Cariboo. Later, like all other stampedes and rodeos of any size, its competitions became open to all comers. Williams Lake was jumping in 1920. Hotels, restaurants and businesses were going up like wildfire. Bill Smith had a restaurant; Bob Henderson built a store; Fred Bucholtz provided a bakery; George and Bill Smith created the Grand Central Hotel; Jack Elliott created a meat market; and Hand Lee started up a rooming house. The P.G.E. station and freight shed were also completed, using lumber provided by Harry Curtis who had bought George Moore's sawmill on the mountain. Entertainment was not lacking. T. A. Moore provided a dance hall on the second floor of his store, and built a pool hall that was run by Newt

Claire, Ted Weyneberg and M. F. Johnson, the last named taking the business over later. Since by no means all the travellers used the P.G.E., Herb Smith built a livery stable and feed store and Sam Marwick, the blacksmith of 150 Mile, moved into town and was one of the busiest people there.

At the beginning of 1921 the town was still booming, and the authorities were now beginning to feel that some attention should be paid to the situation. The first government agent, R. M. Gusty arrived. He was the town's first Magistrate and worked out of Henderson's store until the courthouse was built in 1924. Frank Gallagher was in charge of the police department; he operated from a log cabin at the old Borland House. James Boyd, the district forester also had his office in the Borland. The United Church and Manse were built this year, the Rev. A. D. McKinnon being the first minister. Until the fall of 1920 the town's children were taught in a room at the Lakeview Hotel; the school then was built. As each building was completed the town went on a spree. Every completed building was made the excuse for a party and a dance, and optimism was so prevalent that one of the Williams family from Horsefly moved into town and started a garage even though there were at the time only three cars in town. Williams Lake, in fact followed the usual Cariboo pattern by growing with almost helter skelter rapidity. The streets were not any better looked after than those of early Barkerville and many of the businesses were linked together, as in Barkerville, by boardwalks some height above the mud. It was in 1921 that Williams Lake suffered the fire already mentioned. It took place in July and it was followed by heavy rains that kept up all through August and into the fall and winter. The town was a sea of mud; the roads were almost impassable; five horses were needed to pull a load up the Oliver Street hill to a building site. Nevertheless the townsfolk continued to work with optimism and confidence, and accepted whatever came their way with either rejoicing or equanimity. The first patient in the new emergency hospital and nursing home in the Weetman house next to Elliott and Mellish's equally new meat market was a man called Achieson who had been shot by Angus Black who ran a draying business. Achieson died and Black was given twelve months for manslaughter. 150 Mile was no longer the leading settlement in Cariboo and T. J. Hodgson moved his Chilcotin Mail and Freight Line down to Williams Lake from there. He had started at 150 Mile in 1914 as a sub-contractor for the B.X. and then in 1916 had got the mail contract for the Chilcotin country delivering mail from the 150 to the Chilcotin country. He changed from horses to automobiles at this period, his first vehicle being an old Thomas Flyer which was obliged to cope with the steeper grades by going up them backwards. The main telephone and telegraph office was still at 150 Mile with Hope Patenaude operating it, but Claude Barber opened up another office in Williams Lake.

Throughout the twenties Williams Lake continued to boom. When prohibition ended in 1922 the town got its first liquor store run by Walter Slater. In 1924 Red Hellier started to supply electricity to local residents from his private power plant which he used to operate the movie theatre he had opened. In 1925 Bill Smith built the first Stampede Hall with money he raised from selling shares to supporters; it remained in use until it burned down in 1956. The Masons built their Masonic Hall in 1926 and leased part of it to the new liquor store. The Anglican Church was built in 1928, and in 1929, the town being almost ready for incorporation, three temporary village commissioners were created in order to organize an election. This they did and as the decade ended Williams Lake had its first Board of Village Commissioners, W. S. Western, M. F. Johnson, and J. D. Smedley. The first meeting was held in the Oliver theatre which had been named after Prime Minister Oliver who had picked out the site for the town.

Williams Lake was thus created by the railway, just as Clinton and 150 Mile had been created by the road and Soda Creek by the river-boats. And just as Soda Creek had dwindled when the ferry traffic was replaced first by that on the road that bypassed it on the way to Quesnel, and then by the new railway also, while Quesnel grew and prospered, so now 150 Mile dwindled in importance having been by-passed by the railway and overshadowed by the importance of Williams Lake which, in the time of Gus Wright, it had over-shadowed itself.

This rhythmic rise and fall of settlements and townships is typical of Cariboo. It seems almost as if the country were dominated by the spirit of continual change, by some shape-changing power which, in every decade since the beginning, chose to alter the nature of the country and send the inhabitants of it moving from one place to another, either in search of gold, or in search of the permanent city which once appeared to be Keithley, once Barkerville, once Quesnel, and then Williams Lake. Of these Williams Lake has proved to be the most permanent centre, having retained and increased its importance over the last fifty years, and now it seems to be established quite irre-movably as the heart of Cariboo.

CHAPTER SIXTEEN

The Last Strike

The arrival of the P.G.E. and the rise of Williams Lake put paid to the career of 150 Mile and also reduced the volume of road freight considerably. It also, however, made Cariboo an even more available market to southern business, for goods could now be brought all the way into the heart of Cariboo by rail. Indeed, for some years there was no other way to reach Cariboo, for the construction of the P.G.E. had entailed the destruction of many parts of the Cariboo Road, especially in the Fraser Canyon. Consequently, from the beginning of the twenties until 1926 there was no direct road link between Cariboo and the coast. This presented problems for the salesmen travelling into Cariboo with their cases and hampers of samples. They were now obliged to get to Cariboo by rail and then to hire transport, or to ship their automobiles by rail to Cariboo on flat-bed rail cars. The automobile came into general use by the salesmen in the twenties, and several of the old stagecoach drivers became drivers of hire cars out of Ashcroft. Fred Peters, Ernie Knight, and Len McCarty were three of them. The average car was not really suited to the carrying of large quantities of samples, so two Vancouver drygoods firms, Mackay Smith, Blair Ltd., and Jas. Thomson & Sons converted Cadillacs into what J. R. Hall in the 100 Mile House *Free Press* described as "a cross between today's station wagon, a panel truck and a police paddy wagon." The drivers of these cars always took at least two spare tires of the 37" x 5" size required, and extra gas in four gallon cans, for there were few gas stations in Cariboo. They also, with good reason, carried a shovel, an axe, and a coil of good strong rope. There were no organizations to help in emergencies in the twenties, and travellers who ran out of gas were obliged to face long walks for help. The only car dealer around was Mark Drummond who had a Ford Agency in Ashcroft, though before the twenties were over Johnston Bros. in Quesnel began a dealership in Chevrolets. As in the wagon train days stopping places were required for overnight stays, and J. R. Hall recalled Cunningham's at the 74 Mile, Crosina's at 153 Mile, Pollard's at Clinton, Tom Lee's at Alexis Creek, and one of the very best, the Forbes place at 122 Mile House. The stopping places were also often stores at which business could be done. The only place with garages in Cariboo during the middle twenties was Williams Lake. The pioneers of automobile travel had, indeed, as rough a time of it as their predecessors of the stagecoach days. J. R. Hall tells the story of one of his own journeys which was typical of many. He wrote in 1971

We had left Gang Ranch just at dark for the long drive to Clinton. The night was clear and we had been over the same road numbers of times before but for some reason we got crossed up at Meadow lake, made a wrong turn and by midnight knew we had gone astray. A small house was spotted near the road, no lights, but we knocked and learned that in truth we were many miles from Clinton and this was Dog Creek. We had almost completed a circle.

The house was the home of one of the Place family, old-timers at Dog Creek, who took us inside and offered all the hospitality and comforts associated with Cariboo in those days. A small boy was taken from his bed which was turned over to us for the rest of the night ... We had breakfast with the Place family and then found there was no gas in Dog Creek. The truck was out to Lough Raymond on the P.G.E. to haul in more drums but would not be back before night. We made it as far as Meadow Lake and there sputtered to a halt still thirty miles from Clinton. For the second time in twenty-four hours we were in luck as very soon along came Lincoln Hannon, manager of the B.C. Cattle Co., at Canoe Creek who generously provided sufficient gas for us to make Clinton.[47]

The automobile traffic in Cariboo in the twenties was not particularly heavy by today's standards, but it would have been a great deal less but for the Cedar Creek gold rush at the very beginning of the decade. Indeed, as the twenties continued and the great depression of the thirties set in, more and more optimistic gold seekers entered Cariboo. There were men needed to operate the mines that were now using heavy hydraulic machinery brought into the area by the P.G.E., and the Cedar Creek strike had awoken many to the possibility of at least making a living wage from panning the gravel bars of the Fraser and the many smaller creeks. Though not all the refugees from the hard hit prairies could find work, and many were obliged to settle in camps up and down the country and rely upon temporary and casual labour, Cariboo did not suffer as intensely as most other parts of the country and the mood of the people was

[47] *100 Mile House Free Press*, August 1971.

208

cautiously optimistic. Times were hard, but the people of Cariboo were sure they could get by.

No one was more inbued with this spirit of cautious optimism than H. G. Lockwood, the Barkerville lawyer. In 1933 he published a pamphlet entitled *Accurate and Dependable Prospector's and Traveller's Guide to Barkerville of Today. Absolutely Authentic Information.*[48] His preface is worth quoting for its splendid combination of optimism and benevolence. It runs, in part:

This little book is published in the hope that the information it contains may be found of use and benefit to those travellers and adventurers, business men, professional men, miners, prospectors, cheechakos, sourdoughs, optimists, pessimists and the rest of us who have heard and read the marvellous tale of treasure to be found in the Cariboo and particularly in the Barkerville District.

It is published in all humility, not pretending to be a treatise of scientific interest, but endeavouring to present plain facts in a plain way, and to correct a volume of misinformation that appears to have permeated all parts of the continent.

The writer believes that there is gold in the Barkerville area in paying quantities, but does not pretend to a knowledge of the practical side of mining and prospecting. He knows, however, that the old-timers, miners and prospectors of the district feel that they are now coming into their own, and naturally and humanly they are happy about it, and their ebullient spirits cannot be depressed. Hence the people of Barkerville do not know about the Depression. They are going about their preparation for summer's work and business with high heart and no apparent doubts or misgivings but that a kindly and benevolent Providence who has buried gold treasure in their hills and streams will lend His kindly assistance to them in discovering and recovering each his fair share. Their courage and faith and the apparent absence of petty jealousy and pointless criticism afford at this time an example to most of the rest of the world, torn and harassed by worry, fear, doubt and almost despair. It seems to be part of the spirit of the country to offer a helping hand, advice and counsel to those able to use such assistance. In that connection the writer wishes to express his profound appreciation of all the invaluable help and advice given him by all and sundry of whom help and information were sought. Without such freely given assistance and open-handed co-operation, his task would have been impossible; through the generous help received, otherwise insurmountable difficulties were overcome.

His pamphlet is detailed and extremely helpful. He explains that travellers from Vancouver to Cariboo should take a Union Steamship from Vancouver at 9 a.m. on a Monday or Thursday, which will get them to Squamish at 12:45 p.m. Then the P.G.E. train, leaving at

[48] H. G. Lockwood, *Accurate and Dependable Prospector's and Traveller's Guide to Barkerville Today*, 1933.

209

1:30 p.m. (consisting of a sleeper, day coaches, freight and baggage cars) will take them to Quesnel and get them there on either Wednesday or Saturday at 0:05 a.m. The single fare for the whole trip was $16.75, an additional charge of $4.30 being levied for a sleeper. Meals were served at stopping places on the way, breakfast at D'Arcy, supper at Lillooet, the next breakfast at Williams Lake (50 cents, a la Carte). The lunch at Quesnel on arrival was provided by "Earl Malcolm," the genial and accommodating host at the "Cariboo" who charged $3.50 a day for accommodation.

Those travelling by way of Ashcroft are advised to take a stage operated by Mr. Hinkus of Clinton from Ashcroft to Clinton ($2.00) and then take the P.G.E. from Clinton at 2:30 in the morning. They are also told that the Clinton Hotel operated by Mr. and Mrs. Adamson (meal 50 cents, room $1.00) is "wonderfully comfortable."

For all the enthusiasm of his preface, Lawyer Lockwood's comments on the state of business in Barkerville are a little less than enchanting.

Conditions are this much better than "outside," that there are no people receiving relief. Actually very few people have any money, but the storekeepers know all permanent residents, most of whom have either jobs or placer claims, and their credit is good for their normal requirements. There are only about 130 men in the district earning wages at present, and until some other companies are in a position to take on employees, that will be the limit of the payroll. *There are no jobs to be had.*

His advice to motorists is equally daunting:

HINTS TO MOTORISTS INTENDING TO DRIVE TO BARKERVILLE

Don't go at all unless you have money and equipment to last you for some time, or unless you have a job to go to. Rumours and newspaper reports of prosperous business conditions are greatly exaggerated. There is no employment to be had and no money until the big mining companies start to work after snow has gone.

Your travelling equipment, carried in the car, should include a good axe, a shovel and high boots, proof against mud and wet. Rubber boots are recommended, knee high. You may have to shovel snow or mud, or you may have to cut away a fallen tree. Of course you will carry chains, though you may find the going better most of the way without them. The writer recommends "slip-on" chains, four to a rear wheel, especially the new kind that strap around the tire and have double cross-chains. But you cannot use these with disc wheels. A good stout rope will likely be found useful, on occasion, also for towing purposes.

Do not go until snow has disappeared, and the roads are in travellable condition. Numbers of cars are snowed in on the roads already. Even where

210

cars do travel for part of the way, they only do so at night, or in the very early morning while the roads are frozen. It is still cold at Barkerville and frosty at night, and looks like the middle of a hard winter. If you have never done any driving in the snow, you are certain to come to grief in trying to do so. And for the time being there are sections of the road that are absolutely impossible for car or truck, even for trucks with double drive-wheels. This applies particularly to the last fourteen miles or so.

Gasoline costs up to 55¢ a gallon. There are few garages and none at all beyond Quesnel. Gas at Barkerville is 55¢ a gallon. A gallon is the British imperial gallon, of 160 ounces, being 1 1/4 American imperial gallons.

In another part of his pamphlet he adds:

From Quesnel to Barkerville, by car, travel is doubtful. While there is frost at night, go while the frost is in the ground. You will probably be able to get to Stanley, 48 miles. From Stanley to Barkerville is about 14 miles, at present impossible for a car or truck. Even after the snow has gone, the mud may be so deep that a car will not have a chance until the road dries up. . . .

Optimism reasserts itself to some extent in the lawyer's account of Barkerville's businesses.

The ground is well covered as regards general stores, gas stations, electricians, lawyers (there are four established in Barkerville at present and another one reported to be coming in), surveyors and engineers, and a doctor, and restaurants.

There may be openings for a garage selling repairs and parts, either at Stanley or Barkerville. Stanley is some 14 miles out towards Quesnel. When the ground has been proved, there will probably be a good opening for building contractors, carpenters, etc., but at the present time every man is his own builder for the most part.

At present there is no electricity in Barkerville, but the more important buildings are being wired for electricity, and it is understood that a diesel plant will open shortly supplying current at about 25¢ a kw. hour, in operation for the hours of darkness up to midnight.

There is no picture show anywhere closer than Quesnel. The operator of the Quesnel theatre is reported to be considering the establishment of a "talkie" at Barkerville.

Money is scarce, as elsewhere at present. The town is full of people who have little or nothing in cash. There is the usual element of "sports" who follow a rush to any place. Mostly they are having a tight time, and many of them will disappear shortly.

Naturally, any persons contemplating entering on any of the businesses mentioned should first make a trip to look the ground over for themselves, secure a business site and make sure that some competitor is not ahead of them. The amount of business done will be quite limited for some time to come, and the capital investment will be quite substantial in most cases, with little assurance of quick returns.

Lawyer Lockwood lists the names of the various mines and mining companies in the Barkerville area, stating that "All the ground for miles around and including Barkerville is located and recorded, some of it three or four times on account of overlapping claims." His list is not, however, very impressive. Britannia Mining and Smelting Company is reported as "surveying and consolidating their holdings" merely. Cariboo Consolidating Mining Company Ltd. are "developing their property." Consolidated Mining & Smelting Co. are, he says, only "reputed to have claims." After listing a number of other Quartz mining operations he states "The ground seems to be well covered and at the time of writing there is no knowledge of any of the above having lately produced any quantity of gold for shipment." Then, however, in italics, we read

As this booklet goes to press a shipment has arrived from Cariboo Gold Quartz amounting to 1425 ozs troy, worth over $30,000.00.

Cariboo Gold Quartz Mining Co. Ltd. was the creation of Fred M. Wells, and it was his operation which came to the rescue of Barkerville, and indeed the whole of Cariboo, and which caused the P.G.E. which carried his gold shipments to stop losing money.

Fred Wells was a hard rock miner, and he had prospected widely in the Rockies, the Selkirks, and the Kootenays before coming to Cariboo, in search of a good vein of quartz. He spent some time working near Lowhee Gulch on Cow Mountain exploring the Saunders Vein, so called because a miner called Saunders had discovered and worked it for a while in the early eighties. He had little money to drift into the mountain, however, and it was not until he got help from Tommy Nichol, Tommy Blair, and George Turner of Barkerville that he was able to explore far enough to be assured that the vein was a deep one. The geologists were sceptical. They maintained that the boulder he had found on Lowhee Creek, which assayed at $20 to the ton, was simply a freak, having been deposited there by glacial action and having no connection with Cow Mountain. His friend Dr. Burnett, however, came to his rescue, even going so far as to mortgage his home to pay for the necessary equipment and labour, and in 1927 the partners were joined by O. H. Solibakke of Seattle. It is said that it was in July 1929 that they discovered a vein 125 feet deep and 8 feet wide. The geologists' report, however, was still unhelpful and they were thus prevented by government regulations from selling shares in the Cariboo Gold Quartz Company which they incorporated that year in British Columbia. Therefore in 1932, Burnett and Solibakke took Wells to

New York and raised the money there. In 1932 a townsite to house the necessarily large number of miners required by such an operation was surveyed by Major Gooke of Quesnel, and by the end of the year the building of Cariboo's first planned and company-owned town was well under way. The actual mining began in 1933, just as Lawyer Lockwood was writing his pamphlet, and the first year's work brought in $260,841 (Lawyer Lockwood exaggerated a little). Across the way on Island Mountain the Newmont Corporation of New York was also working, with ninety men. Other companies came into the area also, including the Amalgamated, Coronado, Cariboo King, and Burns Mountain, exploring the whole area. Wells itself grew rapidly. There were two thousand people there in 1934. Some buildings were hauled from Barkerville to Wells by Bill Balleaux, who sledged them on a snow road. It is said that one of these buildings was that of the Barkerville lawyer, Hub King, who stayed in his house as it was being moved and maintained that he enjoyed the trip. Wells continued to be a thriving centre of gold quartz mining until the second world war when the market for gold collapsed. By 1936 the Cariboo Gold Quartz Company was producing $6,700,000 a year. Between November 1934 and April 1936 the Island Mountain mine produced $90,000. Though work was almost suspended during the second world war operations began again in 1947 and continued right up to the sixties.

Fred Wells' discovery and the other quartz mines brought at last some profits to the P.G.E. for the gold was freighted by rail and so was the heavy machinery needed for the hard rock mining operation. It also led directly to the Cariboo gold rush of the thirties. This gold rush, somewhat less frenetic than the first, was swollen by the depression and by the provincial newspapers publicizing the gold of Cariboo, possibly in a deliberate attempt to move the unemployed out of the cities. Thus after the development of ranching in southern Cariboo made another of its sudden shifts of direction, and again the northern part of the country became of first importance, and again the cry was gold as it had been in the beginning. 1934 became, indeed, something of a boom year for northern Cariboo. Though Lawyer Lockwood's 1933 Directory of Barkerville which he included in his pamphlet, lists only 86 persons, Fred W. Ludditt states that during the winter of 1932-33 "there were perhaps two or three hundred people living in Barkerville." The difference in the figures may be partly accounted for by Lawyer Lockwood's not listing any Chinese people. He may also have defined "Barkerville" rather narrowly.

Be that as it may, life in Barkerville was very pleasant. Fred W. Ludditt says of the winter of 1932-33.

There were perhaps two or three hundred people living in Barkerville that winter of 1932-33. The town had several stores; the Barkerville Meat Market, Lee Chong's grocery, Campbell's store — which was in the original Hudson's Bay Post, Nichol's Hotel, the Kelly Hotel, McKinnon's store, the post office, the telegraph office, the present St. Saviour's Church, and another church which was actually one of the buildings moved down from Richfield. Mrs Wendel looked after this church for many years. Besides these there were the Chinese Masonic Hall, the Masonic Hall, at least four cafes, the jail and the Theatre Royal. . . .

During the winter months there were numerous activities in the town. There were bridge clubs, teas, church services and bazaars, parties, dances, sledding and skiing. The skiing parties were a particular attraction. A group of us, young men and women, gathered many times on bright, moonlit nights to go on a ski tour. Most often we started at the farther end of the old street, skiing up the long, narrow valley past the Richfield Court House and Summit Rock to Groundhog Basin. Here we stopped and lighted a bonfire where we made coffee and drank it with the lunches we had brought. Sometimes we had a wiener roast and stayed for a time skiing up and down the slopes of Groundhog Basin. Then we would be off again, heading for the mountain slopes of Prosperine, from where we would reach Antler Road, skimming down its two-mile slope past Cochran's house, and so home again. The round trip was a distance of eight to twelve miles. They were nights to remember.

On skis we climbed the hills and traversed the flat stretches, running the long mountain slopes over the crisp snow, now in shadow, now lighted by a bright winter moon. This was the first time that I had heard the term "ski heil" called out, as we started down the slopes from Summit Rock or Conklin Hill . . . at the far end of the town on the slopes to the left at the old Black Jack Mine and that winter there was a ski meet with participants from Quesnel, Prince George and even Vancouver. Lil Magee won the ladies' ski championship and many trophies. Tom Mobraaten won the men's championship. He was later ski pro at Hollyburn Ridge, Vancouver.

The dances were held in the old Theatre Royal. In those days it had the stage and original heavy velvet curtains and dressing rooms with large ornamental mirrors and many other items belonging to the days when it had been built in 1869. Later this building was torn down to make room for the present community hall. At that time these priceless items were auctioned off to raise funds for the new hall. The townspeople spoke of this with deep regret, even years later. During the process of tearing it down it was revealed that five different floors had been laid successively on top of the original one.

Before the Theatre Royal was torn down, a farewell dance was held in the old building. Here we were all gathered, when on the stroke of midnight, what should happen but the old bell broke from its moorings, and came clattering down to land on the floor at the feet of the dancers, narrowly missing Howard Harris' head!

Early in the thirties my brother Ben came to Barkerville. He prospected, too, but his main interest lay in trapping and hunting. By 1934 we had built and comfortably furnished a cabin of our own, supplying it with a woodshed and overhanging roof and porch. This was on the Antler Road, a bit above Cochran's house. Nestled in among the trees, and with a lovely view, it was quiet, removed from the town and yet near enough for convenience.

Those were happy years in the cabin, and in Barkerville, and we became more deeply aware of the countless attractions of the town and its wonderful people. We knew how much we enjoyed the variety of winter activities, and the marvel of the short summer months with the picnics, exploratory trips to favorite historic sites, and trips around the long chain of lakes some fourteen miles from Barkerville. A favorite picnic spot on the top of Mount Murray was reached by following the Bowron Lake road for about three miles, then taking a trail through the trees on the right, and by gradual ascent through the jack pine and the alpine meadows up to the summit. From here one could look along the main streets of Barkerville, and by looking back could see Bowron Lake and River, and the top end of Isaac and Indian Point Lakes, which were part of the Bowron Lake chain. On any Sunday morning a half dozen or more of us would pack a lunch and take off on this inspiring trip; or we might go to Summit Rock, past the Richfield Courthouse and past the old workings of the sixties, to the huge rock which served as a landmark on the road from Stanley to Richfield and Barkerville up to 1885.

I made these trips often with Charlie Ross who was as keenly interested as I in the old trails and the early days. His father had been one of the pioneers of the Chilcotin. On one of the tramps past Summit Rock, Charlie and I came across a stretch of road about three-quarters of a mile long which had been built in 1864, but never used. When constructing the road, the men had somehow miscalculated, reaching a point where the grade would have been too steep for the pony expresses and stage and freight teams. So this section of the road was abandoned and another piece built at a lower grade. We could see the outline of the original road clearly, and walked along its grass-covered length before returning to the trail we were on.

Another favorite place to visit in the summer months was the famous Lowhee Mine which at that time had been in operation for over seventy years and had progressed for a distance of nearly two miles through the mountains. The deep, wide trench sluiced out hydraulically over the years was an amazing and breathtaking sight.

Ben and I were fascinated by all these things, and we dreamed of building a lodge in Barkerville to provide accommodation for the visitors that Barkerville warranted. We pictured the skiing, hunting and fishing and the historic sites that would attract them.[49]

As news of the Wells success reached the outside world more and more miners arrived in the country. Their enthusiasm was increased by Roosevelt's having pegged the price of gold at thirty-five dollars

[49] Fred W. Ludditt, *op. cit.*, pp. 2-5.

an ounce. New mining companies arrived. According to Fred W. Ludditt these included "The Amalgamated, Richfield, Newmont, Coronado, Cariboo King and Burns mountain" though Lawyer Lockwood lists Newmont as already having "interests" in April 1933. Although in that year some of the houses of Barkerville had been moved to Wells, in 1934 new houses had to be built at Barkerville, the population having doubled from two or three hundred to five or six hundred, according to Ludditt, who tells of the liveliness of the town at this time. He recalls Jens Hansen, who was making a living by "sniping" for gold in abandoned workings:

One time when he'd been particularly fortunate he and a few of his cronies had been having a rousing good time from the proceeds at the Kelly Hotel bar, and for several days really whooped it up, when suddenly they ran out of money.

"Never mind, boys," said Jens, "we'll go out and get some more gold." They all trooped out, stopping to pick up pans and shovels on the way. They hadn't proceeded very far up Stouts Gulch, a favorite place of Hansen's, when he came across a really amazing find and called down, "O.K. boys, we've got it made. We can go back." They all stopped and awaited him and he showed them his find — a $500 nugget! In a mere hour after they had left they trooped back to the hotel with enough gold to assure them a solid week's carousing!

It is said that later on Mrs. McKinnon asked, "Where is that lucky Swede?" This name he carried thereafter — the Lucky Swede. . . .

The Labor Day weekend by long tradition was always a favorite celebrating time at Barkerville. These were three days of rollicking fun ending each evening in a dance. Horse racing was held on the long street, which was cleared of people for the purpose. The race started near the old Billy Barker shaft and proceeded to St. Saviour's Church. There might be only six or eight horses involved in the race, but this took none of the thrill out of it. Climbing a greasy pole for the prize of a bottle of liquor was another attraction. There were gold panning contests, mucking contests, the usual broad jump and high jump and various forms of racing.

The highlight of each day's celebration was the arrival of the stage coach, with passengers and mail. The stage was the last one of the original stage coaches of the 1800's and it was pulled by a four-horse team.

Bill Ward walked up and down the street with a megaphone announcing its progress. "The stage coach is nearing Jack of Clubs Lake. It's at McArthur's Gulch." Then finally he announced, "The stage is half a mile out of Barkerville." On its arrival a few "passengers" alighted and the "mail" sacks were taken out. The "passengers" were dressed in oldfashioned clothes and were announced as well-known old-timers. At least once during the three days there would then be a "robbery" with the "bandit" chased, caught, tried and hanged.

On one of these occasions the ill-fated "bandit" was Howard Harris. He was duly chased, caught, put in leg irons and his hands tied behind him.

216

Then the officiating members of the "hanging" put a noose around his neck and threw the rope over a T-bar and pulled him up, making sure his feet were always touching the ground. Just about that time a gang of roisterers, far gone in spirits, came booming along, momentarily scattering the "hangmen" and shouting, "Oh sure, hang him! Come on, let's hang him!"

Howard was of course rescued but he remarked afterwards that it was just a little too realistic for his liking. At times his feet had been barely touching the ground....

Hundreds of people attended the Labor Day celebrations. It was a time of wholesome outdoor fun and of reunion when long awaited friends might return for the occasion. All the chairs and benches on the verandahs of the hotels and stores were occupied, and the old-timers viewing the activities remarked how the old town had come to life.[50]

Barkerville was indeed a lively place in the thirties, and it is reported that in the middle of the decade there were twenty-five or twenty-six bootleggers in full operation in the town. Prohibition was long over, of course, but Barkerville citizens saw no reason to travel to the liquor store in Williams Lake and buy highly priced whisky when they could stay at home and drink the less expensive home product.

Wells itself, of course, was the centre of the boom. By 1934 its population had reached two thousand and was still growing. The new city, the first truly planned town in Cariboo, was everywhere admired. From the beginning it was furnished with its own hospital and with all the necessary stores and businesses, and was indeed a true "company town."

Quesnel also benefited from the new gold rush. In 1932 more town lots were sold that at any time since 1910, amounting in value to nine thousand dollars. New buildings to the value of fifty-five thousand dollars were built the same year and five hundred and fifty dollars was received by the town in payment for business licences. No wonder that Roderick Mackenzie, the M.L.A. for Cariboo said in 1933 that gold was "the brightest thing in British Columbia."

Gold remained one of the brightest things in British Columbia throughout the thirties, but the outbreak of the second world war changed everything, and gold was no longer to be the main hope of Cariboo. Gold had been the shaper of Cariboo right from the beginning. It was gold that had caused the country to be settled and the roads to be built. It was the needs of the gold miners that caused the first cattle ranches to be created. It was gold that decided when and where towns should be created and when they should be abandoned and disappear. In the thirties it was gold that made the

<hr>

[50] Fred W. Ludditt, *op. cit.*, pp. 155-58.

new P.G.E. Railway a paying proposition, and it was gold that protected Cariboo from the worst ravages of the depression. Gold, is indeed, the heart of the Cariboo story from 1859 to 1939, when the second world war broke out. Thereafter the pattern changed and when the gold market failed in the middle of the war, it spelt the end of an era. The old Cariboo was gone; the new Cariboo would be another story.

Modern Cariboo

The war years were poor years for Cariboo. The market for gold dwindled, and the majority of the male population either joined the armed forces or went south to Vancouver to busy themselves in the shipbuilding yards or engage in other war work. There were no more sudden gold strikes, no more sudden upheavals in the fabric of society, and when the war was over the gold mining industry was in poor shape and there seemed little to be optimistic about. At first, however, the returning miners felt cheerful. Gold would "pick up" they thought, but during the later forties first one then another company ceased mining, and the miners began leaving the Barkerville area. In the summer of 1947 the government assay office at Barkerville was torn down, and the old Scott Saloon, which had latterly been the John Hopp office, and which had survived the great Barkerville Fire was also destroyed. In quick succession Chinese dwellings and business premises were broken up for firewood; the Hudson's Bay Post, rebuilt in 1868, was destroyed. Tourists and others ransacked the old buildings that were left standing and carried off documents, old mirrors, and almost anything portable. Barkerville was rapidly becoming a ghost town, and though the Barkerville Historical Society was formed to try and save the place there seemed little hope. When the people of Quesnel formed the Cariboo Historical Society, however, and persuaded other towns to join in, the situation looked more hopeful. The members of the society set about collecting relics, and documents. Fred Ludditt, who had been talking to every official he could find about the necessity of preserving the area ever since 1947 then set up the Barkerville Historic Development Company, the charter being granted in 1953. The usual delays and frustrations followed, but at last, after much publicity had been organized by well wishers of the press, on June 19, 1958, Luddit tells us, "I received a wire from the B.C. Dept. of Recreation and Conservation asking me if I would take temporary charge of the restoration of

Barkerville." From that time on, year by year, new buildings were restored or facsimiles of old buildings created. Restaurants were created for the tourists. Inevitably souvenir shops were created outside the park proper. A summer company was engaged to perform in the theatre and every summer an actor plays the part of Judge Begbie riding his horse up through the new Barkerville to the courthouse where again his words of wisdom and denunciation ring out as they did a century earlier.

The new Barkerville is now just as much a magnet as was the old one, but now the travellers are tourists and not miners. They began coming into Cariboo to see Barkerville and to feel themselves a part of history not long after the restoration began. These new travellers, like the old ones, needed stopping places and needed accommodation and supplies, and Cariboo provided new hotels, shops, motels, trailer parks, and campsites for them. Museums sprang up at many places along the Cariboo Road, largely rebuilt now, and changed into a great highway. The old schoolhouse at Clinton became a museum. At Lac La Hache there is a smaller one, and there is another at Quesnel, and yet another at Cottonwood. Cariboo, during the summer season, the season which the old miners used to work their creeks and their shafts, before travelling south for the winter, is now a tourist area and not a mining one. The great Williams Lake Stampede, now of international importance, brings thousands and thousands of people into Cariboo and from all over the region, together every July. Some of the old stopping houses and ranches are now "Dude ranches." The lure is no longer gold but entertainment and nostalgia.

Cariboo in the post war years did not, however, spend all its energies on looking back and upon capitalizing upon its exciting and romantic past. The great shape changer that broods over the whole region continued to work. In 1947 the first garage at Lord Martin Cecil's 100 Mile House was built and over the next two decades a village grew into being. Some years later Lord Martin arranged for people to buy their properties from his Bridge Creek Estate and no longer lease them, and by the nineteen seventies 100 Mile had become an important stopping place in the centre of Cariboo, replete with hotels, stores, and shopping plazas.

100 Mile was not the only new town to be created in the new Cariboo. Molybdenum mining at Hendrix Lake led to the creation of a mining town just as had gold mining at Wells. Logging companies began to work in Cariboo and their operations cleared more land for

cattle, so that both cattle ranching and logging became even more important to the region. Williams Lake grew ever larger, and these days, travelling the new Cariboo Road from Clinton, now a delightful rather sleepy little town, there are three modern towns to satisfy the needs of the wanderer, and they are placed almost at equal distances from each other, 100 Mile which was born in the 1960's, Williams Lake which was created in the 1920's, and Quesnel which arrived in the 1850's. After Quesnel and the quiet of Wells where mining is all but at a standstill, and the fascinating museum at Cottonwood, the new Barkerville stands. It is as faithful a reproduction of the old Barkerville as could be contrived, and in the summer months it is lively and busy as ever it has been. The real mystery and romance of Cariboo, however, is only faintly indicated by these buildings and these reproductions. It is to be found, not in the museums and the souvenir shops, not even perhaps in the ghost towns and the quiet ruins of Bullion mine, the remaining fragments of Likely, but in the talk of Cariboo people, in their tall stories, some of which I have repeated in this book, and in the way in which they say, so often, with a light in their eyes, "There's still gold in there, you know" and "A man might find gold anytime" and over and over again tell a tale of the unnamed placer miner, an old-timer, who still walks into town once a year and slaps a poke worth thousands of dollars upon the gleaming counter of the modern bank.

Index

223

224

226

OTHER TITLES OF INTEREST FROM SONO NIS PRESS

Robert D. Turner: *The Pacific Princesses*
    An Illustrated History of Canadian Pacific Railway's Princess Fleet
    on the Northwest Coast.

Ian MacAskie: *The Long Beaches*
    A Voyage in Search of the North Pacific Fur Seal.

Ralph Hall: *Goldseekers*
    Memoirs of the Omineca gold rush.

Cyril Edel Leonoff: *Pioneers, Pedlars, and Prayer Shawls*
    The Jewish Communities in British Columbia and the Yukon. A
    Pictorial History.

Terry Reksten: *Rattenbury*
    A biography of the architect of British Columbia's Parliament Buildings,
    with a full account of his murder.

G. P. V. and Helen Akrigg: *1001 British Columbia Place Names*

G. P. V. and Helen Akrigg: *British Columbia Chronicle, 1778-1846*

G. P. V. and Helen Akrigg: *British Columbia Chronicle, 1847-1871*

David Richardson: *Pig War Islands*
    A History of the San Juan Islands.